GLOBAL URBAN GROWTH

Selected Titles in ABC-CLIO's
CONTEMPORARY WORLD ISSUES
Series

Animal Rights, Clifford J. Sherry
Autism Spectrum Disorders, Raphael Bernier and Jennifer Gerdts
Climate Change, David L. Downie, Kate Brash, and Catherine Vaughan
DNA Technology, David E. Newton
Domestic Violence, Margi Laird McCue
Education in Crisis, Judith A. Gouwens
Environmental Justice, David E. Newton
Gay and Lesbian Rights, David E. Newton
Genocide, Howard Ball
Global Organized Crime, Mitchel P. Roth
Global Refugee Crisis, Mark Gibney
Identity Theft, Sandra K. Hoffman and Tracy G. McGinley
Lobbying in America, Ronald J. Hrebenar and Bryson B. Morgan
Modern Piracy, David F. Marley
Modern Sports Ethics, Angela Lumpkin
Obesity, Judith Stern and Alexandra Kazaks
Same-Sex Marriage, David E. Newton
Sentencing, Dean John Champion
Sexual Crime, Caryn E. Neumann
Sexual Health, David E. Newton
Substance Abuse, David E. Newton
U.S. Border Security, Judith A. Warner
U.S. Space Policy, Peter L. Hays, Ph.D.
U.S. Trade Issues, Alfred E. Eckes, Jr.
Women in Combat, Rosemarie Skaine

For a complete list of titles in this series, please visit www.abc-clio.com.

Books in the Contemporary World Issues series address vital issues in today's society, such as genetic engineering, pollution, and biodiversity. Written by professional writers, scholars, and nonacademic experts, these books are authoritative, clearly written, up-to-date, and objective. They provide a good starting point for research by high school and college students, scholars, and general readers as well as by legislators, businesspeople, activists, and others.

Each book, carefully organized and easy to use, contains an overview of the subject, a detailed chronology, biographical sketches, facts and data and/or documents and other primary source material, a directory of organizations and agencies, annotated lists of print and nonprint resources, and an index.

Readers of books in the Contemporary World Issues series will find the information they need to have a better understanding of the social, political, environmental, and economic issues facing the world today.

GLOBAL URBAN GROWTH

A Reference Handbook

Donald C. Williams

CONTEMPORARY WORLD ISSUES

ABC-CLIO

Santa Barbara, California • Denver, Colorado • Oxford, England

Library of Congress Cataloging-in-Publication Data

Williams, Donald C., 1962–
Global urban growth : a reference handbook / Donald C. Williams.
p. cm. — (Contemporary world issues)
Includes bibliographical references and index.
ISBN 978–1–59884–441–2 (hardcopy : alk. paper) —
ISBN 978–1–59884–442–9 (ebook : alk. paper) 1. Urbanization. 2. Cities and towns—Growth. 3. Cities and towns—Developing countries.
I. Title.
HT371.W545 2012
307.7609172′4—dc23 2011049766

ISBN: 978–1–59884–441–2
EISBN: 978–1–59884–442–9

16 15 14 13 12 1 2 3 4 5

This book is also available on the World Wide Web as an eBook.
Visit www.abc-clio.com for details.

ABC-CLIO, LLC
130 Cremona Drive, P.O. Box 1911
Santa Barbara, California 93116-1911

This book is printed on acid-free paper ∞

Manufactured in the United States of America

To Leah, Ben, and Ellie: may you never stop learning as you travel the cities of the world.

Contents

Preface

Urbanization is the physical growth of cities that takes place over time as people settle into a place of relatively high population density. It is a process that is triggered by attractions that built urban environments offer to those seeking out a new way of life. It may also be pushed by less desirable conditions experienced in rural areas related to poverty, undesirable social conditions, isolation, or even war. The establishment and expansion of urban places is always accompanied by a host of challenges for leaders. Where will all of the newcomers be housed? How will these people find their way through the transportation system? Will sufficient urban services (water, sewage treatment, education, etc.) be provided to meet the needs of this teeming population? Cities have always been places of wealth and power. So urbanization also offers many lucrative opportunities to those who control scarce resources such as land or have services to offer newcomers. Enterprising politicians also have much to gain from those in need of assistance as they adjust to the urban environment.

Historical patterns of urbanization in long-established industrial societies like the United States and France contrast sharply with the experience of many developing societies that have only urbanized on a mass scale in the past few decades. The scale of this growth is staggering. It took New York City (the world's largest metropolis in 1950) nearly a century and a half to expand by eight million residents. Mexico City and Sao Paulo, already far larger than New York, will add this number in the next 15 years. The cities of Asia, Africa, and other parts of Latin America are also experiencing similar levels of explosive urban growth. This book is concerned with the rapid expansion of urban areas that has taken place across the world, and especially the type of growth that has occurred within the previous 50 to 100 years. It will discuss what factors have contributed to this phenomenon and explore the many consequences it has for our future. Urban growth is truly a global trend; hence the scope of the book will include all regions of the world. A special emphasis of the book will be charting different growth trajectories in these societies, and varying policy responses.

The challenges posed by rapid urbanization and the growth of cities have long been a popular subject in both academic and popular literature. Upton Sinclair's *The Jungle* is perhaps the most enduring work in this genre. To be sure, the phenomenon of urbanization and the related field of urban studies has long been a subject of specialized inquiry in social science disciplines like geography, economics, sociology, and political science. Many leading universities have interdisciplinary institutes and curricula that bring together insights from these varied approaches. Academic journals on urban studies abound as well.

This book presupposes that its readers know little to nothing about the subject. With this in mind, it is designed to serve as a launching pad for those seeking more information about the subject. It should help to define exactly what the phenomenon of urban growth is all about, and why it has become a major source of public debate and research. This book is also intended to offer a balanced overview. It will marshal the facts, sort out the benefits and the drawbacks for readers, and yet withhold judgment.

The narrative of Chapter 1 provides an overview of urbanization and the challenges associated with urban growth pressures in all societies. These range from growing demands of urban dwellers for access to more services, to problems that arise from high density living such as traffic congestion, affordable housing, water provision, and air pollution.

The United States has experienced an almost fifty-year boom in housing construction, an expansion of shopping malls and office park developments outside of major urban areas that has perhaps only come to a halt recently. This experience is chronicled in Chapter 2, which also takes a look at current public debates surrounding urbanization. In the eyes of environmentalists and planners, the urban growth of the United States represents nothing less than a tragically underrecognized silent crisis in which Americans are rapidly squandering their finite land resources at rates that are simply not sustainable, nor desirable for the greater good of future generations. Chastising a decision-making process mostly under the authority of local government officials, they are calling for an end to uncoordinated, sprawling development patterns and a shift toward public control through planning institutions that function at the regional and state level. Defenders of the status quo from among the business community argue that such controls put a damper on business expansion, job growth, and long cherished personal freedoms.

Chapter 3 explores the phenomenon of urbanization and related policy challenges throughout the rest of the world. The chapter is organized into nine regions that include Latin America, Europe, Russia and the republics of the former communist USSR, Middle East and North Africa, Sub-Saharan Africa, South Asia, East Asia, and Southeast Asia. Each section will discuss the past history of urban development as well as contemporary urban patterns. Trends, issues, and challenges are identified in each with reference to specific examples.

Chapter 4 provides a brief chronology of key developments in the modern history of urban growth around the world. Chapter 5 contains over 20 biographical sketches of people who have been prominent in the study and development of urban policy. Urban-related issues are by nature inter-disciplinary, so the list of academics includes fields like economics, sociology, political science, and geography. The list also has journalists, activists, and politicians who have taken a role in sponsoring new initiatives in dealing with the urban growth challenge.

The data and documents in Chapter 6 give the reader an opportunity to consider some important statistical information as well as the full text of several key urban planning documents that are representative of different approaches to urban growth. Data will include tables that illustrate global, regional, and national trends in urban growth.

The last two chapters are designed for those who want to probe further, and perhaps even consider getting involved personally in the causes and policy controversies associated with urban growth. Chapter 7 contains a comprehensive directory of organizations associated with the study of urbanization, urban growth management and development. The list includes research institutes, private foundations, international entities, and diverse governmental bodies. Chapter 8 offers the reader a glimpse of the rich array of print and electronic resources that are available today. Finally, the book concludes with a glossary of terms and concepts that are important in understanding the urban growth phenomenon.

1

Global Urban Growth

The "Century of the City" has arrived. In 2008, the United Nations announced that for the first time in the history of humankind, half of the world's population of 6.6 billion was residing in cities. This wholesale shift in societies that have gone from a mostly rural way of life to an urban one began more than a hundred years ago in the industrializing nations of Europe, North America, and East Asia. This was matched in a few short decades after 1950 by a similar urban transformation in much of Latin America and the Caribbean. Today, the rest of the world is racing to catch up with these highly urbanized regions. In the developing world, some five million new urban residents appear each month, pushing up the global urban growth rate to 1.78 percent per year. Over the next 30 years, this will mean that world's cities will add another two billion people.

People and Urban Places

One of the most basic characteristics of human society is the tendency for people to desire living in close proximity with one another. Whether for mutual protection, the production of essential material elements of survival, or merely to satisfy innate feelings of mutual belonging, people have followed an almost instinctual need to gather together into communities long before the onset of recorded history. The phenomenon social scientists call "urbanization" (urban growth) is, however, of more recent origin and refers to the movement of people from small, rural village communities dependent on natural resource extraction and agriculture, to larger, more complex, and densely populated communities called towns and cities. This change of place leads to significant alterations in lifestyle with trade, manufacturing, and service provision replacing farm-related activities.

The rise of cities is among the most significant advances in human development over the previous 7,000 years. These urban places, which grew in tandem with surrounding rural villages and hamlets, have historically provided the space for a whole range of important cultural innovations. With large numbers of people living in close proximity to one another and able to engage in highly specialized activities, cities served as centers for diverse cultural activities and social interaction, as vital engines of economic production and consumption, as promoters of technological advancement, and as seats of administration and government. The concentration of surplus food and other items of value have served, in turn, as the basis for trade and commerce with the wider world. These factors were as much in operation for ancient Mesopotamia, Egypt, and China, as they are today in urban places across the globe.

How are urban places and urban growth to be distinguished from rural places? Most people live in close proximity to one another, but at what point does a village becomes a town, and when does a town become a city? Population size a convenient means to distinguish urban from rural places, and is, in fact, the most common measure used by governments. Through the annual collection of census data, populations are typically sorted into urban and rural categories. This rather simple distinction is, however, complicated by the fact that countries follow differing formulas for determining what constitutes urban settlement. In Denmark, any community of more than 200 inhabitants is classified by the government as urban. In the United States, urban status is conferred on places with 2,500, while it is 5,000 in Ghana, 10,000 in Switzerland, and 30,000 in Japan! In India, urban places are further distinguished by the requirement that more than 75 percent of the adult male population must be employed in nonagricultural work.

Administrative classifications are further complicated by the fact that people living outside of recognized urban boundaries in so-called "rural areas" may actually live in rather high densities. Such communities may be in the process of incorporation into recognized urban boundaries over time, or may exist in legal limbo indefinitely, as has been the case in many rapidly urbanizing areas of the developing world. To overcome such difficulties, researchers prefer to utilize the concept of "functional urban region" in which people living in relatively high densities who are functionally integrated with a single urban place are included as part of a larger urbanized area. Geographers have long distinguished "city regions" with a hierarchy of urban places that surround a primary high-order service center. In the United States, these are known as Standard Metropolitan Statistical Areas (SMSA), while in the United Kingdom, the term "daily urban systems" is utilized in the context of the movement of labor from outer ring areas into central city districts. At a wider level, "conurbations" are distinguished where the functional influence of multiple central cities that were once separated have merged together over time. The term "megalopolis" has been applied to still larger urbanized regions that cover hundreds of miles and tens of millions of residents. The functionality of such regions such as the Boston–Washington corridor in the United States, and Tokyo–Osaka corridor in Japan, is made possible by the existence of highly efficient transportation and communication linkages that pull such large numbers of places together.

More important to an understanding of the urban growth phenomenon, it should be acknowledged that the urban–rural distinction is one that ultimately depends on how people perceive the places they inhabit. To the average person, a "city" is a place where there are opportunities unavailable to them in a rural setting thanks to presence of far greater numbers of persons in close proximity. Cities present people with the daily opportunity to meet and interact with a far more diverse community engaged in many more activities and fields of endeavor than one encounters in rural areas. Cities are bustling, active, and often overcrowded places where one's fortune can be made—or lost—in a hurry.

What Purposes Do Cities Serve?

Cities are exciting and dynamic places that are at the forefront of change in a society. They are attractive to new and potential residents as a home, a place of employment and economic opportunity, and a setting for many vital forms of social interaction that bring them into contact with others through both work and leisure. More broadly, cities can be categorized on the basis of the most dominant functions they serve in the context of wider "urban systems." These encompass the immediate hinterland of cities—surrounding areas that depend on the city for essential services, as well as more distant locations. At regional, national, and global scales, cities are connected in important ways, forming a hierarchy of interconnected functions.

Cities do not all serve the exact same purposes. The economic base that underlies urban growth in a particular location can take many different forms. A closer look at the origins and evolution of city growth demonstrates at least three functional categories that have given rise to urban places. First, one of the oldest functions of towns and cities is to serve as a gathering point at which people from the surrounding area come together to buy and sell goods and services. In cities, market activity takes place on a daily basis, supplementing smaller towns where "periodic markets" may be open for business on an intermittent basis only. The intensive interaction of larger numbers of people provides opportunities for cities to serve additional service-related functions such as governmental administration, education, and the provision of health care. At a wider level, a hierarchy of urban placement can be distinguished in which any single large city is positioned in the midst of a network of medium-sized and smaller cities and towns. This spatial ordering is not static, and typically changes over time in the midst of population fluctuations as well as changes in economic and political conditions arise.

Second, cities may also function as a connection point with more distant locations. Cities that serve primarily as transportation centers have grown up around ports, waterways, railroads, and highways that offer people from the surrounding area an opportunity for their raw materials or semifinished products to be collected, processed, and shipped elsewhere. A heavy concentration of such activities in a single place gives impetus for economies of scale in which increased productivity and higher levels of output are possible with the availability of sufficient labor and capital. Such break-in-bulk functions are vital to the efficient operation of markets. Unlike market cities that are typified by their central location, transportation centers emerge in a linear fashion along heavily used routes of communication between places.

Third, other cities can be distinguished in which a single, specialized function stands out among all others. This may take the form of a single industry such as steel manufacturing or coal mining, or it could be a service such as public administration, university education, or health care. Cities located along international borders similarly serve a highly specialized function uncharacteristic of most other urban places. To whatever degree cities are capable of sustaining these basic functions, they will continue to prosper and grow. Cities may stagnate and contract when these functions are no longer served well, hence diversification and flexibility may be essential to retain vitality. The increasing interconnection between places around the globe—globalization—is triggering rapid changes that have greatly impacted the fortunes of cities around the world.

Cities are sources of wealth and future prosperity. Countries in which most of the people reside in cities tend to have higher incomes, more healthy and educated populations, and are better able to withstand the fluctuations of the global economy. In today's technology-driven world with ever-changing and complicated consumer tastes, cities are potential wellsprings of talent and innovation. In this regard, the growth of urban areas that is encompassing more and more of the world's population represents one of the most significant trends in human history (Brugmann 2009).

Why Do People Prefer Cities?

The growth of urban populations results from both the natural increase of existing urban populations, and net in-migration from people arriving from elsewhere. Most of the explosive growth in Europe and North America a century ago, and in the developing world in recent decades is attributable to the second of these factors. This is because second-generation urban residents (and later generations) show a tendency to prefer fewer children. The decline in birth rates that occurs in industrializing societies is known as the "demographic transition." It is attributable to a host of reasons associated with urban living in the modern era. People once dependent on farm-related incomes no longer see the need for large families in the crowded conditions of the city, where children are expected to attend school and mothers frequently pursue employment outside of the household. Greater access to health care, better hygiene, and the decline of ritual obligations associated with rural life and large family size are also key factors in reducing birth rates of urban populations.

So why are people moving in such large numbers to the cities of the world? The decision of rural dwellers to leave their homes and migrate is shaped by both negative "push" factors, and more positive "pull" factors. In countries undergoing very rapid rural-urban migration, the hard and difficult life of the countryside stands in stark contrast to the allures of the city. Many rural dwellers endure severe poverty due to the small size of their farm plots, which may be exacerbated by rural population growth as well as environmental limitations. Insecure tenancy relations with landowners and other forms of labor exploitation are common complaints as well. These conditions are compounded by the neglect of governments in delivering adequate public services such as education and other needed infrastructure in rural areas. Assistance programs to farmers, if they exist at all, typically benefit only large-scale commercial landowners and may, ironically, render even more unfavorable conditions for peasants who could find themselves removed from the land they have worked for generations. Such conditions may be worsened in the context of lingering ethnic-, racial-, and gender-related discrimination, along with strife and disorder associated with civil wars and refugee migrations out of rural areas.

In stark contrast to these hardships, the busy hustle of the city offers an opportunity for migrants to find a new life, however difficult that may be. Workers willing to work hard for little pay and endure crowded, unsanitary living conditions are needed at every turn in the cities. Spare hands are necessary to manufacture, carry, and sell goods all across the city. Workers are also needed to build and maintain roads and construct the new buildings going up to accommodate burgeoning populations. Others will be called upon to clean, cook, and look after the welfare of already established higher-income residents. Wage and employment differentials with rural areas can be significant, but even more, the longer-term prospects of a better life for oneself and future generations keeps many rural transplants in place. Access to neighborhood schools, modern hospitals, clean water and electricity, public transportation, and a host of other public services are other, more tangible benefits available to city dwellers as soon as they arrive. The thriving commercial and entertainment sectors, as well the potential to experience a more open social environment, provide additional attractions to migrants.

Young adults are the most common rural dwellers to migrate to the cities. Their unmarried status and lack of economic and social standing in their sending community allows them the most returns for their effort. They also demonstrate more flexibility in adapting to the challenges of the urban setting, which is filled with extreme hardships for new arrivals. Most resort to living in crowded slums or in the streets as they search for employment, and then be willing to work long hours under difficult conditions. These are conditions most easily tolerated by those who are willing to sacrifice all while still young in anticipation of a brighter future. Migrants may also be disproportionately male in those parts of the world where unmarried women are expected to remain at home to look after family obligations.

The distinction between rural and urban classifications may become blurred in those circumstances were a pattern of circular migration is evident. Here, family members return back to the home community regularly after working for months at a time in the city. There are multiple outcomes possible with this migration strategy. One is to ultimately make a permanent return to the rural village after a decade or two of work in the city has resulted in substantial savings. Acquiring land to farm or starting a new business in the home village may become real possibilities to those who have succeeded in this strategy. The viability of this option, however, may be undermined by the difficulty returning laborers have in securing employment after each visit home. Work may be no longer available, or employers may refuse to rehire workers who show high rates of absenteeism. Remaining in the city, on the other hand, results in increased social costs to migrants, who experience strains in their relationships with relatives who continue to demand that they honor obligations at home. Such circumstances may lead to the alternative outcome, which is permanent relocation to the city. Others may arrive at this outcome simply because conditions in the rural community have worsened during their absence. A decline in the availability of land to farm, or even the outbreak of civil strife may be evident under these circumstances. The absence of welfare benefits such as old-age pensions, difficulty in finding suitable work, and the high cost of living in the cities may mean this trade-off is a difficult one for older urban migrants who find they must rely on an entirely new social network in the urban setting.

Challenges of Urban Growth

Cities are ever-changing. The size of an urban population, its composition, and the relative well-being of its people are variables, not constants over time. Urban systems are deeply influenced by shifts in economic conditions that occur at both the national and global level. The economic base of an urban region must concomitantly adjust to guarantee survival. For established urban areas in the advanced industrialized countries of Western Europe, North America, and East Asia, concerns over changes in the composition of their urban populations resulting from foreign immigration are matched by more profound questions about chronic urban poverty and a decline in once vibrant industrial manufacturing economies. For much of the rest of the world, such challenges are compounded by the need to somehow accommodate the large numbers of people from rural areas that are crowding into cities that lack the capacity to absorb them.

Of first importance, all urban areas of the world are faced with pressing needs brought by hundreds of thousands, if not millions of residents for essential public services. Thriving urban communities need an adequate provision of clean water, electricity, smooth-running mass transit systems, sewage disposal, education for their children, parks and recreation for residents, and dozens of other essentials—most of which must met by regional and local authorities. Cities require massive budgets to accommodate such needs. Diverse and growing regional economies provide needed revenue bases to undergird massive public expenditure. Hence, there is much at stake in the competition among rival urban regions for business and employment.

General perceptions about the quality of life experienced by residents are a less tangible, but nonetheless a critical concern for city leaders. Decisions about whether to invest in local business, shop in stores, and purchase homes are shaped by perceptions of street crime, gang activity, and violence in schools. Air and water pollution, visual blight associated with deteriorating or abandoned buildings, and vulnerability to natural disasters also impact public perceptions in important ways.

A final challenge of urban growth is the capacity for governments to cross jurisdictional lines and work together to address shared policy concerns. In urban regions, problems like air pollution, traffic congestion, affordable housing, unemployment, and so many other issues are not limited to the confines of political boundaries. Neighboring communities are tied together in a thousand ways as residents themselves cross such boundaries on a daily basis as they commute to work, engage in shopping, and seek out entertainment. The need for cooperation, especially among communities with differing levels of resources, is lacking. Adjacent governments see one another as rivals, more often working toward contrary purposes than seeking out ways to work together.

References

Brugmann, Jeb (2009). *Welcome to the Urban Revolution: How Cities are Changing the World.* New York, NY: Bloomsbury.

Pacione, Michael (2009). *Urban Geography: A Global Perspective.* Third Edition. New York, NY: Routledge.

World Bank (2009). *World Development Report 2009: Reshaping Economic Geography.* Washington, DC: The International Bank for Reconstruction and Development.

2

Urban Growth Pressures and Sprawl in the United States

Background to the Current Crisis: Land Resources and Public Policy in the United States

The United States has long celebrated its productive farms, ranches, and natural beauty in song and verse. In recent decades though, newly built housing subdivisions, suburban office complexes, shopping malls, and accompanying traffic jams along congested highway corridors and side streets have become as commonplace as white farm houses, red barns, and verdant fields and forests once were. Translated into more emotional terms, the United States is presently in the midst of experiencing an unprecedented loss of open space—productive crop and pasture lands, along with forest woodlands, fragile wetlands, and other natural wildlife habitats.

These trends show no sign of abating any time soon, as Americans continue to move out to new homes on the fringes of metropolitan areas. Even in areas of the country that have seen less dramatic population growth, outward urban expansion into rural areas—a phenomenon known as sprawl—has proceeded at a tremendous pace without letup. For example, in just six years between 1990 and 1996, Little Rock, Arkansas witnessed almost a doubling of its urban area from 109 to 199 square miles, even though its overall population growth was nearly flat during that time period. Akron, Ohio experienced a slight population increase of 3.5 percent, while its urban metropolitan area grew by 65 percent. High growth regions of the Sunbelt states have seen even greater losses of open space. The Austin, Texas region, for example, experienced a 50 percent population increase between 1990 and 1996, while expanding its metropolitan area some 160 percent into surrounding land. At the national level, the U.S. Department of Agriculture (USDA) reported that 14 million acres of prime farmland was lost to urban development between 1982 and 2007 in 48 of the 50 states it surveyed (USDA 2007).

To most Americans, there is nothing particularly unusual about the sight of new houses under construction, and shopping malls and office park developments quickly going up around them. Many eagerly seek out such places for new homes, shopping locales, and business opportunities. In the eyes of critics, however, this kind of real estate development represents nothing less than a tragically unrecognized silent crisis in which Americans are rapidly squandering finite land resources at rates that are simply not sustainable. Chastising a decision making process mostly under the authority of local government officials, they are calling for an end to uncoordinated, sprawling development patterns and a shift toward public control through planning institutions that function at the regional and state level. Might such controls, however, put a damper on business expansion, job growth, and long cherished personal freedoms, as opponents fear? A heated debate is presently under way between advocates of private property rights and government regulation that has moved from local to state and even federal political arenas over the past decade.

Historic Evolution of Urban Land Use in the United States

Why has urban development in the United States followed such sprawling patterns, and what is it about these land-use patterns that create problems for society? In many respects, present day urban development patterns are merely an outgrowth of trends set in motion over the previous 200 years. A closer look at these past developments is needed in order to fully comprehend the current debate over sprawl.

The wide open expanses of wilderness of the New World invited much profitable speculation in land for many early settlers from Europe. From the very beginning though, there were countervailing forces at work. The notion of treating land as a marketable commodity was incompatible with the pre-existing Native American system of land use which was largely based on rights of universal access and subsistence needs. Aside from these claims, often forgotten are contrary forces that were at work among the settlers themselves. European settlers brought with them a long tradition of city planning that dated back to medieval communities in which municipal corporations possessed the independent authority to own and dispose of all vacant lands. Historians now recognize that with the blessing of the crown and colonial governor, much of the early municipal development of colonial North America was surprisingly orderly in the design of residential street grids, open public spaces, public buildings, and market places (Cronon 1983).

After the American Revolution, these traditions began to recede. Urban areas had become politically subordinate to their respective state governments, which now had enormous political clout under the new constitution. Counties were given more authority to act as agents of state government in many aspects of land-use policy, while municipalities and towns were restricted to only those powers granted to them under state charters or legislative enactments. As a consequence, cities no longer possessed any clear authority to control, let alone direct, the development of land within and beyond their boundaries.

The frontier now began to be developed by private land companies that purchased huge tracts, surveyed them, and then sold them off quickly to private citizens. With so much money to be made in speculation and sales, there was little support for restrictive land controls in the thousands of new settlements that were founded in quick succession in the decades that followed. Many early towns were actually planned on the basis of traditional grid designs reminiscent of colonial America, but a combination of rampant speculation and minimal government regulatory restrictions quickly reduced such orderly patterns into jumbles of crowded, noisy streets where residences were mixed with shops, taverns, mills, tenements, tanneries, and the like.

It was out the chaos of these nascent cities that a renewed demand for more orderly growth eventually returned to the political sphere. The rise of the industrial city in the latter half of the nineteenth century attracted people to urban centers seeking employment in the new factories, mills, and foundries. Many were crowded into hastily constructed multistory tenements that grew up around the factory sites. Streets became congested and dirty, and the odor of raw sewage and pall of coal smoke spewing out from factory chimneys rendered city life uncomfortable and hazardous. Land developers subdivided lots, sold what they could, and moved on without regard to the consequences.

Ill-equipped city governments found themselves facing the need to provide order in the midst of this urban chaos. The public was demanding a better quality of urban life that included access to clean water, waste disposal, sewage treatment, public education, adequate transportation, gas and electric power, along with other municipal services. Political pressure was soon brought to bear on state legislatures to enhance the independent authority of cities to govern land use and economic development.

By the last two decades of the nineteenth century, cities like New York and Chicago were enacting building codes and making use of professional design standards to realign streets and construct new sewage systems, water treatment plants, and other services. City governments also began to develop the first land-use zoning systems at this time as well. Their intention was to use the power of regulation to delimit the locations of industrial, commercial, and residential land uses to predesignated zones. This would enhance public welfare, stabilize property values, and better control the future spatial development of the community (Bruegmann 2006).

There were a number of legal challenges brought mostly by real estate interests who feared such laws were threatening their property rights. In 1926, however, the U.S. Supreme Court upheld the legality of this type of zoning in *Euclid v. Ambler Realty,* and soon thereafter model zoning codes were being promoted by reformers all across the country. State after state passed enabling acts permitting their municipalities to engage in planning—some, like New Jersey and Massachusetts, even made it mandatory. Public officials subsequently went to work drawing up master street plans, adopting official maps, and enacting zoning codes to enforce their new regulations. Henceforth, future urban land-use patterns would be indelibly influenced by the guiding hand of locally elected or appointed planning commissions and zoning boards.

Another significant response to the declining quality of life in major urban centers was the gradual expansion of residential settlement outward into suburbs. Until the arrival of the electric streetcar, the residents of cities were largely confined to living within distances of their workplaces that could be reached either by a horse-drawn cab or by foot. While some outer suburbs had developed just after the Civil War, most of these were refuges for the rich who did not have to worry about a daily commute to the city center. Streetcars enabled many more people to escape the crowded and dirty city for the bucolic life of the suburbs. Real estate developers quickly saw the market potential, and began to buy up thousands of acres along the streetcar lines so that they could construct modestly priced housing, most of which was built on uniformly narrow lots within an easy walk of the streetcar line. Advertising made much of the tree-shaded streets, broad open lawns, and leisurely pace of life in a setting where traditionally only the elite would have resided. Suburbs not only represented a place to live, they embodied a romanticized and idealized image of nature in contrast to the dehumanizing aspects of the city (Paton 1995, Bruegmann 2006).

With the growing popularity of the automobile by the 1920s, there was no longer any need to stay close to the streetcar lines. Consequently, urban development patterns began to spread out even more widely than before. The compact retail sales and business areas of pre-1920 era, clustered around the railroad terminals and trolley stops, now began to relocate along busy streets and highway intersections to capture the attention of automobile-bound commuters. This outward progression of the city was enormously costly, especially as residents were now expecting well-surfaced roads for their automobiles along with sewers, public water, gas, and other amenities that reached right up to their doorstep. The only way this more diffuse development could be affordable to homeowners was for local governments to underwrite these costs out of general property taxes. State money was also available, as was federal funding after 1916 through grants to state highway programs.

Some of these early suburbs were absorbed by the older cities as each grew ineluctably toward the other over the ensuing decades. More often, racially segregated suburbs sought to protect and preserve the perceived sanctity that their quiet, orderly suburban havens provided. The residents of these suburbs vigorously opposed urban annexation, hoping to keep out the noise, pollution, immigrant populations, and corrupt governmental institutions that they associated with the big city. State governments responded to these concerns by routinely granting recognition to these politically influential communities as autonomous municipal corporations. Once this status was gained, these suburbs made use of their new zoning powers to adopt ordinances intended to exclude undesirable development such as apartments and small-lot housing that was associated with low-income residents, and unsightly factories (Haar and Kayden 1989).

The Great Depression and World War II provided only a temporary lull in these urban patterns that now were firmly established throughout the United States. In fact, plans were under way to encourage urban growth even while the federal government concentrated on winning the war. This arose from concerns in the Roosevelt administration about the inadequate provision of decent housing for many Americans. The 1940 Census had revealed that one out of every eight urban dwellings had no indoor plumbing, and one out of every seven had no running water or plumbing of any kind. In addition, the nation faced a shortage of over seven million urban housing units by 1945. Subsequent state and federal policies were designed to address these shortages as well as satisfy pent-up demand that had built over the previous 15 years.

Most important were the generous mortgage insurance and loan programs that received a big boost toward the end of the war under the auspices of the Federal Housing Agency (FHA) and Veterans Administration (VA). The FHA provided federal guarantees to private mortgage lenders, lowering the minimum down payment to just 10 percent for homebuyers, and lengthening repayment periods to 20–30 years. The VA offered low-interest mortgages with no down payment required at all of qualified veterans. The federal tax code was also modified at this time to permit mortgage interest payments to be tax deductible. There were other federal and state subsidies as well. Funding became widely available for the construction of new regional airports, interstate highways, and tax-exempt bonds for the construction of schools, water treatment plans, and other public utilities that served the needs of suburbs. Low federal tax rates on automotive fuel also contributed. Thanks to these programs, millions of young families had the wherewithal to leave cramped apartments and duplex houses in older residential neighborhoods and seek out new single-family dwellings in the suburbs. Popular media programs and advertising on television also played a significant part in heightening the prestige of the suburban lifestyle among the upwardly mobile middle class (Jackson 1985).

All of these forces worked to generate a massive expansion of suburban growth after 1945. The 1950 Census indicated that 84.5 million out of 151 million Americans were living in metropolitan areas. The greatest share of this growth was in the direction of suburban communities, which had grown by 35 percent since 1940, while central cities increased by only 13 percent during this time. By 1960, two-thirds of the increase in 28 million people recorded by the census were living in suburbs, which now had a total of 60 million residents compared to just 45 million in the cities.

Urban development patterns would henceforth be guided by the preferences of suburban residents. Most pronounced in these communities was the use of restrictive zoning ordinances designed to shield these suburbs from the real or imagined evils of the older industrial city. Typically, this included minimum lot area requirements of one-half to one acre or more; minimum floor areas that would preclude less than substantial construction; and prohibitions on an array of multifamily housing that would effectively deny entry to any who could not afford to purchase a detached, single-family residence. Over time, central cities became surrounded by a suburban wall of exclusionary zoning that effectively denied entry to lower income groups, many of whom were racial and ethnic minorities. This trend was reinforced by official FHA policy, which for many years endorsed restrictive covenants on deeds that prohibited property from being sold to nonwhites. FHA loan officers were also prohibited from approving loans that would upset the racial composition of neighborhoods. African American migrants pouring into the booming cities during the 1940s and 1950s were steered into overcrowded, deteriorating ghettos where they were joined by Hispanics and other people of color (Lewis 1973).

By the latter half of the 1950s, another trend was occurring as retail businesses began to move out of the vicinity of older city centers and into these outer suburbs. Drawn by newly constructed highways, subsidized public utilities, low taxes, and a growing market of well-to-do suburban residents, retail storeowners found a much more amenable climate to do business. Some sought to relocate in strip plazas that provided them with a highly visible location along the main travel corridors out of the city. Others were attracted to new shopping mall sites, especially those located near the intersection of radial and concentric perimeter highways. With acres of parking lots and easy access for automobiles, suburban consumers saw little reason to look elsewhere to satisfy their shopping needs. A variation on the suburban mall, the "big box" discount chain, also grew rapidly at the confluence of major metropolitan travel routes (Hayden 2004).

This outward development pattern even affected the industrial base of U.S. major urban centers, which had historically served as the traditional mainstay of economic growth and job opportunity. Factories, mills, stockyards, and manufacturing enterprises sought out locations on the urban fringe where taxes were low and land was cheap, or moved out even further to rural areas in the southern states. Warehouses followed as well. Thanks to the newly built highways, distribution enterprises were finding they could more easily move freight by tractor trailers directly to strategically placed warehouses on the periphery of metropolitan areas. There, goods could be broken down into smaller lots for local delivery in the surrounding suburbs. This progression was encouraged by cash-strapped suburban local governments, who offered generous property tax breaks, cheap utility rates, and municipal bonding for roads and other services to lure new employers (Hayden 2004).

The disinvestment in U.S. inner cities was compounded by internal forces working against urban revival. Lacking a sound tax base due to the loss of large employers and a deteriorating urban infrastructure, these areas became afflicted with high rates of joblessness, crime, drug addiction, inadequate housing, and social distress. These problems in turn have triggered a growing set of demands on existing city services that are difficult to meet by beleaguered city officials. Older city governments have nowhere else to turn but to tax existing property owners at even higher rates. Even with substantial federal and state subsidies providing funds for economic development assistance, public housing, city welfare services, and education, the "greener pastures" in the outer ring suburbs seem to look a lot better. With open land available at affordable prices on the urban perimeter, safer streets, better schools and the rest, the alternatives are obvious. As a consequence, in a remarkably short period of time, older downtowns in central cities lost their monopoly position as the regional center of choice for entertainment, commerce, trade, and industry. Meanwhile, clusters of new suburban shopping centers and office parks have displaced these functions, and are evolving into full-fledged cities and new urban forms that have been labeled "boomburbs" and "metroburbia" in recent works (Land and Lefurgy 2007, Knox 2008).

Central city mayors have not gone down without a fight. Supported by those businesses that chose to remain downtown and real estate owners who had suffered big losses, they have vigorously pursued federal and state assistance to save their cities through redevelopment. These plans commonly began with massive clearance projects that entailed the demolition of older, rundown apartment blocks and dilapidated housing. This was followed by urban renewal projects that sought to reinvigorate the city with high rise buildings, indoor shopping malls, and entertainment centers along with spacious parking lots. Inner belt freeways were built at the periphery of these downtown redevelopment zones, with radial linkages leading out to the suburbs so that the middle class and wealthy could quickly move to and from their places of residence. Meanwhile, many of the low income residents displaced by these projects ended up in poorly conceived high-rise apartment projects, or were shunted into already overcrowded housing elsewhere (Hayden 2004).

By the late 1960s and early 1970s, prevailing urban development patterns were coming under increasingly critical scrutiny. The most pressing complaints about this "urban sprawl" came from two political movements who shared little in common at the time: (1) affordable housing advocates who operated from a largely minority base in the inner cities, and (2) environmental organizations who drew upon affluent urban and suburban residents for support.

The 1970 Census showed that more Americans than ever were moving to the suburbs. However, low-income families, especially racial and ethnic minorities, were mostly excluded from this outward movement. Part of the reason for this rising disparity had to do with economics. Those with low incomes or who were dependent upon welfare subsidies—regardless of race or ethnicity—simply could not afford to join their more well-off neighbors in moving out to the suburbs. Housing prices and transportation costs were beyond what these people could afford based on their meager incomes. Exclusionary zoning practices in the suburbs were also to blame, since these ensured that affordable housing would not be available outside the inner cities anyway. Complaints about the inequality of this situation came to a head in 1975 when the National Association for the Advancement of Colored People (NAACP) brought suit against the township of Mount Laurel, New Jersey. The case faulted local zoning for the way in which it deliberately excluded housing opportunities for low- and moderate-income families. The New Jersey Supreme Court decided in favor of the plaintiffs, ordering Mount Laurel to revise its zoning to correct these inequities and setting the precedent for affirmative, inclusionary land-use obligations among local governments throughout the state.

Although other states adopted somewhat similar fair housing laws, the potential impact of these policies was watered down in a U.S. Supreme Court decision in 1978. In *Village of Arlington Heights et al v. Metropolitan Housing Development Corporation*, they ruled that such laws only have a bearing if there is a demonstrated proof of intent to discriminate through exclusionary ordinances—a legal standard that has been difficult to establish. The fair housing agenda has also been deflected by countervailing political forces in the suburbs. Fueled by fears generated by school busing mandates, a striking number of suburban communities have stood firmly by their right to home rule, even going so far as to pass referenda against the provision of public housing, low-income housing, and multifamily housing in direct defiance of state mandates. Facing this kind of steadfast opposition, inner-city activists have shifted their attention to redeveloping existing minority neighborhoods where they have a natural political base, rather than trying to break into the white majority suburbs.

The other major force opposing urban sprawl emerged out of the nascent environmental movement. Alarmed by the rapid loss of natural habitats and threats of extinction, environmentalists sought to use local planning and zoning codes to restrict further development. Proposals ranged from stopping all further development (no-growth) that was especially pressing in vulnerable wetland environments, to placing restrictions that would slow down the process (slow-growth). Environmentalists in the suburbs were able to find natural allies among fellow homeowners concerned about the loss of scenic open space and historic properties in their communities.

In 1971, the city of Petaluma, California adopted the first significant local growth management policy in response to these sentiments. It imposed a quota of no more than 500 new building permits issued per year as a means to halt the pace of new development. The policy was upheld in federal court in *Construction Industry Association of Sonora County v. City of Petaluma* in 1975. It was found that the concept of public welfare is sufficiently broad to uphold the desire to preserve small-town character, open spaces, low density population, and orderly growth. Another key case in New Jersey at this time challenged the right of the city of Ramapo to impose a zoning ordinance that made issuance of a development permit contingent on the presence of public utilities, drainage, road access, and other public services. The state appeals court ruled in 1972 that this community had the right to determine the pace of its own development in order to better manage its own fiscal resources. These cases set important precedents for future growth management legislation at the local and state levels that began to appear at this time (Platt 1996).

The Contemporary Phenomenon of Urban Sprawl: Costs and Consequences

Sprawl patterns persist throughout the United States, fueled by a host of governmental policies that encourage real estate interests, homebuilders, banks. and insurance companies to underwrite the expansion. Since 1980, suburban population has grown ten times faster than central-city populations in larger metropolitan areas, averaging a net gain of between 2.4 and 2.9 million per year between 1988 and 1996. Almost 80 percent of Americans today live in metropolitan areas, and of these, a growing proportion, now over 60 percent, reside outside of central cities in suburbs. Even so, the highest rates of urban growth today are found in the most distant fringes of metropolitan areas. Dubbed "exurbs," these are typically unincorporated rural areas that can be as much as 40 miles or more from a central city. As more and more Americans move to the suburbs, the more dependent they become on their automobiles to travel to work, for shopping, school, and virtually every other activity.

These trends have had a dramatic impact on the land. Between 1960 and 1990, the amount of developed land in large urban areas of the United States more than doubled while population grew by less than half this rate. This can be seen throughout the country in greater or lesser degrees, with high growth poles like Los Angeles, Seattle, Denver, and Atlanta witnessing an expansion of their physical sizes from 80–100 percent. These trends are also evident even in regions of slower population growth and economic contraction. New York City's population grew by only 8 percent, but its area grew 65 percent in this time frame. Similarly, Chicago population went up only 4 percent, but experienced some 46 percent growth in size. The Cleveland area actually lost population by 11 percent, yet still expanded its land size by 33 percent.

The expansion of urban development ever further out into the fringes of metropolitan areas has brought mixed results. On the positive side, these trends reflect a boom in the suburban real estate market that has lasted for decades almost without interruption. Those who have purchased undeveloped lands on the periphery of metropolitan areas have reaped enormous returns on their investments. Homebuilders, developers, and real estate sales agents who have catered to the large market for spacious homes situated in large-lot subdivisions and multi-acre estate lots have also prospered. They have helped satisfy many consumers who are searching for an escape from the poverty, crime, underperforming schools, and other associated problems of older cities and inner-ring suburbs. Commercial developers have filled related market opportunities by locating shopping malls, office complexes, gas stations, and strip developments within reach of these new suburbs. Elected legislators, board members, and executives representing these localities also have gained much by taking the credit for delivering millions of dollars in federal and state taxpayer subsidies to their suburban constituents in through new highways, freeway interchanges, schools, and utilities that make it all possible.

The development of such large amounts of open space has also attracted backlash against sprawl among a diverse array of critics. Among them are farmland preservationists who point to the rapid loss of productive farmland that has accompanied urban sprawl. National statistics confirm a dramatic loss in farmlands during the second half of the twentieth century. Although rates vary from one state to another, land in farms dropped from 1.2 billion acres in 1950 to just 968 million by 1997, a 20 percent decline. The most dramatic losses occurred during the 1960s, when 7.3 million acres of farmland went of out production on average each year. Since then, averages of 6.3 million acres were lost yearly in the 1970s, 5.2 million in the 1980s, and in the first half of the 1990s, 2.6 million acres per year. While these figures suggest rates of decline have been slowing, the ongoing loss of such large quantities of open land represents a major challenge for preservation advocates (Daniels 1999).

Given the relatively flat, open, and well-drained nature of cultivated and pasture lands, it is not surprising that real estate developers view this land as being the most readily suited for their projects. In turn, the amount of profit to be gained by farmers selling off lands is well above what prevailing markets offer should this land remain in agricultural use. High estate taxes also make the transfer of such land from one generation to another unviable, as do rising property taxes that often accompany the encroachment of housing subdivisions and strip developments located within the proximity of a growing metropolitan region. With the average age of the U.S. farmer surpassing 50, and record numbers of farms being sold off to developers each year, some now question the very survival of farming in certain sections of the country (Daniels and Bowers 1997).

The loss of farmland poses serious consequences for those who depend on agriculture for their well-being. This includes the creditors, seed companies, tractor suppliers, and related businesses that represent the traditional mainstay of many local economies. Once a critical mass of farmers abandons the land, the entire web of support for agriculture quickly diminishes. The further farmers have to travel for feed, seed, fertilizer, machinery, and marketing services, the more difficult farming becomes (Daniels 1999). Added to the human cost, farmland losses most often occur in those regions of the country where soils are richest and most productive. This land, classified by the U.S. Department of Agriculture with its highest rating, presently comprises about 50 percent of all land under production in the United States, and accounts for 56 percent of gross agricultural sales, 86 percent of fruits and vegetables, 80 percent of dairy production, and 45 percent of meat and poultry production. Over half of the nation's 640 leading agricultural counties are either within or adjacent to major metropolitan areas (American Farmland Trust 1994).

The loss of open space also marks the destruction of life-sustaining wildlife habitats that include diverse wetland, woodland, and prairie environments. Even when sprawl leaves patches of green in between subdivisions and shopping plazas, studies show that it contributes to habitat fragmentation that disrupts migratory corridors and breeding patterns. While certainly not benign to wildlife, agricultural lands do provide habitat for grassland species and support migratory birds. The stubble in harvested fields and land lying fallow sustain a variety of diverse species.

Water supplies necessary to sustain wetlands are also threatened due to the need to pull more resources from already overtaxed aquifers in many parts of the country needed to sustain urban development. More serious still are dramatically high levels of nonpoint source pollution that are derived from yard pesticides, fertilizers, nondegradable debris, and other assorted suburban contaminant wastes that flow uninhibited through street sewers directly into local lakes, rivers, and estuaries. Additional harm comes through thermal pollution which results from water being heated on paved surfaces before funneling downstream into wetlands. Warmer water fosters algae growth which in turn leads to a loss of life-sustaining oxygen. When a region reaches a point where just 10 percent of its surface area is covered by impervious surfaces, significant environment environmental impacts accrue. Natural wetlands and riverine systems play a vital role in channeling, absorbing, and purifying rain and snowmelt that otherwise may pose a threat of flooding for surrounding areas. Impermeable surfaces like parking lots, paved streets, and building roofs eliminate the natural absorptive capacity of the soil to minimize the effect of precipitation. Building on slopes, ledges, and inappropriate soils further worsens the chances of erosion, and in the worst cases, fosters dangerous mudslides (Squires 2002, Barnett 2007).

A growing level of dissatisfaction about sprawl is also emerging from the very people who have chosen to reside in the suburban fringe. Part of this resentment comes from rising tax rates. As more and more residential housing is constructed in remaining open space, local governments find it necessary to raise the property tax burden on existing homeowners and businesses to accommodate the need for expansion of schools, roads, water, and sewage lines, electrical utilities, along with public safety services like police, fire, and emergency medical care. Many suburban residents also complain of a decline in the quality of life that initially drew them to purchase a home in such localities. Each additional housing and commercial development brings more traffic, turning connector roads and local highway systems into overcrowded nightmares filled with endless stops and starts (Gonzales 2009).

The quality of life for these suburban residents is also deeply affected by the design features of the subdivisions that they inhabit. In the pursuit of privacy, single-family units are usually spread apart by large lots along winding roads that often lack even a sidewalk to connect them. Houses are positioned along with shrubs and trees in a manner designed to minimize contact between residences. Potential outdoor gathering points that might bring neighbors together such as porches and sun decks are universally located in the rear of homes, facing empty backyards. Other places that could engender casual association with neighbors such as stores, restaurants, parks, and schools are situated far out of walking or even bicycle distance. Moreover, the high cost of housing and lack of available mass transportation to lower-income communities ensures that such residents also rarely interact with people who come from different ethnic, racial, and economic classes. Decades after civil rights laws were put on the books, the outer ring suburbs remain among the most racially segregated areas of the country. Some critics even contend that the design of these communities leads to social stress, purposelessness, and even acts of civic disengagement that lead to violence (Duany, Plater-Zyberk and Speck 2001, Wasik 2009).

Making Better Use of the Land: The Debate over Controlling Urban Sprawl

The controversial side effects of urban sprawl have been recognized for over 30 years by professional planners and policy experts. This section provides an overview of various policy strategies for containing sprawl, describing programs in some detail as well as the debates that have been sparked by them.

Containing Sprawl through Local Zoning

Communities experiencing rapid urban growth have found themselves overwhelmed by the enormous fiscal burdens created by new development occurring around them. Each new home and business has to be served with public water, sewage connections, access roads, as well as police and fire protection. The anticipated tax revenues from new construction are inadequate to cover these costs, so the burden must pass to others in the community. Faced with pressing financial concerns, local governments have two options: (1) raising property taxes, or (2) making use of growth management tools that are designed to mitigate the impact of future development. Given the general public disposition against higher taxes, it is not surprising that growth management has become a more desirable alternative for municipal and county governments since the 1970s. What forms of growth management have been adopted by local governments, and how effective have they been in containing sprawl?

There are a variety of instruments that local governments can utilize to better manage sprawl-induced growth patterns. The imposition of large minimum lot sizes, frontage requirements, and bans on multifamily dwellings in local zoning codes can have the impact of limiting the number of newcomers into an established community. Districts zoned for business can contain a variety of restrictions that keep out unwanted commercial development. However, these restrictions have not stood up well in the courts. They face opposition from real estate companies and developers since they can substantially limit their investment options and financial returns (Porter 2007).

An alternative is to shift costs for infrastructure to expansion to developers. Revenue gained from impact fees can be used to defray the costs of extending public infrastructure to new projects. Performance bonds are a similar means of covering infrastructure costs. These require developers to provide a lump sum up front at the beginning of a project that will cover the cost of all public infrastructural improvements. Once the project is completed, the local government reimburses the developer should all of the specified components be properly in place. Incentives are sometimes incorporated into these agreements to award developers with density bonuses, more flexible design, and more expeditious processing of approvals should they comply with community growth management objectives.

Comprehensive plans compel developers to work within a more forward-looking community vision that has been previously agreed upon by the community. Such plans can determine exactly what kind of growth a community desires, how it is to be paid for, and where it should be located. To ensure compliance with these plans, periodic project reviews can be mandated. These allow local planning boards to rate the acceptability of a project according to a predetermined point system based on features of the plan. Urban growth boundaries can also be incorporated into these plans. The metropolitan areas of Portland, Oregon, Minneapolis–St. Paul, and San Francisco have all established greenbelts as part of a larger regional comprehensive plan adopted by contiguous local governments.

There is no solid consensus today that local growth management laws actually achieve the goals intended. Property rights advocates contend that restrictive laws cause more harm than good by distorting the otherwise rational decisions made by consumers and producers in the real estate market. Restrictions have the effect of causing the cost of housing in newly developing areas to go up, thereby limiting the choices of lower-income home buyers seeking to move out to the suburbs. They also punish existing landholders unfairly by placing restrictions on their range of options, an especially unjust outcome for those individuals who had made their investment in land long before the regulations were adopted (Staley and Scarlett 1997).

Others argue that these measures have done little to stem the tide of urban sprawl any way. In fact, they charge, in some cases they even make it worse. Government efforts that circumvent the local real estate market merely encourage so called leapfrog development. This occurs when developers who encounter an overly restrictive regulatory environment in one town simply move out to the next community, worsening the problem of suburban sprawl in the long run. Leapfrog development has serious ramifications for all neighboring communities, even those seeking to limit growth. Facing fierce competition for new sources of tax revenue from neighboring communities that seem to be permitting more development brings pressure on elected officials to relinquish development controls. With the need to build new schools and roads and expand other essential services, local officials find it difficult to resist the temptation to avoid compliance with comprehensive plans in the hope that it will raise more tax revenues (Downs 1994, Staley 1999).

Statewide Prescriptions for Sprawl

Over the previous 20 years, the inadequacies of local growth management controls have led advocates to call for greater state-level involvement in combating sprawl. The logic behind this strategy is compelling. State agencies may be in a better position to regulate the impact of sprawl on regional transportation networks and environmental quality since problems like traffic congestion, air pollution, and water runoff extend far beyond local boundaries. They also possess the legal reach to sort out complicated political and economic issues that are generally beyond the ability of limited jurisdictions. States further possess the financial leverage and constitutional authority to get results. They can offer either inducements or mandates requiring local governments to develop land-use plans (De Grove 2005).

For several decades, efforts have been underway in all 50 states to advance more comprehensive land-use planning and growth management at the regional and local levels. In the years between 1971–1974, Oregon, Vermont, and Florida embraced statewide planning laws, following in the footsteps of Hawaii, where these concepts had been on the books since 1961. California and North Carolina also adopted strict land-use laws to regulate development in their coastal areas. Colorado also undertook limited state oversight in areas deemed to be of statewide importance.

Of all of these early initiatives, the most ambitious antisprawl strategy was enacted in Oregon. State law requires all local governments develop a comprehensive plan that establishes growth boundaries and adheres to statewide goals. State agencies are granted substantial regulatory powers to write and enforce rules and oversee the approval process of local plans. Although this strategy has not been without its critics, Oregon was able to bring together an initiative that overcame longstanding concerns about balancing state priorities with local oversight and implementation (Abbott et al. 1994).

The momentum toward further state involvement abated as opposition mounted in the mid-1970s against what were seen as unconstitutional state incursions on local authority. In its most extreme form, opposition stemmed from worries that state governments would override local zoning that prohibited unwanted facilities, such as power plants, prisons, trash incinerators, or wastewater treatment plants. The movement also diminished as development pressures abated due to high interest rates, inflation, and energy concerns. Still, even those states that did not opt for statewide growth management reforms did pass a multitude of laws that focused on either specific geographic areas or specific land-use issues such as farmland preservation, coastal zone management, floodplain regulation, housing, and solid waste disposal. In the absence of state-administered remedies, several powerful regional planning institutions also came into effect that include the San Francisco Bay Conservation and Development Commission, the Cape Cod Commission, and the Pinelands Commission in New Jersey.

Once development pressures resumed after both the early 1980s and 1990s recessions, additional waves of growth management laws have came into existence around the country. Eight states adopted growth management laws of varying magnitude and scope between 1984 and 1991. Florida led this trend with a series of tough growth laws adopted in 1985. The primary instrument in Florida became the principle of "concurrency" that was required in all mandated local comprehensive plans. New development is not permitted unless local plans demonstrate that the utilities, transportation, and other public infrastructural facilities are present or fully funded in time for projects to be completed. In 1986, New Jersey created a state planning commission to formulate a statewide development plan. Local governments henceforth were encouraged to develop their own growth management plans in conformity with the state plan through a negotiated cross-acceptance process. In New England, Maine, Vermont, and Rhode Island all followed suit in 1988 by mandating that their local governments adopt plans consistent with a statewide growth plan. This was particularly significant in Vermont, which already had in place nine regional planning agencies that review and permit developments of significant regional impact. Georgia, Washington, and Maryland enacted similar state laws in 1989, 1991, and 1992 respectively. Although these latter cases differ in details, most require consistency between local plans and state growth management goals, and often insert county or regional planning agencies as a new force for managing growth (DeGrove 2005).

New initiatives again came on to the scene in the late 1990s in several states as growth pressures renewed. Maryland adopted a "Smart-Growth" law in 1997 that channels all future state financial subsidies to areas of the state that are best suited for it. Zones designated by county governments as Priority Funding Areas are targeted for state subsidies while rural areas are set aside for open space preservation. Tennessee adopted a law in 1998 requiring its counties and municipal governments to develop comprehensive plans with urban growth boundaries in place. Once drawn up, state funding is relegated to designated growth areas with these boundaries. Other states simply sought to aggressively increase their commitment to open space preservation in 1998. New Jersey approved a measure to spend $1 billion over 10 years to preserve half of the state's remaining open space, while Arizona pledged an unprecedented $220 million for the same purpose while also tightening local planning requirements.

The decade following the year 2000 did not witness any additional states adopting similarly comprehensive initiatives. Resentment toward new state mandates has been growing, especially in the area of land-use controls. Instead of sweeping legislation, radical overhauls of zoning and restrictive policies, smart-growth initiatives have become more surgically targeted. Open space acquisition, changes in zoning laws, and the redirection of state funding for infrastructure following smart-growth principles are among the areas of the greatest activity. For example, in 2002, Pennsylvania governor Tom Ridge made a strong commitment to protecting green space from suburban sprawl through a five-year, $650-million Growing Greener initiative, which provides funding for protecting open spaces and cleaning up abandoned coal mines. Massachusetts governor Mitt Romney launched several initiatives to better coordinate growth policy through the state agencies responsible for housing, transportation, the environment, and energy. Under a "Fix it First" policy, Romney put a halt to most new roadway construction until urban infrastructure could be repaired; offered cities and towns financial incentives to change their zoning to allow more dense development in town centers, downtowns, and sites near train stations; and changed the way state capital funding is distributed so it goes to places that have planned or instituted smart-growth initiatives. His successors like Democrat Deval Patrick have built on these accomplishments with new programs tied to achieving greater energy efficiency. Michigan governor Jennifer Granholm blocked new highway construction in favor of repairing existing roads in urban areas, and established financial incentives to redirect investment into older cities.

Perhaps, the most significant state initiative came from California governor Arnold Schwarzenegger, who signed a greenhouse gas reduction law in 2008 that linked air quality standards with smart-growth planning. The law establishes a Strategic Growth Council that will award grants and other encouragement for smarter growth in California communities. In addition, developers receive regulatory relief in return for adherence to local "sustainable community strategies" that involve natural resource protection, more affordable housing, mass transit, sustainable land-use planning, and incentives for inner city revitalization. In spite of the recession that began at the end of 2008, new state initiatives continue. Most recently, the state of New York adopted the Smart Growth Public Infrastructure Policy Act in 2010 that requires state agencies to create Smart Growth Advisory Committees that would evaluate public infrastructure investments based on the smart-growth criteria.

Are statewide prescriptions for sprawl the answer? Any measures designed to bring state agencies into local land-use decisions are sure to invite contentious politics, especially in those states with a strong tradition of local home rule. Resentment often runs high when state bureaucrats are given unprecedented new responsibilities that mandate local compliance. Debates over land use are complicated by a mix of groups representing real estate, banking, commercial development, farming, property rights, and environmental interests, many of which have close ties and assistance from much larger national counterparts who see these state arenas as just one more battleground in a larger national effort.

The biggest objection from opponents is that state involvement in planning constitutes an unwarranted degree of interference in a process that is best suited to local government. They contend that state planning officials, environmental activists, and state courts insert outside agendas into a process that is better left to those who will have to live with the consequences. In response, mandated components of state growth management planning have frequently suffered from underfunding by legislatures and governors sympathetic to such complaints. In the case of Maine, the legislature completely withdrew its previous commitment to mandatory planning mechanisms a year after their adoption as a result of a backlash orchestrated by a variety of commercial interests and citizen's groups who feared losing local autonomy. Taken as a whole, the effectiveness of comprehensive land-use planning has come into question in recent years. Critics contend that plans rarely correlate with reality, and are more often ignored in the breech than followed by local planning boards and zoning authorities (Siegan 1997).

Preserving Rural Lands from Urban Sprawl

Is there any way to protect farmland that lies at the periphery of rapidly growing urban areas? Once urban development begins to creep into a rural area, property valuations rise that trigger a hike in taxes for landowners. Farmers face growing pressure to leave as commuters find their slow-moving farm equipment a nuisance on the road, and transplanted urbanites complain about the dust, smell, and pesticides they use on their fields. Farmland preservationists argue that some policy instruments do exist that can help. Bolstered by growing public concern about saving the family farm, a number of policy strategies have been tried by state governments since the mid-1970s.

The primary reason why farms are being sold for development has to do with the potential return these sales have for landowners. Why would any farmer want to continue to work the land for a return of $2,000–$3,000 per acre when a real estate developer will pay them $20,000–$30,000 per acre? The only way to offset these market pressures is to employ either disincentives to potential developers, or incentives to farmers to remain on the land. Disincentives include any policy that discourages real estate developers, potential home buyers, or business owners from locating in an area that has been set aside for agricultural uses. Agricultural zoning is one way to send this message. Local officials are authorized in virtually all states to designate a particular area in their community as being restricted to farm-related uses, combined with large minimum-lot size of 30, 50, or even larger acreage. Typically, these designations also include a significant setback around farm operations to act as a buffer zone between the farm and surrounding urban lands. While effective in the short run, there is no guarantee that this zoning will remain in place for a long period. Eventually, many farmers seek to relinquish their protected status, since zoning does not in any way enhance the existing market values of their land.

Another disincentive consists of right-to-farm laws that presently exist in 47 of the 50 states. These laws legitimize the practice of farming in an area by providing legal protection against nuisance suits that involve standard farming practices. Homeowners must put up with the discomforts of farming or leave the area. As with agricultural zoning, these instruments do nothing about rising property values, tax rates, and market forces that render farming increasingly unprofitable when development encroaches.

Incentive policies seek to provide a financial gain to those farmers who choose to keep their land in production. One type of incentive offered by all 50 states allows a preferential property tax assessment that reduces state and local taxation. As long as farmers keep their land in production, they will continue to enjoy lower tax rates. While this may be welcome relief, the amount saved in taxes is usually not offset by the large sums offered by developers. Tax breaks also do not guarantee that the land will be held as open space in perpetuity. They may even be part of a deliberate strategy by farmers who are seeking a tax break until the right price comes along. Even more persuasive incentives are programs give farmers the opportunity to reap the full market value of their land while remaining in full production. Fourteen states have enacted purchase of development rights (PDR) programs. Farmers are given the opportunity to receive a one-time cash payment (often accompanied by preferential tax inducements) for the full assessed market value of their farm in return for a permanent pledge to keep land in agricultural uses. The state government purchases the development rights by means of a conservation easement that is affixed to the deed for the land. While not required to do so, it is hoped that the farmer will use much of their financial gain to re-invest in the farm to keep it competitive, either by upgrading farm equipment or paying down related debts. Should the farmer decide to sell the land, it must remain in agricultural production by whoever takes it over, or revert to local authorities who then maintain it as open space.

Another variation is transfer of development rights (TDR) programs. This instrument differs in that it includes incentives for potential real estate developers to locate their projects in already existing urban areas. Under TDR programs, a local government issues development credits to local farmers equal to the value of their assessed land. The farmer then offers these for sale to developers. Once sufficient credits are in hand, developers are permitted to begin their projects in growth zones previously set aside for high-density urban uses. The advantage of these programs is that they enhance the capacity and clout of local government planning efforts by accomplishing the twin goals of preserving open space and funneling new development into appropriate areas. These programs work best in communities where concerted efforts have been made to develop comprehensive plans for future land use; otherwise land is preserved in isolated patches (Daniels 1999). Nonprofit land trusts also have been established to save agricultural land, in addition to conserving wetlands, wildlife habitat, shorelines, scenic views, and even historic properties. These organizations trace their origins back to the previous century, but have proliferated since 1976 when donations to land trusts were made deductable in federal taxes.

Open space preservation has sparked a heated debate in recent years. Critics contend that the decline in farms is not occurring primarily as a result of cities crowding out agricultural production. Rather, a host of other factors are at work that include changes in the global structure of agricultural markets that have brought stagnant commodity prices, growing costs of technology and other inputs, and the emergence of large-scale corporate farming interests that have driven down production costs around the country. The precise accounting of farmland losses over time is further muddled by federal programs that in the past have paid farmers to take crops out of production as a means for stimulating prices. Finally, advances in productivity attributed to better harvesting techniques, more intensive irrigation usage, higher yield seed varieties, enhancements in fertilizer, pesticides and other technological gains along with improved distribution and storage mean that existing farmland will be sufficient to meet the needs of the agricultural sector (Staley 1999).

The contention that there is a net loss in open space has also been contested. Presently, more than a third of the total land area of the United States is under public ownership or private conservation easements. U.S. Department of Agriculture statistics show that upwards of 95 percent of the total land area in the United States remains rural—either as forest, desert, cropland, or pasture—and less than 5 percent of all land is devoted to urban uses. Individual states do vary tremendously, with some having between 25–35 percent of total land area urbanized, but the national state-by-state average remains just 5.2 percent (Staley 1999).

Fighting Sprawl by Reclaiming Central Cities

Another way to counter the outward progression of sprawl development is to refocus public and private investment on deteriorating downtown districts and adjacent inner-ring suburbs. The hope is to reverse the forces that are pushing money and jobs out of central cities, but is there any policy that could reverse this trend?

Planners and urban reform advocates seeking to revive inner cities contend that the answer is "infill development." After 30–40 years of steady decline, inner cities usually have a large supply of old mills, factory buildings, and warehouses lying vacant. Many are aesthetically beautiful brick structures that are well served by existing water, sewer, gas, and electric utilities, as well as excellent high-speed road and rail networks. They also benefit from a centralized market location in the midst of large population concentrations, as well as nearby residential neighborhoods that desperately need employment opportunities (Barnett 2007). With relatively little investment, many of these buildings can be converted over to new uses that fill under-served market niches in downtown economies. Examples include incubators for new high-technology industries, manufacturing businesses, and even space for craft workers and artists. Others can be refurbished to provide loft apartments for people who work in the downtown area and wish to avoid long commutes out to the suburbs. Restored buildings have been acquired by community organizations and converted to low-income apartments or congregate housing for the elderly. Restaurants, small shops, and upscale commercial establishments can also been relocated into these buildings. Since older cities are situated along a major waterway, a logical connection can be made with waterfront development and accompanying park lands (Moe and Wilkie 1997, Flint 2006).

One major barrier to infill development in every older community is the presence of toxic waste contamination in abandoned industrial sites, known as brownfields. A survey of 180 older cities sponsored by the U.S. Conference of Mayors concluded that more than 178,000 acres of brownfields existed within the boundaries of these communities—an area equivalent to the combined total of land occupied by Atlanta, Seattle, and San Francisco. The survey also found that should these sites be properly cleaned up and developed, it would add additional tax revenues of between $955 million and $.2.7 billion annually, along with 675,000 more jobs for inner city workers. The major hurdle blocking such promising development are strict environmental rules imposed by stringent state and federal standards. Only in the last several years has the federal government begun to work with state agencies to modify existing environmental regulations and offer extra grant funds targeting cleanup efforts in these neglected sites.

Urban advocates further contend that inner city revival will never occur without the presence of an efficient rapid-transit system that links its residents to the outer rings of the metropolitan area. Otherwise, the shortage of low-wage labor in the suburbs and overabundance of unemployed workers in the inner city will be difficult to overcome. Highways that open access to the urban periphery provide little assistance to residents of the inner core who cannot afford to purchase automobiles that make such a daily commute possible. An expansion of bus systems further out into distant suburban locales, supplemented by the construction of new light rail lines would facilitate the movement of commuters both into and out of large metropolitan areas (Rusk 1993, Lucy and Phillips 2006).

Not everyone agrees with these proposals. Critics question the assumption that high rates of urban development on the metropolitan fringe constitute the fundamental root of the problem. They argue instead that ill-advised policies pursued by big city governments in tandem with state and federal subsidies are to blame for the exodus of jobs, businesses, and residents. The real problems lie closer to home in the form of excessive rates of taxation and inefficient and overstaffed city government departments that fail to administer schools competently, respond inadequately to rampant criminal misconduct, and engage in corrupt enforcement of housing and building regulations. Flawed public welfare policies that provide no stimulus to work are also a factor as well in these analyses. The fact that large numbers of upwardly mobile middle- and upper-income citizens are fleeing the city for life in the suburbs is a completely rational act, they contend, given the many push factors at work. The rising number of ethnic and racial minorities who are choosing to reside in outer ring suburbs is cited as evidence that this calculation is not entirely motivated by racial considerations.

The answer is not better planned cities, but cities that are freed of heavy-handed governmental control and subject more to market forces. To this end, critics call for policy prescriptions that are designed to spark competition and innovation in the delivery of urban services. They also hope to free up land resources by reforming zoning laws that are full of restrictive regulatory entanglements. This would create an environment that would encourage investment and entrepreneurial activity while reducing the influence of political calculations. Public subsidies for transit systems are viewed as wasteful and costly to the taxpayer, especially in an era when people prefer automobile travel and long commutes to their homes in the suburbs. Free market advocates, therefore, seek to privatize these services and permit the private sector to better meet the needs of consumers (Savas 1987l, Shaw and Utt 2000, Inman 2009).

Improving Life in the Suburbs

Life in the suburbs is not as ideal as real estate developers would like us to believe. Millions of Americans residing in low-density subdivisions that are far removed from work, shopping, school, recreation, and other amenities must spend inordinate amounts of time in their cars and minivans on a daily basis. Long commutes and hours stuck in traffic jams swallow precious time that could otherwise be spent with family, friends, and far more productive activities. They are also an inefficient use of energy, and take a toll on the family budget. The large-lot homes and wandering street patterns also keep people apart from those who reside in their own neighborhoods and inhibit neighborly interaction.

Critics blame zoning controls for encouraging sprawl. Such rules mandate that all the components of human settlement be strictly separated. Places of employment are rigidly separated from residential localities. Neighborhoods are separated by lot sizes, and so on. Much of this separation is based on priorities dating back to the early decades of the twentieth century, when residential areas needed to be protected from unregulated industrial enterprises. In more recent decades, separation continues based on the assumptions that all people are inclined to prefer automobile transportation, and have a natural disinclination against high density housing (Elliott 2008, Dunham-Jones and Williamson 2008).

Discontent with suburban development patterns has led to a new approach known as New Urbanism. Supporters share a conviction that planners and architects should follow an imperative to build community, and in the process, completely rethink and refashion existing zoning controls and outmoded urban planning concepts. The neotraditional form of development they hope to create possesses many attributes common to town planning before the era of automobile dependence that ended by the late 1940s. Critical to the success of these designs are much higher housing densities and more compact buildings that place both residences and commercial buildings within easy walking distance. Often cited in these designs is the "quarter-mile standard": the maximum distance that the average person will walk in order to get to important local destinations on a routine basis. Where this design principle is in operation, an entire array of shopping needs, professional services, dining, as well as visiting with friends can and should be undertaken without the need for a car and associated costly transportation infrastructure. Smaller streets organized into more compact grid patterns and allowance for on-street parking help to slow traffic down, making the streets safer for pedestrians and bicyclists. Parallel parking is encouraged except under the most extraordinary circumstances since this provides both a protective barrier for pedestrians and often eliminates the need for parking lots, which in of themselves are extremely destructive of the social fabric. This kind of transit-oriented planning then makes energy efficient bus and light rail commuter lines more easily accessible to the public as well (Dunham-Jones and Williamson 2008).

New Urbanists claim that tighter community bonds are encouraged by these designs which function to bring people out of their homes and closer together through daily face-to-face interaction. This can be achieved by making room for multiple-use development, which allows larger family-size homes to be located adjacent to more affordable multifamily homes and even apartments located over garages. Smaller yards and front porches bring people physically closer to their neighbors, as well as to passerby on the sidewalk and street. Commercial districts, parks, schools, libraries, and other public facilities are important gathering points for community interaction, and are located by design within close proximity of residences as well. Over all, the benefits are that people of very different backgrounds come into close proximity on a regular basis where tolerance and mutual respect are likely to be cultivated. It also assists law enforcement efforts, since residents are more likely to be aware of activities in their neighborhood (Morris 2005, Elliott 2008).

The New Urbanist critique of suburban living and prescriptions for higher density urban development has not been accepted universally. Those who disagree contend that more compact urban designs lead to crowded urban landscapes have more buses plying the streets, increases in traffic volume, reduced travel speeds, and greater air pollution. Higher housing densities further lead to increased housing costs and a worse crime rate than what is found in lower density suburban communities. Rather than rejecting low density suburban sprawl, free market advocates suggest that this form of development is an important contributing factor in achieving the high standard of living enjoyed by Americans. Growing reliance on the automobile for transportation has enhanced the efficiency of labor markets, since the relatively free movement they engender permits workers to better connect with employers who desire their skills. "Big box" retailers and shopping malls offer lower prices to consumers, and the technological revolution is allowing people to both work more and more out of their homes located in low-density suburban or rural locations where they do not have to worry about the many problems associated with urban life (O'Toole 1996, Cox 1999, Gordon and Richardson 2000).

Recent Trends in the Debate over Sprawl

The Smart-Growth Movement

The debate over urban sprawl has never represented a clean distinction between the forces of the free market and the regulatory state. Rather, they constitute rival notions of appropriate governmental intervention in the free market. Should the government continue to offer generous tax breaks, lending policies, and other inducements to developers that underwrite new development on the periphery of metropolitan areas? Or, should it redirect these subsidies to the inner cities and require that landowners and business entrepreneurs adhere to a variety of development restrictions that save the taxpayer money and preserve open space?

Concerns about sprawl and calls for growth management have been on the rise in U.S. politics in recent decades. Growth management has become popular among conservationists environmentalists, and urban reformers who are pushing for greater public investment in inner ring communities. Much less organized, but equally important are growing numbers of suburban residents themselves who are distressed by the loss of open space, rising traffic congestion, overcrowded schools, and worried about the rising taxes in their communities (Flint 2006).

Since the early 1990s, so-called "smart-growth" coalitions have formed around the United States based on the new consensus that seems to be emerging on sprawl. They espouse a philosophy that better regional planning and cooperation in metropolitan areas can bring positive outcomes for all concerned parties—environmentalists, advocates for affordable housing, farmland preservationists, banking interests, home builders, and real estate developers alike. While there are a wide variety of initiatives presently included under the smart-growth label, a few common elements are readily apparent. All seem to call for restricting public subsidies to more compact, higher density urban development on the metropolitan fringe. They also favor greater public investment in mass transit systems, and more substantial public and private investments in older, central city neighborhoods. Underlying these proposals is a strong faith in the notion that regional cooperation is vital in achieving these goals. By working together, older cities and newer suburbs that surround them can achieve the twin goals of suburban growth and urban revitalization. This is certainly the base upon which several recent statewide anti-sprawl initiatives have been built. In turn, a flurry of diverse urban coalitions have appeared in metropolitan areas promoting the smart-growth agenda, along with regional conferences, state legislative committee hearings, and considerable media attention (Bollier 1998, Flint 2006).

The Property Rights Challenge

Growth management has long faced a challenge from both citizens and business interests that perceive it as an attack on individual freedoms. The property rights movement came into existence to address growing concerns over federal environmental laws, state planning statutes, and restrictive growth measures. Alarmed by the ability of regulatory agencies to set restrictions on private land without compensation as guaranteed under the Fifth Amendment, groups at both the national and grassroots' levels were launched to deter or block uncompensated "takings."

These efforts were aided by an increasingly sympathetic majority on the U.S. Supreme Court in the 1980s. In particular, the court affirmed the validity of uncompensated takings claims among plaintiffs in two key decisions handed down in *Lucas v. S.C. Coastal Council* in 1992 and *Dolan v. Tigard* in 1993. In addition, many states have passed property rights laws to offer some means of redress for alleged grievances. In so-called "Look Before You Leap" (LBYL) laws, a takings liability analysis (similar to an environmental impact statement) is required by law. This exercise an assessment of the likelihood that a state or local regulatory action may result in a constitutional taking, alternatives that would reduce the impact on private property and reduce the risk of a taking, and an estimate of the financial cost for compensation if the action is determined to be a taking. Another measure designed to safeguard property rights is called takings quantification laws. These provide a trigger point after which inverse condemnation is presumed to have occurred—typically, this is set at 50 percent of the value of the property or more. Such laws automatically entitle property owners to compensation when evidence is provided demonstrating that the value of a property has been reduced by environmental laws or land-use zoning (Yandle 1995).

Federal Smart-Growth Initiatives

Does the federal government have a role to play in managing urban growth? Direct federal involvement in land-use issues has been a sensitive topic since these regulatory powers have traditionally been relegated to the states and their local governments. Consequently, few initiatives have been successful. For example, urban development grants established in the mid-1950s once mandated the creation of regional planning agencies, but these were stripped of funds and finally dismantled in the late 1960s after years of lobbying by local officials who resented this intrusion into their own jurisdictions. In 1970, a bill was introduced in the U.S. Congress calling for the creation of state-level land-use planning agencies that would prepare comprehensive inventories of natural resources, analyze economic trends, and prepare statewide land-use plans. Even though the National Land-Use Policy bill was pushed as an effective tool for accomplishing popular environmental policy goals, it too went down to defeat by a coalition of private business interests and local governments that feared a loss of local control (Plotkin 1987).

A more indirect means of action that has proven to be more acceptable involves the transfer of federal dollars to the states. Existing programs that fund the construction of new highways and roads, environmental protection, federally backed insurance for home mortgages, and tax policies that underwrite suburban home building can all be modified to address concerns over sprawl. The Intermodal Surface Transportation Efficiency Act of 1991, for example, mandated both regional planning and a consideration of mass transit alternatives in larger metropolitan areas. Incremental policy adjustments such as these were collapsed together into an entire platform launched by President Bill Clinton coinciding with the release of its fiscal year 2000 federal budget. The "Livability Agenda," championed by Vice President Al Gore, offered state and local governments a host of resources for containing sprawl, neighborhood revitalization, and fostering greater commitment to civic and community values. Better America Bonds were among the most significant instruments in this package of proposals. These committed almost $10 billion in bond authority to preserve open space, protect water quality, and clean up urban brownfields through partnerships among local governments, private land trusts, environmental organizations, and businesses.

The Lands Legacy initiative provided an additional $588 million for the purpose of land acquisition, open space planning grants, and farmland protection.

This ambitious effort to involve the federal government in a coordinated smart-growth agenda ended with the election of George W. Bush to the presidency. However, there were some initial indications that the administration was sympathetic to at least some of this agenda. For example, the Environmental Protection Agency (EPA) was headed by former New Jersey Governor Christine Whitman who was a strong proponent of smart growth in her state. Norman Mineta, who headed the U.S. Department of Transportation, had a record of past support for light rail initiatives. The 2003 transportation bill, TEA-3, did in fact reflect some of these priorities. However, funds were directed elsewhere. Reflecting the priorities of the Republican-controlled Congress, emphasis was placed on freeing up small businesses, homebuilders, real estate investors, and potential homebuyers from onerous tax burdens and regulations (Hendrickson 2004). In the 2004 election, former Vermont Governor Howard Dean attracted some attention and the endorsement of several prominent mayors by attacking Bush's policy of "neglect" and promising a $100 billion "urban affairs agenda" to address longstanding concerns. After winning the presidential nomination, however, fellow Democrat John Kerry decided not to feature urban issues in his campaign.

The national debate shifted back toward cities and urban issues with the presidential nomination of Barack Obama, a former grassroots community organizer from Chicago, in 2008. His platform promised a host of new initiatives to address affordable housing and community redevelopment. These issues, in turn, were wrapped up in bigger concerns related to health, clean energy, and the environment in his campaign platform. In the midst of the collapse of financial markets and the onset of the recession in 2008, housing foreclosures and insecurity came to the forefront of debate. The economic recovery bill adopted in the waning days of the Bush administration included massive new spending plans that could be redirected into a comprehensive smart-growth strategy.

Shortly after taking office, President Obama announced his intention to include smart-growth strategies in his plan to revive the U.S. economy and steer the private sector toward the development of clean energy and green jobs. Adopting the same "Livable Communities" label used by the former Clinton administration, cabinet departments were instructed to attack aspects of urban sprawl in the larger effort to revive the national economy. This effort was led by Ray LaHood, a long-serving Republican member of Congress and enthusiastic backer of smart growth who headed the Department of Transportation. His "Partnership for Sustainable Communities" launched an ambitious agenda that included the following:

- Provide more transportation choices. Develop safe, reliable, and economical transportation choices to decrease household transportation costs, reduce our nation's dependence on foreign oil, improve air quality, reduce greenhouse gas emissions, and promote public health.
- Promote equitable, affordable housing. Expand location- and energy-efficient housing choices for people of all ages, incomes, races, and ethnicities to increase mobility and lower the combined cost of housing and transportation.
- Enhance economic competitiveness. Improve economic competitiveness through reliable and timely access to employment centers, educational opportunities, services and other basic needs by workers, as well as expanded business access to markets.
- Support existing communities. Target federal funding toward existing communities—through strategies like transit oriented, mixed-use development, and land recycling—to increase community revitalization and the efficiency of public works investments and safeguard rural landscapes.
- Coordinate and leverage federal policies and investment. Align federal policies and funding to remove barriers to collaboration, leverage funding, and increase the accountability and effectiveness of all levels of government to plan for future growth, including making smart energy choices such as locally generated renewable energy.
- Value communities and neighborhoods. Enhance the unique characteristics of all communities by investing in healthy, safe, and walkable neighborhoods—rural, urban, or suburban (DOT 2009).

The centerpiece of this new agenda are the Transportation Investment Generating Economic Recovery (TIGER) grants that gave the U.S. Department of Transportation authority to allocate $1.5 billion in grants for innovative transportation projects across the country. The projects, funded by the American Recovery and Reinvestment Act (ARRA) were connected to the creation of jobs as part of the economic revitalization. Selected projects must foster job creation, show strong economic benefits, and promote communities that are safer, cleaner, and more livable. HUD awarded tens of millions of additional dollars in Sustainable Community Challenge Grants to help support local planning designed to integrate affordable housing, job creation, and public transportation. These proposals were derided by skeptics who criticized them as wasteful boondoggles that shifted too much authority of state and local planning to the federal government (Utt 2009).

New Trends in Urban Growth

In the midst of a slow, painful recovery following the wake of the worst economic recession since the Great Depression of the 1930s, new trends in urban growth now seem to be emerging. A shift toward redevelopment of urban centers has been tracked in recent studies, which show sluggish construction in the outskirts of suburbia. The U.S. Environmental Protection Agency (EPA) suggests that a "fundamental shift" has begun in the real estate market. In 26 of the nation's 50 largest metropolitan areas, their research demonstrates that the share of residential construction taking place in central cities more than doubled since 2000. The previous emphasis on single-family homes has shifted toward large, multifamily developments such as apartment complexes and blocks of condominiums, according to the study. Construction of single-family homes fell to about 600,000 units in 2008, down from 1.7 million three years earlier. High-density residential construction remained flat at about 200,000 units, the same number of units built before the "housing bubble" burst in 2008. This shift appears to be at least partly due to changing demographics. In denser urban centers, aging baby boomers have been joined by young people who remain unmarried and have chosen to not have children (EPA 2010).

References

Abbott, Carl, Deborah Howe, and Sy Adler, ed. 1994. *Planning the Oregon Way: A Twenty-Year Evaluation*. Corvallis, OR: Oregon State University.

American Farmland Trust. 1994. *Farming on the Edge: A New Look at the Importance and Vulnerability of Agriculture near American Cities*. Washington, DC: American Farmland Trust.

Barnett, Jonathan, ed. 2007. *Smart Growth in a Changing World*. Chicago, IL: American Planning Association Press.

Bollier, David. 1998. *How Smart Growth Can Stop Sprawl*. Washington, DC: Essential Books.

Bruegmann, Robert. 2006. *Sprawl: A Compact History*. Chicago, IL: University of Chicago.

Cox, Wendell. 1999. "The President's New Sprawl Initiative: A Program in Search of a Problem." *Heritage Foundation Backgrounder* (March 18) No. 1263.

Cronon, William. 1983. *Changes in the Land: Indians, Colonists, and the Ecology of New England*. New York: Hill and Wang.

Daniels, Tom. 1999. *When City and County Collide: Managing Growth in the Metropolitan Fringe*. Washington, DC: Island Press.

DeGrove, John M. 2005. *Planning Policy and Politics: Smart Growth in the States*. Washington, DC: Lincoln Institute of Land Policy.

Downs, Anthony. 1994. *New Visions for Metropolitan America*. Washington, DC: Brookings Institution and the Lincoln Institute of Land Policy.

Duany, Andres, Elizabeth Plater-Zyberk, and Jeff Speck. 2001. *Suburban Nation: The Rise of Sprawl and the Decline of the American Dream*. New York, NY: North Point Press.

Dunham-Jones, Ellen, and June Williamson. 2008. *Retrofitting Suburbia: Urban Design Solutions for Redesigning Suburbs*. New York, NY: John Wiley & Sons.

Elliott, Donald L. 2008. *A Better Way to Zone: Ten Principles to Create More Livable Cities*. Washington, DC: Island Press.

Environmental Protection Agency. 2010. *Residential Construction Trends in America's Metropolitan Regions*. Development, Community, and Environment Division Working Paper. Washington, DC.

Flint, Anthony. 2006. *This Land: The Battle over Sprawl and the Future of America*. Baltimore, MD: Johns Hopkins University.

Garreau, Joel. 1991. *Edge City: Life on the New Frontier*. New York: Doubleday.

Gordon, Peter, and Harry W. Richardson. 2000. *Critiquing Sprawl's Critics*. Policy Analysis Paper #365. Washington, DC: Heritage Foundation.

Haar, Charles M., and Jerold S. Kayden. 1990. *Zoning and the American Dream: Promises Still to Keep*. Chicago, IL: American Planning Association.

Hayden, Delores. 2004. *Building Suburbia: Green Fields and Urban Growth, 18202000*. New York, NY: Vintage.

Kimberly Hendrickson. 2004. "Bush and the Cities." *Hoover Institution Policy Review*, No. 126.

Inman, Robert P., ed. 2009. *Making Cities Work*. Princeton, NJ: Princeton University.

Jackson, Kenneth T. 1985. *Crabgrass Frontier: A History of Suburbanization in the United States*. New York, NY: Columbia University Press.

Knox, Paul L. 2008. *Metroburbia, USA*. Rutgers, NJ: Rutgers University.

Kunstler, James H. 1996. *Home From Nowhere: Remaking Our Everyday World for the Twenty-First Century*. New York, NY: Simon and Schuster.

Lang, Robert E., and Jennifer Lefurgy. 2007. *Boomburbs: The Rise of America's Accidental Cities*. Washington, DC: Brookings Institution Press.

Langdon, Philip. 1995. *A Better Place to Live: Reshaping the American Suburb*. Amherst, MA: University of Massachusetts Press.

Lewis, Eugene. 1973. *The Urban Political System*. Hinsdale, IL: Dryden Press.

Lucy, William H., and David L. Phillips. 2006. *Tomorrow's Cities, Tomorrow's Suburbs*. Chicago, IL: American Planning Association Press.

Moe, Richard, and Carter Wilkie. 1997. *Changing Places: Rebuilding Community in an Age of Sprawl*. New York: Henry Holt.

Morris, Douglas E. 2005. *It's A Sprawl World After All: The Human Cost of Unplanned Growth—And Visions of a Better Future*. Vancouver, BC: New Society Publishers.

O'Toole, Randal. 1996. "The Vanishing Automobile and Other Urban Myths." *Different Drummer* (Spring) 3: 2–62.

Paton, J. John. 1995. *The Suburbs*. New York, NY: McGraw-Hill.

Porter, Douglas R. 2007. *Managing Growth in America's Communities*. Washington, DC: Island Press.

Savas, E. S. 1987. *Privatization: The Key to Better Government*. Chatham, NJ: Chatham House Publishers.

Shaw, Jane S., and Ronald D. Utt, eds. 2000. *A Guide to Smart Growth: Shattering Myths, Providing Solutions*. Washington, DC: Heritage Foundation.

Siegan, Bernard. 1997. *Property and Freedom: The Constitution, the Courts, and Land-Use Regulation*. New Brunswick, NJ: Transaction.

Squires, Gregory D., ed. 2002. *Urban Sprawl: Causes, Consequences, and Policy Responses*. Washington, DC: Urban Institute Press.

Staley, Samuel R. 1999. *The Sprawling of America: In Defense of the Dynamic City.* Reason Public Policy Institute. Policy Study No. 251.

Staley, Samuel, and Lynn Scarlett. 1997. *Market-Oriented Planning: Principles and Tools.* Reason Public Policy Institute. Policy Study No. 236.

United States Department of Agriculture. *Summary Report: 2007 National Resources Inventory* (December 2009).

Utt, Ronald. 2009. "Obama Administration's Plan to Coerce People out of Their Cars." Heritage Foundation Reports Web memo #2536.

Wasik, John F. 2009. *The Cul-de-Sac Syndrome: Turning Around the Unsustainable American Dream.* New York, NY: Bloomberg Press.

Yandle Bruce, ed. *Land Rights: The 1990s' Property Rights Rebellion.* Lanham, MD: Rowman & Littlefield.

3

Urban Growth around the World

More people than ever before are living in cities today. This is the result of a steady expansion of urban places that is presently every country of the world which has resulted in a quadrupling of the world's urban population since 1950. In 2005, 3.17 out of 6.45 billion people resided in cities, and current trends show this number rising to almost 5 billion by 2030.

This growth creates new opportunities as well as numerous pressures that call for policy action, but these challenges differ around the world. As was shown in the United States in Chapter 2, in the advanced industrialized societies of Europe, East Asia, and the former Soviet Union, growth in sheer numbers is no longer a major cause of concern. On average, cities in these places are growing by only 0.75 percent per year. Rather, policy attention in the developed industrialized world has shifted to the need to revitalize declining urban areas while finding ways to accommodate expanding low-density urbanization taking place around the peripheries of cities. The loss of open space and threats to the environment are major concerns in these places today.

In the developing world, the need to accommodate the movement of huge rural populations into the cities far outpaces any other concern. The sheer size and scope of this is staggering. According to the United Nations, 324 cities with a population of over 750,000 registered growth of more than 20.0 percent between 2000 and 2010. The fastest-growing city among this group was Abuja, Nigeria, which experienced a 139.7 percent increase, followed by the Yemeni cities al-Hudayda (108.1% increase) and Ta'izz (94.0% increase). Regionally, 53.1 percent of these places were located in Asia Pacific, 24.4 percent in Africa and the Middle

East, 16.0 percent in Latin America, and the remaining 6.5 percent were in North America, Australasia, and Western Europe.

Measured on a regional scale, growth concerns are most pressing in Sub-Saharan Africa, where 45 countries average an annual urban growth rate of 4.58 percent. Southeast Asia comes next with a growth rate of 3.82 percent, while Western Asia (the Middle East) is expanding at 2.96 percent. South Asia's urban growth is 2.89 percent, and North Africa is only slightly lower at 2.48 percent. The only part of the developing world where urbanization has slowed down close to developed world levels is in Latin America. But even here, urban growth will not peak until 2015 when it is projected that 81 percent will be classified as city residents. Taken as a whole, the cities of the developing world are facing massive challenges related to employment, public health, transportation, pollution, and a host of other issues. This is especially evident when it is understood that today, one out of every three people who live in cities resides in a slum, and 90 percent of this population is located in the developing world. In the following section, we will explore the theme of urban growth in both worlds.

Urban Growth in the Developed World

Western Europe

The roughly two dozen countries of Western Europe comprise the largest urbanized region in the world, with an average of 75 percent living in cities and towns. This region has a very old urban tradition, with roots going back to the Middle Ages. Flourishing long distance trade and growing specialization of local regions in the European economy gave impetus for cities to develop and grow by impressive proportions hundreds of years ago. The establishment of global trading empires and the concentration of administrative, banking, and mercantile functions furthered the urbanization process so that by the eighteenth century, cities like Paris, Vienna, London, and Amsterdam were setting the standard for the entire world in art, architecture, and urban planning. The spread of manufacturing associated with the Industrial Revolution in Northwestern Europe stimulated urban expansion on an ever-widening scale.

The structure of older cities was radically altered in the rush to accommodate all of the new factories, foundries, and mills that sprang up. Older districts were cleared away to make room for factory complexes, port expansion, and railroad networks needed to move large quantities of raw materials, goods, and people in and out of densely populated areas. At a wider level, there were a range of services needed to maintain and promote new industrial growth: public transportation, housing for workers, schools, water, commercial districts, and countless other services and amenities. As the Industrial Revolution progressed, rising concerns about traffic congestion, noise, pollution, and interferences with the quality of life led to the first efforts to develop city planning. With an already well-established tradition of urban governance, reforms were adopted and new institutions were introduced to implement planning controls that it was hoped would better regulate growth. Growth was still quite haphazard in the nineteenth century, and it would take a new set of reform laws that originated in the twentieth century to really begin to establish the framework in place today. Inspired by visionary European architects like Raymond Unwin in Great Britain, Ernst Gloeden in Germany, and Le Corbusier in Switzerland, after World War II, it was hoped that growth would be directed into new town—"garden cities" that would be carefully planned and developed in non-urban locations interspersed with green belts of protected land (Pacione 2009).

Germany was the first to adopt building regulations, land-use controls, standardized procedures for expropriation of property, and systems of municipally owned public enterprises in the 1920s. Great Britain and the Netherlands were also early innovators in developing centralized systems of planning and regulation at the national level as well as subsidizing public housing and planning out new towns. Sweden and Switzerland followed with similar policies using a strategy that was more decentralized at the local level. In contrast, less industrialized countries of Western and Southern Europe saw little need to regulate much slower urban growth. For example, France did not begin to rigorously enforce its system of centralized land-use planning as its rural population began to move into growing industrial cities in the 1950s.

Urban growth rates in Western Europe accelerated in the two decades after 1945 in the postwar economic boom, reaching a peak in the 1950s when urban expansion averaged 3.3 percent per year. This caused a crisis in housing capacity due to the lack of building in the 1930s as well as extensive war-related damage in urban areas. Governments responded with massive investments in urban redevelopment and basic infrastructure. For example, Great Britain set out to construct 28 "New Towns" around London and other large cities in rural areas that lacked agricultural value. In time, some 1.4 million people were provided with new housing in these communities, and motorways and public housing were developed through both public and private investment (Alexander 2009).

Western Europe's postwar expansion took place in the context of surprisingly modest population growth. Since the mid-1950s, European cities have expanded an average of 78 percent whereas population has grown by only 33 percent. By the 1970s, population growth was dropping steadily, falling below 1 percent by the 1980s, and reaching an average of just 0.12 percent by 2000. Significant changes in the composition and size of households, families, and child rearing have also occurred over this time. The average household size is 3 persons with one-fourth of homes having only one person, while rates of divorce and cohabitation are high. These trends have triggered a dramatic expansion in the number of households as more and more people are living alone rather than as couples or with children. Great Britain, for example, is anticipating a 19 percent rise in the number of households in the country by the 2020 (Richardson and Bae 2004).

What does urban growth look like in Western Europe today? On the outer periphery of cities, a steady process of expansion along transportation corridors and accompanying suburbanization of formerly rural areas is occurring. This sprawling growth has eliminated the stretches of farmland and small villages that once separated cities, so that urban areas have coalesced into "conurbations," urbanized areas of a million or more inhabitants that now number almost 40 across the region. Most of these urbanized areas remain politically fragmented (Couch et al. 2005). Only a few of these clusters of cities are formally organized into a single metropolitan government like the 33 boroughs that comprise the Greater London Authority. Most function independently with little coordination among them. An example is the vast Rhine-Ruhr district in Germany that includes Dusseldorf, Duisburg, Essen, Wuppertal, and Dortmund and some 11.3 million residents. Another is the Randstad (ring city) urbanized region in the Netherlands where the four large cities of Amsterdam, Rotterdam, The Hague, and Utrecht, combined with adjacent developed urban areas comprise 7 to 10 million inhabitants, depending on how this urban region is delineated.

Most Western European cities were hit hard by the post-1960s deindustrialization trend. The closure of heavy manufacturing industries as a result of financial restructuring and relocation to less costly locations led to massive job losses in these places, decreasing tax revenues, and a host of related social ills. The shift to a service-based, high-tech economy has had a differential impact on the older central cities of Europe. Some, like Munich, Berlin, Rome, London, and Paris have been revitalized through a new emphasis on retailing, white-collar office functions, governmental administration and tourism, but many smaller industrial cities have struggled to find a new niche in the global economy. One successful effort to embrace this kind of growth that offers a model to other cities in Europe is the Munich Perspective, which was adopted by the city in 1998. The document is the culmination of years of discussion among diverse constituencies that has committed this thriving urban center to a vision of sustainable growth that promotes cultural diversity, tolerance, economic opportunities, and creativity (Munich Perspective 1998).

The outward expansion of urban areas has been triggered by both prevailing market forces and the willingness of governments throughout Europe to underwrite the costs of infrastructural expansion. New investment in thriving sectors like information services, high technology industries, and distribution has been directed toward the periphery of large urban areas where new businesses have located to capitalize on lower land costs and better access to transportation. The movement of business has been accompanied by an expansion of housing, as people have exchanged more enclosed quarters of the city for free-standing apartments and detached houses of adjacent suburban areas (Basse 2010). These trends have been accelerated by "retirement migration," in which older people leave such areas for smaller towns in the countryside or coastal belts on the Mediterranean periphery. All of this has contributed to a gradual decline in the quality of life in city centers, with derelict and abandoned factory sites and decaying public housing estates now commonplace.

In all European countries, the case can be made that city centers are worth saving. Given their historic role as political and administrative headquarters, they continue as a focal point for white-collar employment. City cores also remain a force in the cultural life of Europeans, attracting people from near and far to enjoy the arts, entertainment, and retail establishments. Education and health care are also important growth points for central cities. Flowing in to these places are foreign immigrants, who are willing to move into older, rundown urban districts of West European cities. Many of these new arrivals are of childbearing age, and typically have higher birth rates than national averages. This trend, however, has not cancelled out the net population loss from the cities, but it has minimized it. An additional category of people moving into the cities are younger, often single adults who are seeking to reside closer to universities, places of employment, entertainment, and cultural diversity. In either case, these new residents have helped to bring much-needed investment, revitalization, and energy to neighborhoods that were written off by more affluent citizens earlier (Phelps et al. 2006).

Urban sprawl has had the most marked impacts in areas with high population densities such as the coastal regions of the Low Countries, southern and western Germany, northern Italy, and the greater London and Paris regions. Cities in these areas have a planning tradition that promotes spacious, less compact garden suburbs. In much of the rest of Europe, cities have traditionally been more compact. Sprawl has been especially evident in low-cost investment magnets like Portugal, Spain, Ireland, and eastern Germany that have experienced accelerated growth due to outside investment as well as EU structural funding. The expansion of tourism and second-home building in already highly populated coastal strips in the Mediterranean region has been a major source of sprawl in these outlying regions. During the 1990s, coastal urbanization leaped ahead 30 percent faster than adjacent inland areas. The Mediterranean coast is particularly vulnerable to the side effects of urban sprawl. Identified as one of the world's 34 "biodiversity hot spots," dozens of rare and unique species are threatened by loss of habitat and the siphoning off of water resources for expanded urban uses as well as agriculture. In Spain, for example, the massive increase in golf courses has led to over-extraction of groundwater, triggering saltwater intrusion from the nearby ocean. Scenic mountainous regions favored by good transportation and communication with adjacent lowlands have also been under severe urbanization pressures in countries like Germany, Austria, Italy, and Switzerland. These mountain ranges are universally recognized as the main source areas for water for surrounding lowlands and also have very sensitive ecosystems under threat. Taken as a whole, the growth of urban areas and associated infrastructure throughout Europe consumed 8,000 km^2 of land in the ten years between 1990 and 2000, a 5.4 percent increase that is equivalent to the entire territory of the state of Luxembourg (EEA 2006).

Eastern Europe and Russia

Until the end of World War II, most of Eastern Europe and Russia was considerably more rural and less affluent than Western Europe. Urbanization was limited to relatively small provincial capitals and market towns. The era of communist rule altered this pattern. Government investment was poured into the development of new industrial centers connected by expanded rail networks. Central planning directives from Moscow advocated locating industries away from already established cities like Budapest and Berlin in order to maximize control over design. As a consequence, entirely new cities sprouted up in remote locations with inducements offered to rural workers to migrate to these places. In spite of these plans, larger cities that predated the communist era continued to grow since they had advantages such as better infrastructure, more skilled workers, and served as administrative nerve centers necessary to coordinate elaborate industrialization plans.

Cities developed in the era of state socialism took on very distinct patterns. Since the main focus was on meeting ambitious industrial production targets, most investment went into developing mines, transportation networks, factories, and related support facilities. Housing for workers was provided almost as an afterthought, with people crowded into nearby dormitories or older tenement buildings. In the post-Stalinist era, greater priority was given to housing, although state investment was never sufficient to entirely meet demand. By the 1960s, the outer fringes of industrial cities were being developed as "microregions" consisting of vast high-rise apartment blocks built to a standard design, along with shops and parks. Housing blocks were built in an unadorned and starkly uniform fashion to minimum space standards. Priority was placed on preserving agricultural land near cities to meet food production targets, so densities were kept high in these estates, and mass transit favored over private vehicular traffic. Consequently, urban sprawl was inadvertently minimized during the communist era (Pacione 2009).

Socialism contributed to an urban transformation of Eastern Europe and Russia. By 1989, 61 percent of the population of the 14 countries of Eastern Europe and the 15 formerly associated with the Soviet Union resided in cities with 100,000 or more people with 29 percent in cities of over 1 million. Today, only the Czech Republic is on a par with Western Europe as the sole country from this region with over 70 percent of its population urban, but the rest of Eastern Europe is catching up quickly.

The end of state socialism and introduction of market economies throughout the region is now exposing the urban areas of Russia and Eastern Europe to all the effects of globalization. The restitution of private property, privatization of state-owned assets, and openness to outside investment has deeply influenced patterns of urbanization. Once compact cities are now spreading out into the surrounding countryside. A big change from the earlier era has been the expansion of office space to accommodate the explosion in demand for commercial, retail, and office space. Growing employment opportunities in service fields like banking, retailing, real estate, and information technology have created a premium on such facilities. Foreign retailers have led this activity, which was initially concentrated in older city centers, but now is moving to affluent new neighborhoods located on the periphery of larger urban areas. Privatization of outdated industrial properties, many of which have serious environmental and aesthetic concerns, has resulted in some conversions to housing or commercial development. More often, however, these districts are left alone in preference for more distant locations situated along transportation corridors. However, this kind of growth has not been uniform. Cities that are best linked to the expanding service sector are projected to grow with new job opportunities and expanding foreign investment. On the other hand, the collapse of the industrial sector after the fall of communism hit urban areas dependent on a single heavy industry or mining complex particularly hard. Communities hit with high unemployment, environmental contamination, and poorly functioning urban services have experienced a net out-migration of able-bodied workers. Housing remains a critical issue. Between 20–40 percent of all housing in Eastern Europe and Russia consists of complexes with more than 2,500 dwellings—a figure that averages just 5 percent for Western Europe. Conditions in these estates are generally poor and deteriorating, with low energy efficiency, neglected maintenance and repair work, and limited technical infrastructure. This, too, is triggering an expansionary dynamic as new housing is located far outside these crowded districts (Hamilton et al. 2005).

The situation is brighter in European Union member states of the region that are experiencing significant new investment in manufacturing attracted by lower operating costs and taxes than Western Europe. Newly invigorated city governments working with private investors have undertaken redevelopment projects in downtown districts to accommodate this growth. Greater awareness of environmental quality and a desire for more attractive, livable cities is contributing to the development of a host of new amenities ranging from parks and theaters to stadiums and refurbishment of historic monuments. The need for institutional reforms remains very great, however. Strategic planning is largely absent and little regional cooperation is occurring, hence urban growth is taking on a haphazard character that threatens economic competitiveness in an increasingly globalized economy (Hamilton et al. 2005).

Future Directions for Europe and Russia

Urban sprawl has become a major concern of European policy makers in recent years. A variety of studies and increased awareness among the general public have brought calls for changes in public policy. In Great Britain, for example, an Urban White Paper was released by the government in 1998 offering a range of planning and housing initiatives at the local level. Communities were encouraged to increase urban densities and give priority to reusing urban areas rather than undeveloped green sites for new development. Similar directives have been emanating from Germany and several other northern European countries. In spite of these intentions, the forces of urban decline remain difficult to reverse. Surveys reveal that public fears of urban decay and preferences for a more tranquil suburban lifestyle outweigh positive incentives in older urban neighborhoods. People continue to associate high rates of violent crime, bad schools, traffic, and pollution with densely populated urban districts. The bulk of private investments in property and real estate over the previous 20 years continue to favor suburban housing, shopping centers, and business parks (Richardson and Bae 2004).

Is it possible that the European Union will serve as a vehicle for collective action aimed addressing regionwide urban growth pressures? A growing consensus seems to be emerging in the affirmative (Lewyn 2009). The European Environment Agency report titled "Urban Sprawl in Europe: The Ignored Challenge" published in 2006 offers a compelling argument in favor of this approach:

> Typically, in Europe today, cities flow imperceptivity across their immediate boundaries. This process is at different stages of development in different countries, but it occurs everywhere. At the same time, the responsibility for land use management remains divided between different administrations and this fragmentation of management, frequently exacerbated by the political tensions of neighboring administrations, may lead to incoherent and uncoordinated land use management. (EU 2006, 39–40)

Policy action at the European Union level will have to overcome considerable institutional barriers. Past treaties and agreements have traditionally consigned land-use planning decisions to member states, which in turn defer to regional and local authorities. On the other hand, substantial investment in economic development and infrastructure targeting economically distressed urban communities and underserved rural areas is directed through the EU's Cohesion and Structural Funds. In addition, new highways and infrastructure built as part of the Trans-European Transport Network are a major stimulus for new development that sprawls into the countryside. This program alone will be spending 225 billion euros in 30 projects by 2020. The direct involvement of the European Commission in environmental regulation also offers possibilities for greater engagement. Several of its functions directly impact land-use planning, such as analyzing the environmental impact of proposed developments, coastal zone planning, and river basin management.

In recognition of the close correlation between land-use planning and EU policy, the European Spatial Development Perspective (ESDP) was released in 1999, calling for regionwide policy action to promote balance and cohesion, improved competitiveness, better access to markets and knowledge, as well as wiser management of natural and cultural resources. Its impact was somewhat limited, as it was only intended to offer recommendations related to policy options for planning agencies. More recently, "integrated spatial development" has been addressed by the Territorial Agenda of the EU that aims at mobilizing the potential of European regions and cities for sustainable economic growth and more jobs (EEA 2010).

Japan and East Asia

Japan shares much in common with other industrialized societies. Its urban population expanded dramatically in the early decades of the twentieth century in the context of the country's rapid push to industrialize, jumping from 34 percent at the end of World War II to over 50 percent by the 1960s. This percentage is projected to increase to 80 percent in the next decade. As Japan has become more urban and affluent, it has experienced a dramatic drop in fertility rates as well as rising life expectancy. Today, birth rates are so low that population growth is expressed in negative terms at -0.191 percent. In 2005, Japan's population declined for the first time, two years earlier than predicted. Some 80 million of the nation's 127 million people are concentrated in an urbanized region that runs along coastal plains and interior valleys of Honshu and into adjacent areas of northern Kyushu. Leading all other areas is the metropolitan region centered at Tokyo, with upwards of 34.6 million people, while the metro region around Osaka–Kobe–Kyoto is over 18 million, and Nagoya metro region has over 8.7 million. Space is highly restricted in these crowded urban areas, with overcrowded roads, housing shortages, and heavy pollution. With the gradual restructuring of its manufacturing base over the past two decades, these urban areas are now also experiencing problems associated with derelict industrial areas.

Japan has found innovative ways to manage the expansion of its urban areas so that high densities can be maximized on very limited land areas. In so doing, the country sets the global standard for "smart growth" and energy efficiency. Public transit systems carry some the highest rates of per person use in the world. In Tokyo, for example, 63 percent of passenger miles are traveled by public transit through an efficient system of commuter heavy rail, subway networks, and street-level buses. This comes as a result of a longstanding tradition that promotes investments in public transit while discouraging automobile use through taxes and underinvestment in roads. With roads that are crowded and inadequate parking spaces for drivers, public transit is widely preferred as the quicker and more inexpensive way to travel city routes (Sorenson 2002).

Higher densities are further managed through permissive zoning of urban land. Although the country has enforced city planning since 1919, a tradition of official toleration for mixed land uses has always existed. In urban areas where space is at a premium, attempting to segregate residential, commercial, and industrial districts is an impracticable use of limited resources. Integrated building complexes that mix together commercial, office, residential, and even recreational uses in a single space are therefore common. Stores and shops built into the front of residences and narrow, pedestrian-friendly streets linked to residential areas enable many to hold onto the tradition of walking and shopping in their own neighborhood rather than traveling longer distances. Open space protection is a high priority, with a large collection of protected forests and park lands. Local governments are compelled by a strong ethic to protect and promote farming as well, even in the midst of highly urbanized areas where available land is scarce. Intensive farming in relatively small plots interspersed among urbanized neighborhoods serve as truck farms that supply fresh orchard fruits and vegetables to the community. Rice paddies remain commonplace in urban fringe locations where sufficient water is available. Expansion into the countryside often follows a called Land Readjustment (LR), where a preexisting, irregular pattern of agricultural land holdings is rearranged into regular building plots and equipped with basic urban infrastructure such as roads and drains. A percentage of each landowner's holding is contributed to provide land for roads and parks, and for some plots to sell to pay the costs of the project (Sorenson 2002, Sorenson et al. 2004).

Japan's neighbors in East Asia, South Korea, and Taiwan share many of the same characteristics. Both are highly industrialized urban societies at the leading edge of technological development and manufacturing. They also share a similar demographic profile, with low fertility rates and nearly stagnant population growth. Like Japan, a single metropolitan region dominates these countries. The city of Seoul and its surrounding area of South Korea are home to 25.5 million people; 48 percent of the country's total. The Taipei-Keelung metro area of Taiwan is home to 6.7 million or 29 percent of the country's 23 million people. Both of these countries have followed Japan's lead in seeking to guide urban growth into higher density, mixed use zones (Chou and Chang 2008).

In spite of these practices, urban sprawl remains a serious concern in the affluent, highly urbanized societies of East Asia.

The tradition of tolerant land use control has provided many opportunities for sprawling development that lacks basic infrastructure like roads and sewers, and has led to a backlog of infrastructure projects for local governments situated on the fringes of larger urban areas. The proliferation of new highways and other infrastructure supportive of automobiles over the past two decades is attributable to schemes designed to boost flagging economic growth. Shopping centers surrounded by large parking lots—a sight heretofore unknown in Japan, are now being built across the country (Sorenson 2004).

Canada

Urban growth in Canada resembles the United States in many respects. In expanding urban areas like Toronto, Calgary, and Vancouver, low-density suburban housing tracts and peripheral commercial strip development have been "swallowing up" open space for decades. The basic assumption that most travel will remain dependent on automobiles remains fully in place. Older industrial districts and adjacent urban communities suffer from joblessness, social breakdown, and a lack of new investment. Affordable housing is at a premium at a time when the Canadian government has reduced subsidies for public housing (Hodge & Robinson 2001).

In response to these trends, several provincial governments have adopted legislation that promotes regional planning and even the amalgamation of contiguous municipalities. One example is CityPlan, a comprehensive plan put together by the city of Vancouver over three years between 1992 and 1995. It is designed to reinvigorate older communities and guide future growth following sustainable principles that create a more "livable region" by protecting the region's green zone for agriculture and recreation, slowing urban sprawl, and cutting down on automobile travel by creating more complete communities. Local planners and municipalities now have tools to better regulate and control land use through a host of "smart-growth" measures such as changes to zoning that permit smaller lot sizes, in-fill development, mixed uses, and the conversion of abandoned land to new uses. However, real estate development remains subject to economic imperatives and the perceived tastes of the consumer market. Cultural traditions based on the assumption that the country's natural resources are inexhaustible retain a powerful hold on Canadians (Sorenson et al. 2004).

Urban Growth in the Developing World

The "developing world" comprises those countries that experienced the economic, political, and social impacts of imperialism from the sixteenth century onwards. While some regions like Latin America achieved independence from colonial rule in the first decades of the nineteenth century, others endured this status until after World War II. Either way, the fate of these countries was largely determined by the powerful nation-states of Europe, the United States, and Japan. Today, one of the most enduring legacies is a much lower standard of living that continues to lag behind the diversified, high-tech economies of the former imperialist powers.

Urbanization in Historical Perspective

Cities and urban civilization are nothing new in the countries of the developing world. The world's first cities appeared in the Middle East, India, and China not Europe or North America. The modern cities of the developing world today, however, are very much a product of social, political, and economic forces launched in recent centuries. From colonial times forward, cities played a vital role in the chain of surplus extraction, exporting raw materials while importing European manufactured goods. At another level, cities served as administrative centers used to monitor and control subject populations. New transportation infrastructure like ports and railways were put in place, while older structures and street patterns were selectively replaced to meet the needs of colonial administrators and business interests. Hence, cities represent a combination of older patterns alongside modern grid designs, monumental architecture, courthouses, offices, parks, and wide boulevards modeled on a European design. Separate residential districts were set aside for expatriates with amenities provided at a standard associated with the home country. Elsewhere, little urban development was pursued, and in many cases, local populations were even restricted from entering cities. Finally, the high degree of centralization established during this era further instituted a pattern of "urban primacy" in which a single city came to dominate all aspects of life.

Cities began to expand at a very rapid pace across the developing world after the end of World War II. In Latin America, countries undertook ambitious industrialization plans that attracted rural migrants. Elsewhere, departing colonial administrations in the newly independent states of Africa and Asia meant an end to residency restrictions and other laws that had limited indigenous business expansion. With the aid of international loans and foreign assistance, governments throughout the developing world invested resources in their urban areas to promote ambitious economic development schemes, university-level education, and expand the provision of health care and other urban infrastructure (Cohen 2004).

Today, urban growth in developing countries shows no sign of slowing down. While there is considerable debate among experts over the precise way in which numbers are being tabulated, few dispute the overall trends. Every month, approximately five million new residents enter the cities of Africa, Asia, and Latin America, absorbing some 95 percent of all global urban growth. In the decade of the 1990s, cities in the developing countries averaged an annual growth rate of 2.5 percent. At current rates, the urban population in the developing world will number 5.3 billion people, with 3.3 billion in Asia and another 1.2 billion in Africa by 2025. In contrast, the countries of the developed world (including the former republics of the USSR) will experience only a slight increase in urbanization from 900 million to 1.1 billion (UN-HABITAT 2008).

Cities of the Developing World Today

The growth of cities in the developing world offers many contrasts from earlier phases of urbanization in the developed nations of Europe, North America, and Japan. For one, industrialization is not the primary draw for migrants to the cities. While cities do offer opportunities in manufacturing and related support services, the rate of industrial growth lags far behind the migration rate in most of these countries. Workers are most likely to find employment in the informal sector through trading, processing, and distribution of goods, as well as service activities. It has been estimated that as much as 70 percent of all jobs are in the cities of Latin America, Africa, and Asia are in the untaxed, unregulated informal sector. The consequences are severe: cities that suffer from a shortfall in tax revenues are incapable of expanding needed infrastructure such as transportation, utilities, public safety, and education to accommodate growing demands (Davis 2006).

In the past two decades, restructuring of the global production cycle has offered new opportunities for industrialization in countries like China, Mexico, Vietnam, and Indonesia. These and a growing number of neighboring countries have become magnets for low-wage assembly work in factories and mills financed by foreign investors and corporations. However, the sheer numbers engaged in this work are far smaller in comparison to the more labor-intensive industrialization of the nineteenth century. In fact, much of the actual factory work is contracted out through the informal sector, and in many cases, makes use of underage labor and especially women who have few rights or representation by labor unions. Another difference is that migration to the cities of the developing world has been larger in volume and more rapid than what occurred in the late nineteenth and early twentieth centuries. Additionally, for those who arrive, there is greater accessibility to educational institutions and better health care, as well as new opportunities linked closely to the expanding global economy such as cell phones and the internet (Neuwirth 2006, Brugmann 2009).

Finally, massive slum areas of spontaneous, unplanned settlement dominate these urban areas, accounting for half or more of all housing. Slums at this scale and magnitude dwarf similar types of settlement in nineteenth century in Europe and North America. The widespread occurrence of slums has been attributed to both the sheer volume of persons seeking residence in cities as well as traditions of poor governance. While most developing countries inherited a top-down, highly centralized governmental administration that has the legal power to regulate land use, much of the actual development of real estate is done outside of the boundaries of these laws. Hence, traditions of widespread avoidance of the law and official corruption deeply impact the way cities have grown in the developing world (Cohen 2004, Brown 2010).

Life in the Slums

The archetypical city in the developing world today follows a predictable pattern. The central core is built around a well-planned street grid with modern office blocks and government buildings surrounded by expensive apartments, upscale retail districts, and parks. Emanating outward from this elite district are transportation corridors, with adjacent industrial and middle-class residential areas. Interspersed throughout this urban landscape are a vast collection of slums that are situated in less desirable living spaces, but also extend outward into the metropolitan periphery. Wherever there is available space, people take up residence. The growth of slums in the developing world exceeds any scale set in previous eras of rapid urbanization in the developed world. In 1990, there were 715 million slum dwellers worldwide, by 2000, this population had escalated to 912 million with a projection that this number will reach an astonishing 1.4 billion by 2020.

How is a slum or shantytown defined? This is a difficult question because these communities are made up of people who have no legal right to the land they are occupying. Hence, they are often referred to in planning documents as "informal settlements" or "unauthorized townships," if they are recognized at all. Residents commonly live in substandard housing in communities that are poorly served by public infrastructure. Such services that exist (electricity, water, etc.) are usually improvised by residents themselves. Focusing on this dimension, UN-HABITAT has defined slums as "a settlement in an urban area in which more than half of the inhabitants live in inadequate housing and lack basic services" (2006, p. 21). In this formulation, slum households face one or more of five types of deprivation, all of which pose serious risks to people residing in these places.

Lack of durable housing

The conventional definition for housing that lacks durability is any dwelling that does not have a permanent floor. Statistics show most countries have impressive percentages of durable housing under this interpretation, although some 133 million people's homes do not measure up to this standard. Since few countries collect statistics related to the durability of other parts of homes, such as roofs and wall materials, most agree that the figures for nondurable housing are grossly underestimated. In Nicaragua, for example, 65 percent of all homes had permanent floors in 2005, but only 9 percent also had adequate roofs and walls. The disparity in Bolivia is 84 percent and 28 percent. Also missed is the fact that many nonpermanent homes (as much as 1 in 4) are located in hazardous areas prone to flooding or mudslides. Others may be located in dangerous proximity to contaminated soil and water associated with industrial pollution, toxic waste, and effluent from sewage and garbage dumps.

Lack of sufficient living area

A lack of sufficient living space is defined as any home where three or more adults must share a bedroom in common. This form of poverty tends to be difficult to survey because people in slums often move from place to place, finding shelter with family and friends. Overcrowding of this type is associated with poor ventilation and hygiene, and is directly related to increases in rates of disease transmission, greater child mortality, and higher levels of negative social behavior. Conditions in slums are worsened since outdoor air is contaminated by motor vehicles in nearby streets. Industrial emissions can add to this toxic mix as well. Forms of indoor pollution generated by solid biomass fuels used for cooking and heating poses an additional threat, since they release irritants that increase the risk of contacting acute respiratory illnesses. In 2003, the United Nations reports that approximately 401 million people lived in housing that did not have enough floor space to accommodate the number of people residing in these dwellings. This constitutes 20 percent of the world's urban population (UN-HABITAT 2007).

Lack of improved water

Water delivered through pipes rather than by open pools and rivers is considered to be "improved" and thus suitable for human use and consumption. Under this measure, official figures reported to the United Nations by member countries show that 95 percent of the world's city dwellers were estimated to have had access to improved water in 2002. These figures can be very misleading, however, since there is no guarantee that its provision is in sufficient quantities, nor may it be affordable or necessarily free from waterborne parasites and other impurities. Slum residents commonly must make use of communal pipes that are shared by hundreds of neighbors and often have to resort to purchasing water from vendors. Even those fortunate enough to have taps running into their homes may have to endure recurrent water stoppages or low pressure.

Lack of access to improved sanitation

The absence of facilities providing for the sanitary disposal of human waste was a daily reality for 2.6 billion people (42%) in the year 2000, according to UN estimates. While most of this population is rural, 506 million city residents (25% of the world total) lack adequate sanitation—a statistic that encompasses not only the absence of household flush toilets, but also poorly designed sewage lines and treatment facilities. Lack of access to improved sanitation is a serious health concern. Those with inadequate sanitation are more likely to be exposed to a range of illnesses associated with waterborne parasites and food contamination. Poor hygiene associated with this problem further leads to higher rates of morbidity and child mortality. It is also impacts human dignity as people living under such conditions must endure daily intrusions into their most private affairs. This especially impacts women, who are subject to more restrictive cultural traditions of modesty than men. It is not uncommon for women to wait in long lines during the day to gain access to public toilets, or endure the danger and difficulty of seeking out toilets at night hours.

Lack of secure tenure

The people who have constructed shelter and operate businesses in slums exist in legal limbo. Residents generally have no formal rights to their property and operate businesses without permission. As a consequence, municipal authorities often have little tolerance for these people. Slum communities are regarded as eyesores, environmental threats, and havens for criminal activity. Powerful political and economic interests may also see such areas as holding great potential for redevelopment. Hence, slum populations face a real threat of eviction at any time. Slum clearances are usually carried out absent any prior notice by local governmental authorities, and are usually accompanied by brutality and violence. Those evicted from their homes face the loss of substantial personal investments in time and money, and have an uncertain future on the street.

Most people who reside in slums are there by personal choice. For some, especially new migrants, it offers an affordable residence in a location that is within a reasonable distance from places of employment. For others, the high density of residents translates into a large base of customers for their shops and eateries located within its confines or nearby. Slums may also provide readily available labor for factories, warehouses, and other unregulated enterprises that are also operating within its boundaries or in nearby districts. The close quarters and need for cooperation among residents typically fosters strong bonds among these communities, with a leadership structure and informal set of social conventions. Women and ethnic minorities may even find more opportunities in the freer social environment than the rigid one they left behind in rural villages (Neuwirth 2006).

No two slums are identical. Gradations among communities usually develop based on the amount time a slum has been existence. Those that are newly established face great uncertainty and are vulnerable to being demolished by local authorities at any time. They usually lack any public services, so residents have no electricity or clean water, and must dispose of garbage and waste in local canals and streams. In more mature slums, dwellings have become more substantial as single-room shacks are replaced by sturdier, multistory brick buildings. Dirt paths may become paved, and residents have the option to pay for access to electric utility lines, pipeborne water, and sewerage services that are extended into its neighborhoods.

Growth and Evolution of Slums

While slums offer a means of survival for desperately poor urban residents who really have no other alternatives, municipal governments traditionally have viewed slums as nuisances. They consist of unauthorized and potentially unsafe structures filled with transients who pay no property taxes and pollute the surrounding area with sewage and trash. At worst, they are seen as dens of criminals and regarded with disdain. At best, they are tolerated as an acceptable place where the poorest residents can fend for themselves rather than bother in established neighborhoods. There is also the view that such places are merely temporary holding areas for people who will move on once they earn enough money to find better accommodations elsewhere. As the needs of the city change in the future, slums can be cleared and the land utilized for other types of development as has been the case with Dharavi, a thriving slum in Mumbai, India.

Urbanization is not a uniform process in the developing world. It is taking place in the context of highly variable political, economic, social, and cultural factors. In the section that follows, these differing patterns will be traced in the context of Latin America, Africa, the Middle East, South and Southeast Asia.

Latin America

Latin America comprises 38 countries that stretch from Mexico and the Caribbean islands south to Argentina and Chile. The population of Latin America and the Caribbean was 569 million in 2007, representing 8.5 percent of the world's total. While some Latin American countries are continuing to experience relatively significant population growth, the trend has been toward a slowing down of growth. The region's population doubled between 1960 and 1990, rising to some 440 million people, but has come down in recent decades as these societies become increasingly urbanized. At present, the average rate of population growth for the entire region is just 1.5 percent with the mean number of children (fertility rate) down to 3, which is half of the rate in 1960. Figures vary considerably across the region. The Southern Cone nations of Argentina, Chile, and Uruguay, plus Venezuela and most Caribbean island states fall well below this figure. More rural, underdeveloped countries like Guatemala, Bolivia, and Nicaragua remain over 2 percent.

No other region of the developing world has experienced the high rates of urbanization found in Latin America. Today, 77 percent of the region resides in urban areas, and this figure is projected to rise to 85 percent by 2020. There is a long urban tradition in this region and many cities have historical legacies reaching back hundreds of years from the colonial era. Nonetheless, urban populations were relatively small until the 1940s, when a general exodus from the countryside began. Urban growth rates peaked in the 1960s when cities grew an average of 4.6 percent annually, and have since slowed down to 3 percent. This move to the cities was triggered by rising opportunities in urban areas stimulated by government policies and foreign investment that favored industrialization in these locations. Extreme inequality in rural areas and general neglect on the part of governments to extend modern services into the countryside further pushed migration to the cities (UN-HABITAT 2008).

A significant proportion of the urban population in this region tends to be concentrated in a single metropolitan region that serves as the capital city as well as the main economic and cultural center for a country. Examples of this tendency include Montevideo, Caracas, and Lima. In 2000, one-fifth of the urban population resided in cities of five million or more. Four of these urban areas constitute mega-cities (population over 10 million). Mexico

City is ranked second in the world with 19 million, Sao Paulo ranked fourth at 18.8 million, Buenos Aires ranked nineth at 12.7 million, and Rio de Janeiro ranked thirteenth with 11.7 million. In recent years, these dominant cities have not experienced the rapid growth as in years past. In 2005, urban growth averaged just 1.7 percent across the region, and this figure is projected to drop to less than 1 percent by 2015. Much of this trend was reflected in the contracted growth in larger cities, of which two-thirds experienced growth rates of less than 2 percent. This was offset to some extent by smaller cities with populations between 100,000 and 500,000, which have experienced a higher rate of growth at 2.6 percent per year. Between 1990 and 2000, these small cities attracted half of all new urban dwellers. The spread of democracy throughout the region has contributed to this growth, as this had led to a significant increase in infrastructure spending from governments that have become more responsive to public input from diverse constituencies. Deliberate efforts by governments to decentralize functions, promote regional planning, and industrial delocalization by public and private investors have also contributed to this trend. So too has been the attractions of small communities, which offer an alternative to the high-cost business environment of the large cities, as well as relief from pollution, congested roads, crime, and other social ills. These policies have been most successful in Mexico and Brazil (Cohen 2004, Brunn et al. 2008, UN-HABITAT 2008).

Sub-Saharan Africa

The cultural area of Africa located south of the Saharan Desert comprises 47 independent states that include the large island of Madagascar and several island chains located in the Indian and Atlantic Oceans. The population for this entire region was 749 million in 2007. An average population growth rate of 2.5 percent for the region reflects the high regard and value children have in enhancing family status and their utility as a workforce and a source of security. Fertility rates average 4.7 children per female across the subcontinent in societies that are still overwhelmingly rural. This is the world's least urbanized region, with an average of just 31 percent of the population residing in urban areas.

Cities are growing at faster rates in Sub-Saharan Africa than any other region of the world with an urbanization rate that averaged 3.3 percent between 2000 and 2005. What is propelling this flood of migrants into Africa's cities? One reason is the extreme contrast between rural and urban life in the region. Few Africans living outside the large cities receive basic services such as electricity, pipe borne water, paved roads, and other public services. The finest educational institutions, hospitals, and such important public infrastructure as airports and governmental offices are also concentrated here. As important are more diverse and lucrative job opportunities unavailable outside the cities. In some parts of Africa, another reason for the push into cities has been threats to survival in surrounding rural areas from drought, crop failure, and famine. In a region troubled by political violence, guerrilla warfare, and civil unrest, it is not unusual for those seeking refuge to start a new life in the region's cities where more people of many different cultures live side by side. This has been the principal stimulus for urban migration in war-torn nations like Sudan, Somalia, Côte d'Ivoire, and the Democratic Republic of Congo in recent years, and in past years, Liberia, Chad, Sierra Leone, Angola, and Mozambique.

Urbanization in Sub-Saharan Africa tends to be concentrated in a single primate city. Typically located on the coast, these cities are often the national capital as well as the principal center for commerce, trade, industry, and culture. More than half of the urban population of Africa are found is in large cities between one and five million, compared to one-fourth in Latin America and one-third in all of Asia. The region has 17 of the world's fastest growing cities of more than one million, among which Nairobi, Addis Ababa, and Dakar lead the list. Growing at an even faster rate are smaller cities between 100,000 and 500,000, which average over 4 percent growth in the 1990s—the highest recorded in the world.

Africa's cities have developed around an urban core established during the colonial era. Expansion beyond this administrative and commercial zone was stimulated by the establishment of industrial zones which it was hoped would foster an industrial manufacturing revolution. While a small number of upper-level managers, bureaucrats, and senior politicians were favored with carefully planned housing estates along tree-shaded streets, the massive inflow of new arrivals otherwise overwhelmed limited budgets. Resources were either not available or misallocated so that roads, sewers, electric grids, water systems, schools, housing, and other vital services never kept up with the huge demand. In subsequent years, African cities have faced deteriorating conditions as more and more people continue to arrive. Conditions have worsened over the previous two decades as debt-ridden governments have experienced an evaporation of foreign investment, and stagnating growth due to overreliance on agricultural and mineral exports.

Cities in Africa today have lost a lot of the luster and appeal they once had. Beyond the small number of middle- and upper-class residential districts, most people must find a home in slums. Today, African cities have the dubious distinction of having the highest rate of slum growth in the world. Slums are expanding at a rate of 4.53 percent per year, which is just behind the total urban growth rate of 4.58 percent. In sheer numbers, this represents a population that grew from 101 million to 199 million between 1990 and 2001, and this figure is expected to double again to nearly 400 million by 2020. Slums house almost 72 percent of the population and thus, must be regarded as the norm rather than the exception. Even worse, the quality of life in Africa's slums is the lowest in the world when compared with other regions and governments have little wherewithal to address the deplorable conditions of these communities. As these cities expand, growth pushes ever further outward to places where migrants can find cheap land and escape planning regulations. Encroachment into rural areas has led to conflict and ethnic rivalry among indigenous landowners. The absence of infrastructure such as electricity, sewerage, and piped water in these new zones of settlement poses further challenges that simply must be addressed (Cohen 2004, UN-HABITAT 2007).

Middle East

The Middle East encompasses a band of territory 6,000 miles long and 3,000 miles wide that stretches from Morocco on the northwest coast of Africa all the way to Afghanistan in Central Asia. This includes 21 countries and the Palestinian territories, which totaled around 500 million people in 2007. Three of the largest countries; Turkey, Iran, and Egypt, account for almost half of this population and the two largest cities as well: Istanbul and Cairo. The Middle East is the location of the world's first permanent urban settlements, and today these cities still remain clustered near sources of surplus water in this otherwise mostly arid region.

For several decades, much concern was expressed about the high rates of population growth in this region, especially in light of scarce water resources and arable land. Within the past decade, however, population growth rates have begun to shift downward, falling to an average of just 1.9 percent by 2000. There is considerable variation in urban and rural contrasts, with on overall average of 56 percent the people residing in urban areas. The oil-rich Gulf States, Israel, and Lebanon are the most urbanized and have much lower growth rates that are close to 1 percent. Countries like Egypt and Syria that remain heavily dependent on labor-intensive agricultural exports have maintained a fairly steady rural-to-urban ratio in spite of the explosive growth of their cities. Others like Afghanistan and Yemen have less than 30 percent urban, and are experiencing rapid rates of change. Egypt, Sudan, Afghanistan, and Yemen all have growth rates well above 2 percent. There is considerable debate in the region about whether it is desirable or not for governments to promote family planning, and as in the case of Saudi Arabia, even strong resistance based on prevailing interpretations of Islam.

Increased levels of urbanization in the region have been the most dramatic in the oil-rich states of the Persian Gulf, Arabian Peninsula, and North Africa. Saudi Arabia jumped from 24 percent urban in 1980, to 81 percent in 2000, Kuwait went from 56 percent to 100 percent, while Oman was just 5 percent urban in 1980, but is 71 percent today. Much of the oil wealth flowing into these countries has been invested in coastal cities with ambitious plans to modernize and diversity local economies. New industries, and expanded service sector as well as educational institutions, hospitals, and other public infrastructure have been concentrated in these urban centers. This activity has resulted in critical labor shortages in the Arabian Peninsula that has added a steady migration of migrants from abroad to already fast-growing cities. In the United Arab Emirates and Kuwait, an estimated 80–90 percent of the urban population is foreign-born. Israel is also an immigrant magnet, attracting newcomers from the worldwide Jewish Diaspora. Urban growth has also been accelerating due to a tide of refugees seeking safe haven from nearby conflicts. The Israeli-Palestinian conflict has been the biggest cause for forced movement, with over 700,000 people resettling into neighborhoods and camps located in urban areas of Jordan, Syria, and Lebanon. More recently, the civil war in Iraq triggered an exodus of another half million people into neighboring countries (Cohen 2004, Brunn et al. 2008).

The rapid urbanization of Middle Eastern societies over the past four decades presents serious challenges to governments that are hard-pressed to accommodate the needs of so many people. Added to conventional demands like sewers, electricity, and transportation is the critical question of water provision. Nowhere is this problem more acute than in the large cities of Egypt, where waste and refuge are dumped into canals that are also used for bathing and drainage for industrial effluent. The rising number of cars has created severe problems with congestion and air pollution as well. Many governments have responded to these demands with major new investments. Egypt, Tunisia, and Morocco have all been recognized by UN-HABITAT for either maintaining or even reducing rates of slum growth through increased public spending on improved sanitation, water provision, and housing (UN-HABITAT 2008).

South Asia

The seven countries of South Asia are located on the Indian subcontinent and surrounding islands. Like the Middle East, this region experienced rapid population growth in the 1960s and 1970s that has dissipated more recently. Although this is still a very rural region with an average of just 28 percent of its people classified as city dwellers, population growth rates have fallen below 2 percent for all countries except Pakistan, and average is 1.7 percent today. The region comprises one-sixth of the world's population, and India stands out as the regional giant, with 1.13 billion of the region's total of 1.5 billion people in 2007. Pakistan and Bangladesh constitute much of the remainder, with 169 million and 144 million respectively.

South Asia will account for much of the global growth of cities in the decades to come. Already, there are over 450 million people, and this number is projected to almost double to 840 million by 2030. Over 60 cities in South Asia have metropolitan populations numbering over one million, and almost 400 more that are at least 100,000. India has some of the largest cities in the world; the metropolitan regions around Mumbai and New Delhi are each estimated to hold over 20 million people, while Kolkata (Calcutta) is over 13 million and Chennai (Madras), Bangalore (Bangalooru), and Hyderabad are each well above five million.

Growth of these large cities has declined in recent years. In their place, medium-sized cities of between 1 and 5 million like Kanpur, Pune, Jaipur, and Surat are averaging far more rapid annual growth above 2.5 percent. This trend can be explained as a reaction to the growing congestion, pollution, and relatively higher business costs in the largest cities, and the more favorable conditions in smaller cities that have more favorable conditions and better communication links. Another factor favoring this class of cities is their relative proximity to the distant fringes of India's larger cities. This is illustrative of a wider trend in Asia called the "doughnut effect" where urban expansion is emanating from ever-expanding, interlocked rings in between cities. Pakistan replicates India's pattern of multiple, competing urban centers. Leading them all is Karachi in the south with 12 million in its metro area where a terrific 5 percent growth rate continues unabated. The rest of South Asia demonstrates the more conventional developing world pattern of urban primacy, with a single large city dominating the life of the country. Of these, Dhaka, the principal city of Bangladesh, is experiencing 4 percent rates of growth and now has over 13 million in its metropolitan area (Dwivedi 2007).

Slum conditions are common in South Asia's cities. India is home to over 100 million slum dwellers—a number that accounts for 17 percent of the world total. Bangladesh and Pakistan are also notable for high rates of urban poverty. Bangladesh counted over 30 million slum dwellers in 2001—85 percent of its total urban population, while Pakistan had more than 35 million, accounting for 74 percent of its city dwellers. Taken as a whole, Bangladesh, Pakistan, and Nepal continue to lag behind India and Sri Lanka in addressing slum growth (Cohen 2004, UN-HABITAT 2008).

Southeast Asia

Located at the meeting point between the Indian and Pacific Oceans, the diverse collection of tropical peninsulas and islands that comprise the 11 countries of Southeast Asia illustrate many similar urban patterns. While all of these countries share a common experience deeply imprinted by European colonial rule, they took divergent paths at independence. Some like Thailand and Singapore embraced global markets and welcomed foreign investment; others like Vietnam were isolated for a time under communist rule. Today, all are in a race to develop through global market competition and are experiencing rapid-paced urbanization. Each is seeking to out-muscle the others in the race to become the next manufacturing hub for Asia. As such, enormous resources are being pumped into a few cities that serve as growth magnets. Yet the majority of the 574 million people of Southeast Asia remain largely rural, with urban populations that average just

38 percent across the region. The modern city-state of Singapore is an exception to this rule. There is a sharp bifurcation in living standards, marked by a fast-rising minority of 25–40 percent now living in large urban centers on the coasts and a much larger rural population engaged in subsistence-related production. A growing middle class in these cities enjoy access to a solid infrastructure, good schools, and other benefits. For the rest of the population, opportunities are limited. Today, other than the city-state of Singapore, only the tiny oil-rich Sultanate of Brunei and Malaysia have moved to a position where over half of their population are urban.

The rapid pace of urbanization and inadequate infrastructure and investment has meant that slums remain a significant part of the urban landscape in Southeast Asia. Few countries other than Thailand stand out as having made significant progress in addressing its slums. The number of people living in slum conditions in the country fell from over 2 million to just 119,000 between 1990 and 2005, according to UN statistics. This success is attributable to the government's long-standing commitment to improving housing for its urban poor. Indonesia and the Philippines have managed to keep slum growth rates low, while Cambodia experienced a high annual increase of 6 percent in the growth of its slums (UN-HABITAT 2007).

China

China is a nation of vast proportions. Fast-paced development and its growing role in the global market place it second only to the United States in economic clout. Its population of 1.32 billion makes it home to one out of every six people worldwide, yet its size is projected to decrease in the decades to come. China's population was growing at a rapid 3 percent pace in the 1960s and 1970s when the Communist government imposed its draconian one-child policy. The lingering impact of this policy remains in an exceptionally slow 0.5 percent growth rate that will lead to a projected contraction in total population in the future.

While the size of China's population has stabilized, its cities are experiencing record rates of growth. China today is in the midst of the largest single shift in population in the history of the world. As many as 150 million people have left the countryside for life in the cities, and an estimated 300 million more will make this move by 2030. As recently as 1978, 80 percent were still residing on the farm. Today, China's urban numbers have risen to over half a billion: 44 percent of the total, and this number is set to reach 50 percent soon. Urban growth averaged 3.9 percent per year between 1990 and 2000, and continues today at 2.7 percent with little sign of slowing down. Cities like Chongqing, Xiamen, and Shenzhen are currently expanding at an amazing 10 percent per year. Of the 100 fastest-growing large cities of over one million in the world, 33 are located in China. When this number is expanded to include the world's 324 fastest-growing cities between 2000 and 2010, 84 were Chinese.

Only three decades ago, the official position of the Chinese government was to actually discourage urbanization, especially in the country's coastal cities that were the traditional outposts of alien culture and capitalism. What forces have been behind China's explosive urban growth? One cause is an abrupt change in public policy. The shift away from a state-directed economy and a more permissive attitude toward private investment and market capitalism have allowed the county's large cities to return to their former status as China's main centers of trade, commerce, and industrial production. Special Economic Zones situated in coastal enclaves have been given extra latitude to experiment with new partnerships involving local governments, private investors, and foreign companies—a status that has now has expanded to include interior cities. Added to this has been a strongly pro-urban focus in public spending. The Chinese government has pumped vast resources into its urban infrastructure, modernizing and expanding the capacity of its cities to accommodate the expansion of business enterprises and the new population of urban workers necessary to help these firms succeed in regional and global markets. Nowhere has this growth been more impressive than Shanghai, which has reverted to its former status as China's premier center for international trade, commerce, banking, and finance. Its metropolitan population has pushed above 17 million and continues to grow as new mass transit systems, expanded seaports, airports; rail and road networks all expand its boundaries ever further into the surrounding delta. Residents in prosperous coastal cities earn on average five times more income per capita than those residing in China's interior provinces.

Generous public spending has not favored more remote interior towns and farm-dependent villages that house two-thirds of the population. Official policy regulates where a person may choose live, deterring further rural-to-urban migration. The "hukou system" that requires a residency permit to live in cities is no longer as rigidly enforced as it once was, but still is important for access to public services such as schools, health care, and housing. For those who are classified as "peasants," it is difficult to receive permission to reside in the largest, most prosperous cities where opportunities and pay are the best. They retain rights in rural land in their home villages, but are not permitted to trade this land, which is possible in urban areas today. Hence, inequality between rural and urban areas is rising, making it difficult and unpopular for the government to contain urban migration (Hsing 2010).

Infrastructure in China's cities has not kept pace with such explosive growth. In absolute numbers, China today is home to the world's largest slum population—totaling some 196 million, which constitutes 20 percent of the world total. About 38 percent of its urban residents endure at least some of the deprivations associated with slums. Substandard and overcrowded housing is frequently found in older inner-city areas, some of which have been cleared away to be replaced by new urban development. Peripheral urban zones on the fringes of the large cities have also witnessed slum growth. Much of this results from a high cost of living in the cities and the lack of affordable housing—an issue that has been neglected by policymakers until recently. One new program that marks a shift in attention to this issue involves "equity grants" in which the government auctions leases to developers willing to build housing for those living in substandard conditions.

Like cities in many other developing countries, Chinese urban areas face growth-related challenges with air and water pollution. Problems are so severe that it holds the dubious distinction of having 16 of the world's 20 most polluted cities. Water shortages are worsening in the dryer regions of northern and western China, giving impetus for large-scale water diversion projects that are drawing away funds that could otherwise be utilized for slum alleviation (Brown et al. 2010).

Future Directions in the Developing World

The explosive growth of cities throughout the developing world is symptomatic of deeper changes at work in these societies. The relative poverty and inequality of rural areas associated with low-value raw material production contrasts sharply with the higher standard of living and diverse opportunities available to people in the cities. In spite of the risks involved and crowded conditions of shantytowns, the bustling metropolis offers more chances to succeed than in the countryside. Given this state of affairs, governments face significant challenges with limit budgets. As people crowd ever more into the cities, there is a pressing need to stretch city services to help migrants succeed. As an alternative, greater investment in rural areas might improve life enough to induce some to remain on the farm. While international development agencies and the United Nations once pressed governments to consider more rural investment, the focus today is on expanding essential urban infrastructure. There is neither the political will nor the scope of resources today to meaningfully address the huge backlog of infrastructure improvements for rural dwellers. Hence, organizations like the World Bank are urging investments in urban areas as the chief priority. "If local and national policies do not change, much of the imminent urbanization will be characterized by more slums. Hundreds of millions of new slum dwellers will suffer from the relentlessly inhuman conditions that affect the already very large population living in slums" (World Bank 2008, p. 20).

What Can Be Done about Slums?

What can be done to alleviate the conditions of the urban poor? One of the most important ways to address the concerns of the urban poor is giving residents a real voice in politics. Democratic reforms are essential as a means of empowering the people with access to a free and unrestrained news media, the right to political organizing, and selecting their representatives at all levels. Through such mechanisms, slum dwellers can make their concerns known to politicians, bureaucrats, and judges in the courts and hold them accountable when they are pushed aside and ignored. City planning conducted in an open and inclusive manner—ideally in the context of a fully functioning democratic system—can offer a place at the bargaining table for representatives of the poor right alongside financial and commercial real estate interests that traditionally dominate decision making. Past practice has shown that there is no guarantee that objective criteria will rule the day. Powerful party patrons and wealthy campaign donors still hold a lot of clout. However, patronage politics can still work favorably in the interests of the poor, who ultimately hold their votes in the balance. Including entire communities in the planning process is never easy in any country. Achieving a coherent consensus can be difficult as slums are not homogenous. There are many diverse interests that encompass ethnic differences, different levels of poverty, landlords, and even criminal elements.

Even with the best of intentions, finding sufficient funding to upgrade urban slum districts is a serious challenge for many developing countries. Plans and promises must be backed with adequate resources that are needed for costly projects like constructing new sewage treatment systems, paving roads, extending electric utilities, and piped water into underserved neighborhoods. Too often, municipalities are forced to rely on national governments, which are pulled in many different directions and often utilize unwieldy top-down approaches with local governments to finance debt. Domestic capital markets are often underdeveloped or restricted by national laws, and therefore, much in need of liberalization. Even in the poorest countries, there is potential local investment capital available in pension funds, insurance companies, and with private investors should the right legal conditions be established. One way forward is for city governments to work through broad-based partnerships. Planning can potentially bring together all stakeholders that include real estate developers and financial institutions alongside nongovernmental organizations and community groups. Cooperation with outside aid donors may also work to bring additional funds into the picture (Pieterse 2008).

Another important reform is for city governments to pursue policies that enhance the security of tenure for slum dwellers. Otherwise, the threat of eviction and removal is ever-present—a reality that will inhibit investments people would otherwise make to improve their homes and property. From a political standpoint, enhancing tenure rights must begin with an acceptance that those who have built homes and improved the land illegally have established a claim that overrides other prior private or public rights to the same land. Once this is established, land registration and titling is necessary. This is not a simple process, since rival claims may arise that will need public hearings or even judicial action to remedy.

Even with titles firmly in place, other complications may arise. Usually, zoning and building regulations must be rewritten or less stringently enforced to accept existing buildings that often are not up to code and lot sizes that may be smaller than what is normally accepted. This is especially important should homeowners seek loans to improve or expand their property. Freehold title may also be problematic if an up-to-date land registry is not in place and local bureaucrats and courts do not enforce a consistent and fair regulatory framework. Finally, slum dwellers must accept the reality that they will be asked to pay property taxes on properties that were previously untaxed.

An alternative is for governments to make vacant land elsewhere in the city available to slum dwellers that face pending eviction from their homes. In these so-called sites and services programs, land can be platted out in advance, with adequate roads, utilities, and other improvements made to accommodate those who will be compelled to settle there. While these kinds of programs seem to offer an acceptable trade-off for the urban poor, they always have one significant shortfall: location. Municipal officials can typically only find land on the distant outskirts of the city to locate these new housing estates. In the absence of readily available transportation, the poor are left without the means to support themselves, as they had when living in a slum in or around districts where low-wage employment was to be found. As a consequence, relocation programs have been controversial, and quite often result in failure. The World Bank does not favor relocation unless existing slum areas are built on fundamentally unsafe or unsound land that is vulnerable to natural catastrophe (World Bank 2009).

Turning to the International Community

Can the international community contribute to alleviating slum conditions in the developing world? The United Nations and World Bank have long called attention to this issue as a critical matter of concern. In 1976, the UN Conference on Human Settlements (Habitat I) highlighted serious problems cities were facing with pollution and overcrowding, but mainly focused on the need to more evenly spread development to underserved rural areas. Slums were viewed as an unfortunate side-effect of misguided policies and should be discouraged by shifting more resources to rural communities. The "Global Strategy for Shelter" adopted in 1988, turned away from rural areas and pressed for more adequate housing and living conditions among the growing population of urban poor. It called on governments to remove obstacles and constraints on the private sector, and promoted the adoption of low-cost self-help housing assistance programs for slum dwellers. In the 1990s, the World Summit on Sustainable Development introduced the concept of "sustainable urbanization" while the second UN Conference on Human Settlements

(Habitat II) committed 171 governments to a pledge to provide "adequate shelter for all." With the adoption of the Millennium Declaration in 2000, time-bound targets and a system of data measurement and reporting were adopted to commit member states to poverty reduction, health and gender quality, education, and environmental sustainability by 2015. Included among the declaration was Goal #7, target 11, which called for achieving a "significant improvement in the lives of slum dwellers" by the year 2020. For the first time, this established a clear, time-bound target and authorized UN-HABITAT to focus the energies of member states on slum-upgrading programs.

International nongovernmental organizations have taken up the cause of slum dwellers worldwide. Among a host of relief and development agencies, perhaps one of the most innovative is Shack/Slum Dwellers International. Led by Jockin Arputham, himself a longtime slum dweller and activist from India, the organization works to assist and inspire slum dwellers to get organized for political action while also promoting a variety of self-help strategies (Neuwirth 2004). In the future, it is very likely that these partnerships will hold the greatest prospects for addressing slum conditions in otherwise resource-short nations.

Private Sector Solutions to Slums

The fast growth of cities in the developing world offers many opportunities for foreign investors. As people leave rural areas for the cities, businesses of all description can reach consumer markets far more easily than in the past, when poor roads and inadequate communication networks made access nearly impossible. In addition, a rising middle class centered around government offices, white-collar businesses, and universities are located in these fast-growing cities. This makes large cities the natural market for consumer goods and services aimed at middle- and upper-income households. Opportunities abound for foreign investors to offer solutions to the huge backlog in demand for urban infrastructure and services. Whether there is an interest in indirect financing or more direct marketing of products, there are abundant opportunities for foreign multinationals to partner with local governments, real estate interests, entrepreneurs of all description, and even nonprofits in and around the slums.

References

Alexander, Anthony (2009). *Britain's New Towns*. London: Routledge.

Basse, Ellen Margrethe. "Urbanization and growth management in Europe." *The Urban Lawyer 42* (4; Fall 2010): 385–407.

Brown, Denise Scott and Christina Crane (2010). Asia *Beyond Growth: Urbanization in the World's Fastest-Changing Continent*, San Rafael, CA: ORO Editions.

Brugmann, Jeb (2009). *Welcome to the Urban Revolution: How Cities are Changing the World*. New York. NY: Bloomsbury.

Brunn, Stanley D., Maureen Hays-Mitchell, and Donald J. Ziegler, eds. (2008) *Cities of the World: World Regional Urban Development*. Fourth Edition. New York, NY: Rowman & Littlefield.

Chou, Tsu-Lung, and Jung-Ying Chang. "Urban sprawl and the politics of land use planning in urban Taiwan." *International Development Planning Review 30* (1; March 2008): 67–93.

Cohen, Barney (2004). "Urban Growth in Developing Countries: A Review of Current Trends and Caution Regarding Existing Forecasts." *World Development 32* (1): 23–51.

Couch, Chris, Jay Karecha, Henning Nuiss, and Dieter Rink. "Decline and sprawl: an evolving type of urban development–observed in Liverpool and Leipzig." *European Planning Studies 13* (1; January 2005), 117–136.

Davis, Mike (2007). *Planet of Slums*. New York, NY: Verso.

Dwivedi, Rishi M., ed. (2007) *Urban Development and Housing in India, 1947–2007*. New Delhi: New Century.

European Environment Agency (2006). *Urban sprawl in Europe: The ignored challenge*. European Commission Directorate-General, EEA Report No. 10/2006.

European Environment Agency (2009). *Ensuring quality of life in Europe's cities and towns: Tackling the environmental challenges driven by European and global change*. European Commission Directorate-General, EEA Report No. 5/2009.

Hamilton, F. E. Ian, Kaliopa Dimitrovska-Andrews, and Natasa Pichler-Milanovic, eds. (2005). *Transformation of Cities in Central and Eastern Europe: Towards Globalization*. New York, NY: United Nations University.

Hodge, Gerald, and Ira M. Robinson (2001). *Planning Canadian Regions*. Vancouver: University of British Colombia.

Hsing, You-tien (2010). *The Great Urban Transformation: Politics of Land and Property in China*. London: Oxford University Press.

Lewyn, Michael. "Sprawl in Europe and America." *San Diego Law Review 46* (1; Winter 2009): 85–112.

MUNICH PERSPECTIVE – Our city's future (1998). Landeshauptstadt München. http://www.muenchen.de/Rathaus/plan/stadtentwicklung/perspektive/pm_en_m/41525/index.html.

Neuwirth, Robert (2006). *Shadow Cities: A Billion Squatters, A New Urban World.* New York, NY: Routledge.

Pacione, Michael (2009). *Urban Geography: A Global Perspective.* Third Edition. New York, NY: Routledge.

Phelps, Nicholas A., Nick Parsons, Dimitris Ballas, and Andrew Dowling (2006). *Post-Suburban Europe: Planning and Politics at the Margins of Europe's Capital Cities.* New York: Palgrave Macmillan.

Pieterse, Edgar (2008). *City Futures: Confronting the Crisis of Urban Development.* New York: Zed Books.

Richardson, Harry W., and Chang-Hee Christine Bae, eds. (2004). *Urban Sprawl in Western Europe and the United States.* London: Ashgate.

Sorenson, Andre (2002). *The Making of Urban Japan: Cities and Planning from Edo to the Twenty-First Century.* New York: Routledge.

Sorenson, Andre, Peter J. Marcotullio, and Jill Grant, eds. (2004). *Towards Sustainable Cities: East Asian, North American and European Perspectives on Managing Urban Regions.* London: Ashgate.

UN-HABITAT (2005). *UN-HABITAT's Strategy for the Implementation of the Millennium Development Goal 7, Target 11.* http://www.unhabitat.org/pmss/listItemDetails.aspx?publicationID=1805.

UN-HABITAT (2006). *State of the World's Cities: 2006/7.* London: Earthscan.

UN-HABITAT (2007). *State of the World's Cities 2006/7.* London: Earthscan.

UN-HABITAT (2008). *State of the World's Cities 2007/8.* London: Earthscan.

World Bank (2008). *Approaches to Urban Slums: A Multimedia Sourcebook on Adaptive and Proactive Strategies.* Edited by Barjor Mehta and Arish Dastur. New York, NY: World Bank Publications.

World Bank (2009). *Systems of Cities: Harnessing urbanization for growth and poverty alleviation.* http://siteresources.worldbank.org/INTURBANDEVELOPMENT/Resources/336387-1269651121606/strategy_exec_summary.pdf.

4

Chronology

1800 London is the first city in the world to reach a population of one million.

1853 Baron Haussmann begins a twenty-year project to restructure Paris with broad new thoroughfares that link major subcenters of the city with one another in a pattern which will serve as a model for many other modernization plans.

1867 The City of San Francisco enacts the first land use zoning ordinance in the country to restrict the placement of slaughterhouses and meat-curing plants in the city.

1869 A prototype for the world's first planned suburb is developed outside of Chicago at Riverside, Illinois under the direction of Frederick Law Olmstead and Calvert Vaux.

1877 The U.S. Supreme Court recognized that the public has an interest in the use and development of privately owned land in *Munn v. Illinois*.

1880 The U.S. Census reveals that New York City is the first community in the country to reach the one million population mark.

1888 The first electric trolley is constructed in Richmond, Virginia soon becoming the dominant means of transportation in the United States and a major impetus for the development of suburbs.

1891 The first private, nonprofit land trust is begun in Massachusetts under the name Trustees of Reservations.

1898 Delegates from around the globe gather in New York City for the world's first international urban planning conference.

1901 Charles M. Robinson, a U.S. journalist and pioneering urban planning theorist, publishes *The Improvement of Towns and Cities*, the first modern guide to city planning. New York City creates a tenement house department to administer and strictly enforce its building construction code, becoming a model for similar laws throughout the United States.

1903 Letchworth is founded in southern England as the world's first planned suburban "garden city"—a new design that was to incorporate elements of the country, alongside city life.

1906 Daniel Burnham and Edward H. Bennett prepare *The Plan of Chicago*, the first comprehensive plan for the controlled growth of a U.S. city, and an outgrowth of the City Beautiful movement.

1907 The Connecticut state legislature authorizes the creation of the first permanent locally elected planning board for the city of Hartford.

1909 The first metropolitan regional plan is developed for the city of Chicago under the direction of Daniel H. Burnham and Edward H. Bennett.

1909 The Wisconsin legislature is the first state to enable its local governments to adopt full planning powers. The city of Los Angeles institutes the first major use of land use zoning to direct its future development.

1910 The number of registered automobiles in the country passes the 500,000 mark.

1913 New Jersey becomes the first state to institute mandatory referral of subdivision plats for local government approval, instituting the beginning of subdivision control as a function of city planning.

1916 New York City adopts the first comprehensive zoning code in the nation.

1922 Los Angeles County adopts the first county planning board in the country as means for controlling the direction of suburban expansion.

1924 The city of Kitchener passes Canada's first zoning bylaw. Zoning, traffic regulations, and road widening are top priorities for Canadian town-planners during the 1920s.

1925 Ernst May begins applying revolutionary new urban design techniques to the city of Frankfurt that are quickly adapted to over twenty cities in Germany over the following decade. May later traveled to the Soviet Union to develop new urban planning designs. The planning commission of Cincinnati is the first to adopt a long-range comprehensive plan for a major U.S. city.

1926 The U.S. Supreme Court validates the use of comprehensive zoning for the first time in *Village of Euclid v. Ambler Realty Company,* becoming the constitutional building block for all future zoning ordinances. New York is the first state to provide public funding for the construction of lower-middle-income housing.

1928 The garden-city idea is developed in the United States at Radburn, New Jersey through first use of cluster zoning.

1934 The Federal Housing Administration (FHA) is created, with authority to provide insurance for private

1934 (*cont.*) home loans and establish minimum housing construction standards. The first federally supported public housing project is begun in Cleveland, Ohio. After 30 years of debate, a master plan to guide in planning for regional growth is adopted by the city of Paris, France.

1945 The Pennsylvania legislature passes the first state Urban Redevelopment Act.

1946 The New Towns Act is adopted in Britain, leading to the development of over a dozen new planned communities to accommodate urban growth.

1947 The first large-scale suburban residential housing project is developed at Levittown, New York, subsidized by federal VA and FHA loan insurance programs.

1949 The first Soviet-inspired urban-industrial city plan is implemented at Nowa Huta near Krakow, Poland. The U.S. Congress passes the Housing Act, which authorizes the first federal funds to support slum clearance programs in older cities.

1950 China adopts a new urban planning system designed to build "Socialist Cities" that will aim to increase the industrial labor force, create affordable housing for all, and organize people into communes and work units. Cities will reflect Soviet-style planning elements such as broad central avenues, large squares, and exhibition halls. The U.S. Census reported that suburban population had grown by 35 percent since 1940, while central cities had increased by only 13 percent.

1951 The first "new town" in India is developed at Chandigargh based on a neighborhood plan designed by Le Corbusier.

1956 The new capital city of Brasilia is begun under the direction of Lucio Costa and Oscar Niemeyer, representing a bold redirection of development inward into the Amazon. In the United States, the Interstate Highway Act provides $60 billion in federal funds to assist states in the development of over 40,000 miles of limited-access highways.

1959 The newly independent government of Singapore begins a comprehensive urban development strategy based on the new-town concept that will set the world standard for urban design.

1960 Pakistan begins construction of its new planned capital city of Islamabad as both a strategic move and to symbolically reposition the nation closer to the nation's heartland.

1961 Soon after becoming a state, Hawaii enacts the first comprehensive statewide land use law in the United States which puts all authority over development decisions in the hands of county and state officials.

1962 The population of the metropolitan region of Tokyo is recorded at 10 million, making this the largest urban agglomeration in the world.

1964 The first modern high-speed railroad system, called "Tokaido Shinkansen," opens for service in Japan.

1965 The U.S. Congress creates the federal Department of Housing and Urban Development (HUD), elevating federal urban policy to cabinet-level status.

1969 The U.S. federal government mandates that areawide regional planning agencies review all proposals for local participation in federal urban development programs.

1970 The U.S. Census reports that for the first time, more Americans were living in suburbs than in central cities.

1971 The city of Petaluma, California is the first local government to impose severe development controls

1971 (*cont.*) on sprawl in the United States. Reacting to popular alarm about the loss of rural lands to development and rising property taxes, the Vermont legislature adopts Act 250, which mandates that all large development projects be subject to review by regional commissions.

1972 Navi Mumbai or Greater Bombay, the largest planned city in human history, is begun on the west coast of the Indian state of Maharashtra as a twin city of Mumbai.

In the United States, the *Golden v. Planning Board of Ramapo* of the New York Court of Appeals upholds the legality of a zoning ordinance designed to manage growth. The California state legislature also passes the Coastal Zone Conservation Act, which establishes six regional commissions to prepare coastal plans in cooperation with local governments.

1973 Oregon adopts the Land Conservation and Development Act, the toughest statewide growth management law in the nation. It establishes 19 state planning goals designed to limit sprawl, and mandates that all counties and municipal governments adopt plans in conformity with state goals.

1974 The U.S. Supreme Court rules that school desegregation plans could not cross local government boundaries in *Milliken v. Bradley*, thus insulating suburbs from mandated racial integration and directly impacting the future development of metropolitan United States.

1975 The Mumbai Metropolitan Region is set up as an apex body for planning and coordination of development activities in this urban region. Mumbai has been India's fastest growing city for decades and is presently the fifth largest metro area in the world.

1977 Massachusetts and Maryland are the first states in the United States to set aside public funds for the purchase of development rights to safeguard productive farmland from urban encroachment.

1978 The United Nations establishes the UN Human Settlement Program (UN-HABITAT) after a meeting in Vancouver, Canada in a conference known as Habitat I.

1980 The population of metropolitan Mexico City reaches 13.9 million, an increase of 16.8 million in just 30 years as a consequence of massive rural-urban migration. This span set a new world record in both the pace and scale of urban growth in such a short period.

1982 China relaxes its internal passport system in order to ensure a plentiful supply of labor in newly established economic development zones, triggering the beginning of the largest rural-to-urban migration in human history.

1984 The Mumbai Urban Transport Project is launched by the Mumbai Metropolitan Region Development Authority to bring about improvement in traffic and transport primarily through the expansion of new railway projects.

1985 Florida amends its 1984 law by requiring each local government prepare and adopt local growth management plans consistent with regional and state plans. New Jersey passes a State Planning Act establishing statewide growth management goals, calls for the creation of a state development and redevelopment plan, and classifies all land in the state into categories that are designed to assist local decision makers in locating future development.

1986 The first "World Habitat Day" sponsored by the United Nations is observed with intention of encouraging people across the world to reflect on the pressing needs of urban places and the basic human right to adequate shelter.

1987 China adopts a new national strategy to control urban growth that aims to place strict limits of expansion of

1987 (*cont.*) its biggest cities (500,000+), shifting resources to the development of medium-sized cities (200,000 to 500,000), and especially concentrating on the growth of smaller cities (under 200,000). The newly elected mayor of Curitiba, Brazil, Jaime Lerner, implements a revolutionary urban development strategy that incorporated ecological and social concerns into city growth plans. This included a variety of innovative and successful programs that addressed urban service delivery, water pollution, and urban transportation.

1990 The U.S. Census reports that 102 million Americans—41 percent of the population, are residing in suburbs, while older central cities held just 17 percent. The state of Washington adopts the Growth Management Act which requires all counties facing serious urban growth pressures to prepare comprehensive growth management plans that are in conformity with state guidelines.

1992 Rio de Janeiro, Brazil hosts the UN Earth Summit. Leaders from more than 100 countries agree to the adoption of Agenda 21, a plan of action for sustainable urban development and planning.

1994 In *Dolan v. City of Tigard*, the U.S. Supreme Court rules that a jurisdiction must show that there is a "rough proportionality" between the adverse impacts of a proposed development and the exactions it wishes to impose on the developer.

1995 Malaysia begins construction of two new ambitious "intelligent cities." A new capital city that will be electronically connected to the world through a host of innovative designs is situated at Putrajaya, while Cyberjaya is developed as the center of country's high technology industries.

1996 The United Nations held a second conference on cities, *Habitat II*, in Istanbul, Turkey to assess two decades of progress since the 1978 Vancouver event and set fresh goals for the new millennium. Adopted by

171 countries, the political document that came out of this "City Summit" is known as the *Habitat Agenda* and contains over 100 commitments and 600 recommendations.

1997 Maryland enacts its Smart Growth Act. It mandates all local governments to designate growth areas that are most suited for development or redevelopment, and eliminates state funding for all infrastructure projects located outside of them.

1998 Vice President Al Gore announces the "Livable Communities" initiative, the first comprehensive federal plan to fight urban sprawl through enhanced support for urban planning, land acquisition, brownfields redevelopment, park restoration, and a variety of other components.

2002 UN-HABITAT is recognized as a fully fledged program, and establishes targets to meet its obligations under the Millennium Declaration.

2005 The world's urban population is estimated at 3.17 billion out of a world total of 6.45 billion. Trends projected that the number of urban dwellers will reach almost 5 billion by 2030 out of a world total of 8.1 billion. The population of metropolitan Istanbul more than tripled during the 25 years between 1980 and 2005, rising from 2.7 million to over 10 million.

2006 The planned development of Masdar City is begun by private developers and the government of Abu Dhabi, United Arab Emirates as the world's city to run entirely on renewable energy.

2007 For the first time in human history, more people are living in cities than in rural areas. In India, the newly elected Congress-led government announces it will spend $1.5 trillion over the next decades in funding the development and expansion of India's infrastructure to accommodate anticipated growth.

2008 Since 1990, China's urban population has doubled by over 150 million, and its urban land area has expanded by 150 percent. The urban population of India is recorded at 329 million, reflecting a 61 percent increase over the previous forty years and just under 30 percent of the total population of the country. The urban population in Brazil is measured at 85 percent (164 million) of the country's total population, rising from 60 percent just 30 years earlier in 1978.

2010 The United Nations declares the World Health Day theme will be "Urbanization and Health" in recognition of the health challenges associated with the rising number of people living in cities around the world. The world's fastest-growing cities in the decade of 2000s were found in Asia and Africa. Between 2000 and 2010, urban population grew by an annual average of 3.3 percent in the Middle East and Africa, and by 2.7 percent in Asia Pacific, compared with a global urban growth rate of 2.1 percent. In other regions, urban growth rates were far less, and in Eastern Europe, the urban population actually fell by an average 0.1 percent annually over 2000–2010. Guangzhou, China recorded the largest population growth in absolute terms, growing by 3.3 million between 2000 and 2010. It was followed by Karachi, Pakistan (3.1 million increase) and New Delhi, India (2.9 million increase).

5

Biographical Sketches

Urban growth is truly a global phenomenon today. Every society must find ways to deal with the challenging consequences associated with millions of their citizens living in close proximity to one another. With scarce land and growing pressure on diminishing natural resources, policy practitioners and researchers alike are pressed to find ways to accommodate the need for better transportation, affordable housing, efficient service delivery, environmental sustainability, and many other priorities. This chapter offers an all-too-brief list of a sampling of those individuals who have contributed in extraordinary ways to helping us better understand the nature of these challenges through their leadership in policy roles as well as conducting vital academic research. The list includes a broad range of experts from the United States and a number of countries around the world.

Geoffrey Anderson

Geoffrey Anderson is currently serving as the president and CEO of Smart Growth America, a coalition of nonprofit organizations committed to promoting sustainable urban growth. He came to this position in January 2008 after heading the U.S. Environmental Protection Agency's (EPA) Smart Growth Program for thirteen years. During his tenure at EPA, he was instrumental in creating the Agency's Smart Growth Program, while also helping to found the Smart Growth Network, the New Partners for Smart Growth Conference, and the leading anti-sprawl website smartgrowth.org. In addition, Anderson facilitated acquiring seed funding for the

National Vacant Properties Campaign, The LEED for Neighborhood Development Certification program, and the Governors' Institute for Community Design. He has co-authored numerous publications including: *This Is Smart Growth, Getting to Smart Growth* (Volumes 1 and 2), *Protecting Water Resources with Higher Density Development, The Transportation and Environmental Impacts of Infill vs. Greenfield Development,* and many others. His work also included direct technical assistance, helping with smart-growth implementation in communities nationwide including Cheyenne, WY, Prince George's County, MD, and the flagship smart-growth project Atlantic Station in Atlanta, GA. He received a master's degree from Duke University's Nicholas School of the Environment with a concentration in resource economics and policy.

Jockin Arputham (1947–)

Jockin Arputham was born and raised in the gold fields of Karnataka state, India and moved to Mumbai when he was eighteen to work as a carpenter and building contractor. He became involved in his slum community organizing residents with household waste collection, setting up informal schools, and establishing water connections. Shocked by the sight of fellow slum dwellers facing eviction, he became active organizing them under the belief that strength in numbers would provide residents with the ability to resist injustice. In 1969, Arputham was instrumental in forming the Bombay Slum Dwellers Federation, an organization that eventually to encompass the entire country as the National Slum Dwellers Federation (NSDF). As president of this organization, he helped to organize chapters in 70 cities in India and 23 countries around the world.

In 1985, Arputham linked his federation with the Society for the Promotion of Area Resource Centers (SPARC) to develop a national network of self-help women's collectives. The organization assists women in forming savings clubs, income generation, neighborhood improvement schemes, and new housing projects built in posteviction relocation sites. These combined efforts have given women the tools to obtain housing loans, negotiate with government officials regarding evictions and relocation rights, and promote more attention from municipal services. In 2000, his work was recognized through the Ramon Magsaysay Award for International Understanding in Manila, Philippines. In 2011, the government of India bestowed on Arputham its highest civilian honor, the Padma Shri award.

Jonathan Barnett

Jonathan Barnett, a fellow of the American Institute of Architects and the American Institute of Certified Planners, is a professor of city and regional planning and the director of the Urban Design Program at the University of Pennsylvania. Barnett has served as an urban design advisor to many U.S. cities and federal government agencies. In these projects, he has participated in the design of large urban redevelopment projects, planned communities, and master plans for suburban areas. For over two decades, he has sought to promote urban planning and design initiatives that overcome the growing split between older central cities and fast-growing suburbs that result from sprawl patterns of development.

Barnett's many books are recognized internationally among the leading works in urban design and planning. These include basic texts such as *Introduction to Urban Design* and *Redesigning Cities: Principles, Practice, Implementation*, along with a number of critical commentaries such as *The Elusive City: Five Centuries of Design Ambition and Miscalculation, The Fractured Metropolis: Improving the New City, Restoring the Old City, Reshaping the Region*, and a co-authored work, *Smart Growth in a Changing World*. His newest book is *City Design: Modernist, Traditional, Green, and Systems Perspectives*, published in 2011. He is a *magna cum laude* graduate of Yale University, and has master's degrees from the University of Cambridge and Yale.

Inga Björk-Klevby

Inga Björk-Klevby is a native of Sweden and a leading expert on the challenges associated with urban growth in the developing world. Her background includes working in various advisory and senior management capacities in international finance at the Central Bank of Sweden, the International Monetary Fund (IMF), the World Bank, the Asian Development Bank, culminating with the post of Executive Director for the African Development Bank where she represented Nordic countries, Switzerland, and India.

She was appointed to be her country's ambassador to several countries in Africa including Kenya, Côte d'Ivoire, Rwanda, Seychelles, and the Comoros before taking on work at the United Nations as Permanent Representative to the UN Environment Program (UNEP). In 2006, Björk-Klevby took on the job of serving as deputy executive director of UN-HABITAT in which capacity she has been involved in restructuring the UN Center for Human Settlements. Her main task is to revitalize and oversee the management of the Habitat and Human Settlements Foundation so that it can contribute effectively to the water and sanitation goals and the slum upgrading targets of the Millennium Declaration, as requested by the 2005 World Summit Outcome document. Her long-standing experience with development policies and financing, budget preparations, and debt relief negotiations has served her well in leading new initiatives. Björk-Klevby is an economist by training, and holds a master's degree from the Stockholm School of Economics.

Lawrence Bloom

Lawrence Bloom is a native of the United Kingdom and has served in a leadership role in several different capacities in addressing the challenges of global urban growth. Much of his past career has been in the real estate industry, where he rose to serve on the executive committee of the Intercontinental Hotel Group, managing its $3 billion global real estate portfolio. In this capacity, he created an environmental manual for the Intercontinental Hotels that was endorsed by HRH Prince Charles and is now being used in 4.5 million hotel rooms worldwide. In 1989, Bloom created the Global Action Plan, which is now the charity partner of the Sky Corporation.

Currently, Bloom serves on a variety of different nonprofit boards that are working to manage urban growth. He is vice chair of the Climate Prosperity Alliance, a senior fellow and member of the Board of Directors of Global Urban Development, and chairman of the United Nations Environment Program (UNEP) Green Economy Initiative on Green Cities, Buildings, and Transport. He also is chairman for United Kingdom Affairs of the Intergovernmental Renewable Energy Organization, a member and former chairman of the World Economic Forum's Global Agenda Council on Urban Management, and a member of the Jury for the Globe Award for Sustainable Cities. In addition, Bloom serves as executive chairman of Bhairavi Energies, a private corporation researching and investing in bio-remediation, renewable energy, and clean water technologies.

Somsook Boonyabancha

Somsook Boonyabancha is an architect who has worked to find ways to resolve stalemates between poor slum squatters and real estate developers and landowners. After graduating from the Chulalongkorn University in 1975, she worked for the government in an office devoted to slum-upgrading. Through her work in the Center for Housing and Human Settlements Studies of Thailand's National Housing Authority, Boonyabancha has pioneered a methodology for "land-sharing," an innovation built around mutually beneficial deals negotiated between urban squatters and the owner of the land who wishes to develop for commercial purposes. The slum dwellers get new, better, if more dense housing on a back portion of the plot in dispute, and the owner gets the street-front portion for immediate development. As director of the Community Organization Development Institute (CODI) in Bangkok, Boonyabancha has spearheaded moves to reduce poverty in Thailand's poorest communities.

In 1988, these ideas were moved beyond national borders through the creation of the Asian Coalition for Housing Rights, which is an affiliation of nongovernmental groups working on behalf of slum dwellers across the region. Boonyabancha served as its first secretary, providing leadership that has helped ACHR put an international spotlight on the disturbing problems faced by slum dwellers. The organization seeks to develop new understanding and provide training support initiatives in the field by members. ACHR has evolved into a regional network and representative for Habitat International Coalition for Asia. It has also become the main regional network on human settlements and urban issues consulted by many UN agencies such as UNCHS, UNDP, and ESCAP.

Peter Calthorpe

Peter Calthorpe is recognized as a leading proponent of the New Urbanist perspective. A practicing architect since 1972, he has been a pioneer of innovative approaches to urban revitalization, suburban growth, and regional planning that follow a vision of livable communities in harmony with the environment. In the 1986, he co-authored *Sustainable Communities,* a book that inspired several generations of new thinking in environmental design and helped launch "sustainability" as a defining goal of many ecological efforts. In the early 1990s, Calthorpe developed the concept of Transit Oriented Development (TOD) that was featured in *The Next American Metropolis.* He is a founder of the Congress for New Urbanism, and was its first board president, helping launch a movement that has helped to transform planning and development in the United States. In 2001, he published *The Regional City: Planning for the End of Sprawl* with Bill Fulton, explaining how regional-scale planning and design can integrate urban revitalization and suburban renewal into a coherent vision of metropolitan growth.

Calthorpe's work has included designing regional plans for Portland, Salt Lake City, Los Angeles, posthurricane Southern Louisiana, and Vision California, a statewide plan facilitate the implementation of the state's innovative climate change legislation. He has served on the President's Council for Sustainable Development, and at one time directed the HUD's Empowerment Zone and Consolidated Planning Programs.

Calthorpe has taught at the University of California, Berkeley, University of Washington, University of Oregon, and the University of North Carolina, and is a recipient of numerous honors and awards. He has been cited by *Newsweek* as one of 25 "innovators on the cutting edge." He holds a degree from Yale University Graduate School of Architecture.

Joan Clos (1949–)

Joan Clos is a leading voice in international urban growth and settlement policy today through his service as executive director of the UN Human Settlements Program (UN-HABITAT). He was appointed to this position, which is at the level of undersecretary-general by the UN General Assembly in October 2010.

A native of Barcelona, Spain, Clos has enjoyed a distinguished career in public service that began with his appointment to the Barcelona Municipal Government as director of Public Health in 1979. He won election to the city council in 1983, and from 1990 to 1994 he was deputy mayor in charge of Finance and Budgeting, playing a key role during the 1992 Olympic Games in Barcelona. He was twice elected mayor of Barcelona in the years 1997–2006 at which time he earned a reputation for improving municipal management and for urban renewal projects. One of the most ambitious was the Barcelona@22 program that helped revitalize dilapidated industrial zones. A newly refurbished neighborhood near the old dockyards was chosen as the site for the second gathering of UN-HABITAT's World Urban Forum in 2004. Before appointment to the UN post, Clos served as minister of Industry, Tourism, and Trade and as ambassador to Turkey and Azerbaijan.

At the international level, Clos was selected as president of Metropolis in 1998, and then president of the World Association of Cities and Local Authorities. Between 2000 and 2007, he served as chairman of the UN Advisory Committee of Local Authorities. Between 1997 and 2003, he was member of the Council of European Municipalities and Regions. He has received a number of awards which include a gold medal from the Royal Institute of British Architects in 1999 for transforming Barcelona. In 2002, he won the UN-HABITAT Scroll of Honor Award for encouraging global cooperation between local authorities and the United Nations. Clos is a medical graduate from the Universidad Autónoma de Barcelona.

Wendell Cox

Wendell Cox is principal of Wendell Cox Consultancy, an international public policy firm which specializes in urban policy, transport, and demographics. Cox has an extensive background in this field that began as an appointed member of the Los Angeles County Transportation Commission. While at LACTC, he authored the tax amendment that provided the initial funding for building light rail (Blue Line) and the subway (Red Line) and became a vocal champion for privately contracted transit systems as an alternative to government-run operations. He left LACTC in 1985 to continue his work in promoting competition in urban transportation. He served three years as the director of Public Policy of the American Legislative Exchange Council, where he oversaw the development of state model legislation and policy reports. He drafted the 1988 Colorado legislation that required

20 percent of the Denver transit system to be competitively tendered, the only mandatory competitive tendering law in the United States, and in so doing provided a model for regulations which have been enacted in Europe, South Africa, Australia, and New Zealand. Cox was commissioned by the congressional Millennial Housing Commission to prepare a policy report, Smart Growth and Housing Affordability, and in 1999, he was appointed to the Amtrak Reform Council by the Speaker of the U.S. House of Representatives. He also serves as visiting professor at the Conservatoire National des Arts et Métiers in Paris, where he lectures on transport and demographics.

Cox is perhaps best known for his influential website, known as "Demographia." This resource has been a leading source of information on urban growth and development policy for over a decade, offering extensive data sets compiled by the author, as well as a clearinghouse of articles and commentary on urban growth-related issues. He has served as elected chairman of the American Public Transit Association Planning and Policy Committee and the American Public Transit Association Governing Boards Committee. Cox attended the University of Southern California and earned a bachelor's degree in government from California State University, Los Angeles and a master's degree in business administration from Pepperdine University.

John M. DeGrove (1924–)

John M. DeGrove is a professor of Political Science and a leading scholar and policy advisor on statewide planning and urban growth management laws. For over three decades, he led growth management in Florida and the United States, served on state and national commissions, authored numerous books and articles, and was known as a national authority in planning and public administration.

DeGrove has taught at the University of Florida, the University of North Carolina, and Florida Atlantic University where he served as dean of the College of Social Sciences and co-founded the Joint Center for Environmental and Urban Problems. He has also served as secretary of Florida's Department of Community Affairs from 1983–1985; he was instrumental in the passage of the state's Growth Management Act and the State Comprehensive Plan in 1985. He is a member of the Governor's Commission for a Sustainable South Florida, and has also serves as an advisor to state, regional, and local planning and growth management agencies in fifteen states. He was a founding member and president of 1000 Friends of Florida, the state's growth management watchdog group.

DeGrove has been published widely on the origins and development of growth management policy across the United States in a number of texts that include *Land, Growth and Politics* (1984), *Balanced Growth: A Planning Guide for Local Government* (1991), and *The New Frontier for Land Policy: Planning and Growth Management in the States* (1992). In 2000, he retired from Florida Atlantic University as eminent scholar emeritus in Growth Management and Development, but continued to pursue his research with an updated look at the status of state growth management laws in *Planning Policy and Politics: Smart Growth and the States*, published in 2005.

DeGrove received degrees from Rollins College and Emory University before going on to obtain a Ph.D. from the University of North Carolina in 1958.

Andres Duany (1949–)

Andres Duany is an architect and urban planner who is internationally recognized for the leading role he has played in formulating and popularizing New Urbanism around the world. Duany first began to attract widespread notice through work he and his wife, Elizabeth Plater-Zyberk did through their Miami-based architecture firm. By 1980, they were beginning to popularize the national movement called the New Urbanism, and their innovative designs developed at Seaside, Florida and Kentlands, Maryland. Since then, Duany has completed designs and codes for over two hundred new towns, regional plans, and community revitalization projects as well as leading the development of comprehensive municipal zoning ordinances that prescribe appropriate urban arrangement for all uses and all densities. He is a co-founder and emeritus board member of the Congress for the New Urbanism, established in 1993, and has written and co-written several books that include *Sustainable and Resilient Communities: A Comprehensive Action Plan for Towns, Cities, and Regions* (2011), *The Language of Towns and Cities* (2010), *The Smart Growth Manual* (2009), *The New Civic Art* (2003), and *Suburban Nation: The Rise of Sprawl and the*

Decline of the American Dream (2001). Duany has worked as visiting professor at many institutions and holds two honorary doctorates.

In 2001, Duany and his wife were awarded the Vincent Scully Prize by the National Building Museum in recognition of their contributions to the U.S. built environment. He was featured in the Canadian documentary *Radiant City* on suburban sprawl released in 2006. Duany received his undergraduate degree in architecture and urban planning from Princeton University, and after a year of study at the École nationale supérieure des beaux-artes in Paris, he received a master's degree in architecture from the Yale School of Architecture.

Alain Durand-Lasserve

Alain Durand-Lasserve is a leading voice in France in urban land management in cities of developing countries, tenure upgrading, and tenure security policies. He is currently the director of Research at the Centre National de la Recherche Scientifique in Paris. Prior to this, he served as Scientific Coordinator of the European Science Foundation Network on "Innovative practices and emerging concepts for sustainable urban management in developing countries."

Durand-Lasserve has been responsible for various research initiatives on tenure regularization policies for slum settlements in Asia, Latin America, sub-Saharan Africa, and Arab countries for the French government and other European bilateral co-operation agencies, multilateral donor agencies, and the World Bank. His scholarly work has included organizing several international seminars on urban land tenure issues, tenure security, and local development. In 2002, he co-edited *Holding Their Ground: Secure Land Tenure for the Urban Poor in Developing Countries*.

Lasserve holds a Ph.D. from the University of Paris-Sorbonne.

Gordon Feller

For more than 25 years, Gordon Feller has been a major figure in building partnerships around urban environmental and urban transport issues that link private sector, public sector, independent sector, and academia. Currently, he serves as chief executive officer of the Urban Age Institute, an independent international organization founded in cooperation with the World Bank to help build and develop innovative approaches to complex global problems, particularly where economics and politics and sustainability intersect. Feller's "Meeting of the Minds" annually convenes a select group of corporate and government leaders to assess sustainability and transport.

Feller has written and published approximately 400 articles for newspapers, scholarly journals, and news magazines, including such periodicals as *IBM Magazine, CFO Magazine, Urban Land, Transnational Academic, Financial Times of London,* the *Washington Report,* and *TIME.* His lectures have been delivered at World Business Academy, World Future Society, and many universities around the United States.

Feller holds a bachelor's degree, *cum laude,* from Columbia University and a master's degree in international affairs from Columbia University, also *cum laude.* He graduated Phi Beta Kappa and was the recipient of numerous fellowships and scholarships both as an undergraduate and a graduate student.

Robert H. Freilich

Robert H. Freilich has been a major force in helping to establish legal support for planning, development, zoning, and land-use regulations across the United States, with cases and appeals that have moved through state supreme courts, federal courts of appeal, and the U.S. Supreme Court. In this capacity, Freilich has represented both the public and private sectors and has developed and implemented sustainable green land-use plans and systems for over 250 cities, counties, and states from San Diego to Boston, and Honolulu to the Florida Keys. His most significant case was the Ramapo decision won in the New York Court of Appeals in 1972 that established important precedents supporting growth controls at the local level. He has appeared as an expert planning witness in over 60 cases nationwide.

Freilich is a partner in the nationally recognized law and planning firm of Freilich, Leitner, and Carlisle based in Kansas City, Missouri and Aspen, Colorado. He has represented more than 200 cities, counties, and state governments in a variety of cases dealing with planning, land-use regulations, and litigation defense.

Freilich is currently the editor of *The Urban Lawyer,* a national quarterly journal on state and local government law published by the American Bar Association. He is author of numerous articles on land-use planning, and co-wrote *Case and Materials on Land Use* and *Model Subdivision Regulations: Planning and Law* both of which are essential compilations among legal professionals. Most recently, he has written *From Sprawl to Smart Growth: Successful Legal, Planning, and Environmental Systems*. Published in 2000, this book explores in detail the wide array of policy alternatives being pursued by the state and local governments in the effort to slow down sprawl development.

Freilich has authored numerous legal articles and books that include *From Sprawl to Sustainable Growth: Successful Planning, Law, and Environmental Systems* (2009); *The 21st Century Land Development Code* (2008); and the leading planning and law casebook in the field, *Cases and Materials on Land Use* (2008). He also serves as an editor of the *The Urban Lawyer,* directs the Annual Planning and Zoning Institute of the American Center for National and International Law and the Advisory Board of the Land *Use and Environment Law Review.* He has served as visiting professor of Law at Harvard Law School, the London School of Economics, and the University of Miami School of Law (1996–1997).

Freilich holds an A.B. from the University of Chicago, a Juris Doctor from Yale Law School, and M.I.A., L.L.M., and J.S.D. degrees from Columbia University. He currently teaches in the faculty at the University of Southern California Law School.

Parris N. Glendening (1942–)

Parris N. Glendening became a nationally recognized figure in the smart-growth movement while serving as governor of Maryland. An expert on federalism and long-time member of the University of Maryland, College Park faculty, he entered politics in 1973 by winning election to the Hyattsville City Council, and subsequently held several positions in county government. In this capacity, Glendening was honored by *City and State* magazine as the "Most Valuable County Official" in the nation.

In 1994, Glendening was elected on the Democratic Party ticket to his first term as governor of of Maryland. A major component of his election campaign centered on a sponsoring a new initiative designed to stem the tide of urban sprawl and by so doing, protect existing open space while also reinvigorating neglected urban communities. This was the basis for the landmark 1997 Smart Growth law, which built strongly on an earlier blueprint adopted by the state in 1992. After four years in office, Glendening won his race for re-election to a second term in 1998.

Glendening continues to be a major force in urban growth policy through his service as president of the Smart Growth Leadership Institute, a Washington, DC-based organization that is dedicated to helping state and local elected, civic, and business leaders design and implement effective smart-growth strategies. Glendening earned bachelor's and graduate degrees in political science at Florida State University, completing his studies in 1967.

Sir Peter Hall (1932–)

Sir Peter Hall is currently professor of Planning and Regeneration at the Bartlett School of Architecture and Planning, University College London, and senior research fellow at the Young Foundation. Serving as both an academic and advisor for almost fifty years, he is recognized as one of Great Britain's most respected voices in research and writing about urban growth and development policy. Hall is considered by many to be the father of the industrial enterprise zone concept, which is applied worldwide by city planners seeking to redevelop industry in disadvantaged areas.

Hall has been the author or editor of nearly 30 books on urban and regional planning and related topics that include *Planning and Urban Growth: An Anglo-American Comparison* (1973), *Urban and Regional Planning* (1982), *The World Cities* (1983), *Cities of Tomorrow* (1988), *London 2001* (1989), *Technopoles of the World* (1994), *Sociable Cities* (1998), *Cities in Civilization* (1998), *Urban Future 21: A Global Agenda for Twenty-First Century Cities* (2000), *To-Morrow: A Peaceful Path to Real Reform* (2003), and *The Polycentric Metropolis: Learning from Mega-City Regions in Europe* (2006). He writes regularly on urban topics for the magazines *Town and Country Planning* and *Regeneration & Renewal.*

Hall has served as a key advisor for urban planning, transportation, and redevelopment projects in metropolitan London, the Channel Tunnel, and elsewhere. He received the Founder's Medal of the Royal Geographical Society for distinction in research, and is an honorary member of the Royal Town Planning

Institute and honorary fellow of the Royal Institute of British Architects. He is a fellow of the British Academy and a member of the Academia Europea. Hall holds 14 honorary doctorates from universities in the UK, Sweden, and Canada. He was knighted in 1998 for services to the Town and Country Planning Association, and in 2003 was named by Her Majesty Queen Elizabeth II as a "Pioneer in the Life of the Nation" at a reception in Buckingham Palace. In 2003, he received the Gold Medal of the Royal Town Planning Institute. In 2005, Hall was awarded a Lifetime Achievement Award by the deputy prime minister for his contributions to urban regeneration and planning. He received the 2005 Balzan Prize for work on the social and cultural history of cities since the beginning of the sixteenth century. In 2008, he received the Sir Patrick Abercrombie Prize of the International Union of Architects. Hall is a graduate of Cambridge University where he earned a master's degree and doctorate in 1957.

William H. Hudnut (1932–)

William H. Hudnut has been a leading advocate of urban redevelopment, efficient government and regional policy, growth management, and sustainable development in his career as both an elected public official and a scholar. An ordained minister, he won a seat in the U.S. Congress in 1972 representing Indianapolis, Indiana as a Republican for one term. After losing his race for reelection, Hudnut successfully won the race for mayor of Indianapolis, taking office in 1976 as the first leader of Unigov, the newly merged government of Indianapolis and Marion County. Hudnut's goal was to bring urban revitalization to the city through economic development of the downtown area. He devoted large amounts of the budget on tax incentives, infrastructure improvements, and development projects to attract business to the downtown area which resulted in more than 30 major building projects that included extensive renovations and expansions of city facilities. Many office buildings were constructed, new sports-related programs and projects were completed, and several major companies were committed to staying in Indianapolis.

Nationally, Hudnut's work has won him numerous awards and appointments. He served as president of the National League of Cities and a member of the board for over twenty years. In 1988, he was named *City and State* magazine's Nation's Most

Valuable Public Official. In 1985, he earned the Distinguished Public Service Award from the Indiana Association of Cities and Towns, and in 1986, a Woodrow Wilson Award for Public Service. He has co-authored *Cities on the Rebound* (1998), *Halfway to Everywhere* (2004), and *Changing Metropolitan America: Planning for a Sustainable Future* (2008), and currently serves as Joseph C. Canizaro Chair for Public Policy at the Urban Land Institute.

Hudnut graduated from Princeton University in 1954 and earned a divinity degree from Union Theological Seminary in the City of New York and was ordained a clergyman in 1957.

Bruce Katz (1959–)

Bruce Katz has been a central figure in conducting path-breaking research and exploring policies associated with urban growth and development in the United States. He presently serves as the director of the Center on Urban and Metropolitan Policy at the Brookings Institute in Washington, DC, where he leads research designed to assist leaders in cities and suburbs to better understand demographic, environmental and social trends, economic challenges facing them, and to develop policy strategies that can facilitate transitions that will be of benefit to all.

Before joining the Brookings Institute, Katz served as chief of staff to Henry G. Cisneros, former Secretary of the U.S. Department of Housing and Urban Development. Katz has also served as the staff director of the Senate Subcommittee on Housing and Urban Affairs. After the 2008 presidential election, he co-led the housing and urban transition team for the Obama administration and served as a senior advisor to new Secretary of Housing and Urban Development, Shaun Donovan. Katz regularly advises federal, state, regional, and municipal leaders on policy reforms that advance the competitiveness of metropolitan areas.

Katz's scholarship is widely recognized around the world. He is the editor or co-editor of several books on transportation, demographics, metropolitan trends, and regional governance, including *Redefining Urban and Suburban America* (2006), *Taking the High Road: A Metropolitan Agenda for Transportation Reform* (2005), *Redefining Urban and Suburban America* (2005), and *Reflections on Regionalism* (2000). He is also principal author or co-author of dozens of book chapters, articles, and research papers on urban and metropolitan trends and policy, including publications in the *Brookings Review* and *Atlantic Monthly.* He has appeared as a commentator on a variety of network television and radio programs as well. In recent years, he has lectured about urban and metropolitan issues in countries such as Canada, China, Germany, Turkey, Great Britain, Italy, and South Africa. In 2006, Katz received the prestigious Heinz Award in Public Policy for his contributions to understanding the "function and values of cities and metropolitan areas and profoundly influencing their economic vitality, livability, and sustainability."

Katz received a bachelor's of arts degree from Brown University and a law degree at Yale University Law School.

C. S. Kiang

C. S. Kiang is a leading advocate in China for developing the country's urban infrastructure in an environmentally sustainable manner in the twenty-first century. Kiang holds a variety of positions that enable him to project his vision for a sustainable future. These include serving as vice chair of the Climate Prosperity Alliance, chairman of the Sustainable Development Technology Foundation, and ofof the Peking University Environment Fund. He is also a member of the Advisory Board of Global Urban Development. In addition, he is a member of the World Economic Forum's Global Agenda Councils on Water Security, Alternative Energies, and Climate Change. He serves as an advisor for the Global Elders and for Climate Change Capital, and he is a frequent consultant to private corporations and nonprofit organizations.

In the past, Kiang has held a number of influential positions in academic settings. He previously served as the founding dean of the Peking University College of Environmental Sciences from 2002 to 2006. He was institute professor at the Georgia Institute of Technology, where he served as director of the School of Geophysical Sciences, and of the Office of Environmental Sciences, Technology, and Policy, and as founding director of the Southern Oxidant Study. He also served as head of the Aerosol Program at the National Center for Atmospheric Research. Kiang is a councilor of the World Future Council, a member of the Advisory Board of Environmental Research Letters, and of the Asia Society's International Council. Kiang trained in physics at National Taiwan University and Georgia Institute of Technology.

Miloon Kothari

Miloon Kothari is an influential voice in India as well as in the international arena advocating for the rights of poverty-stricken urban migrants and slum dwellers. Since 2000, he has been serving as the special rapporteur on adequate housing for the UN Commission on Human Rights. His mandate involves presenting an annual report to the Commission on the status of adequate housing throughout the world. These reports also include information about policies and programs that have proven successful in the securing housing for the urban poor in developing countries. Kothari's work has included promoting cooperation among governments to secure these rights, applying a gender perspective to these issues, and encouraging collaboration between governments and UN bodies as well as public and private agencies, civil society, and international financial institutions. He has also been active on issues related to globalization and trade liberalization and their impacts on the right to adequate housing and other related rights. In addition to housing and land rights, he has also been actively involved in works related to human rights dimension on poverty, water, and sanitation.

An architect by training, Kothari also serves as the coordinator for the South Asian Regional Program of the Habitat International Coalition's (HIC) Housing and Land Rights Network, and is founding member of the International NGO Committee on Human Rights in Trade and Investment (INCHRITI). He is also a member of the Leadership Council of the Global Women and AIDS Coalition, UNAIDS.

Gerrit-Jan Knaap

Gerrit-Jan Knaap has made numerous contributions to research on the economics and politics of land-use planning, the efficacy of economic development instruments, and the impacts of environmental policy in the United States. An economist by training, he is a professor of urban studies and planning, and executive director of the National Center for Smart Growth Research and Education at the University of Maryland, in College Park.

Knaap's research in Oregon, Maryland and elsewhere has helped to provide a better understanding of the impact of state-level policies designed to shape local land-use decision making and planning. He is the author, coauthor, or editor of several books: *The Regulated Landscape: Lessons on State Land Use Planning from Oregon* (1992), *Land Market Monitoring for Smart Urban Growth* (2001), and *The Oxford Handbook of Urban Economics and Planning* (2011). Knaap has also published articles in journals which include the *Journal of the American Planning Association*, the *Journal of Urban Economics, Land Economics, Policy Analysis, and Management*; and *State and Local Government Review*. His research has been supported by grants from the National Science Foundation, the Lincoln Institute of Land Policy, the U.S. Army Corps of Engineers, and numerous other federal, state, and local government agencies.

Knaap received an undergraduate degree at Willamette University, and completed his master's and doctoral studies in economics from the University of Oregon. He received additional postdoctoral training at the University of Wisconsin-Madison.

Aprodocio A. Laquian

Aprodocio A. Laquian is recognized as one of the world's foremost authorities on urbanization in developing countries and the policy challenges associated with slums and poverty. He was born in impoverished circumstances in a rural village in the Philippines and moved with his family to the slums of Manila where he experienced firsthand the difficulties of life in a squatter community. While working and attending night school, he developed a passionate commitment to poverty alleviation, community-based activism, urban management reform, and local politics. After attaining a degree in public administration from the University of the Philippines in 1959, Laquian won a Fulbright grant to study in the United States where he pursued a Ph.D. at the Massachusetts Institute of Technology. His pathbreaking research into the role of urbanization in national development resulted in his first book, *The City in Nation-building* (1966). He returned to Manila and taught at the University of the Philippines where subsequent work was published in the book *Slums are for People* (1967) and a monograph, *Slums and Squatters in Six Philippine Cities* (1968). His pioneering efforts in urban community development was supported by the World Bank, which was the first community upgrading and sites and services project in the country. Working as deputy director of the university's Local Government Center enabled

Laquian to conduct training programs for local government officials, help design a new metropolitan government for Manila, and formulate low-cost housing programs for the urban poor.

As an internationally recognized scholar on metropolitan planning and urban poverty alleviation, Laquian was involved in directing grants for research throughout the developing world and also authored numerous books that included *Social Change and Internal Migration* (1977), *Housing Asia's Millions* (1979), and *Basic Housing* (1983). He also directed a social science development project in East Africa and taught urban research courses at the University of Nairobi. Subsequently, Laquian worked for the UN Population Fund in several different countries in Asia and collaborated with researchers studying internal migration and the growth of small towns in China's coastal regions.

Laquian is presently director of the Centre for Human Settlements and a professor emeritus of community and regional planning at the University of British Columbia. His most recent work is *Beyond Metropolis: The Planning and Governance of Asia's Mega-Urban Regions* published in 2005.

Jaime Lerner (1937–)

Jaime Lerner is a leading figure in urban affairs and planning in Brazil with a career that spans both the political and academic worlds. Born in Curitiba, Lerner pursued studies in architecture and urban planning in the School of Architecture of the Federal University of Parana. In 1965, he helped to found the Institute of Urban Planning and Research of Curitiba (IPPUC), and participated in the preparation of an innovative master plan for city of Parana that would accommodate the rapid growth of the metropolitan region. He was elected mayor of the city for three terms (1971–1975, 1979–1983, and 1989–1992) which gave him a key role in overseeing the urban transformation of the city. Lerner's accomplishments included the completion of an integrated mass transportation system that has been acknowledged worldwide for its efficiency, quality, and low cost; ensuing terms of office opportunities for pursuing innovative urban planning; and enhancing social programs. His career in public office continued with election to the governor's office of Parana state in 1994 and reelection in 1998. Working at the state level, he was able to continue to advance a variety of programs and projects related to urban land development and enhanced transportation, sanitation, health, education, recreation, and culture for urban areas of the state.

Lerner's work was recognized by the International Union of Architects with the award of their Robert Matthew Prize for Improvement in the Quality of Human Settlements in 2002. At that same meeting, the Union's general assembly elected Lerner president of the IUA where he served for three years. At present, Lerner is a professor of urban and regional planning at the School of Architecture and Urban Planning of the Federal University of Parana, Brazil. He has been a guest professor at the University of Berkeley, and also served as a consultant in urban planning at the United Nations. Additional distinctions won by Lerner include the United Nations Environment Award in 1990, the 1996 UNICEF Children and Peace Award, The Netherlands Prince Claus Award for Culture and Development in 2000, and the World Technology Award from the National Museum of Science and Industry (London) in 2001.

Born in Curitiba in 1937, Lerner graduated in architecture and urban planning from the School of Architecture of the Federal University of Parana in 1964.

Patricia McCarney

Patricia McCarney is has been an important authority in Canada on urbanization and the growth of cities in the developing world. After completing a Ph.D. in international development from the Massachusetts Institute of Technology in 1987, she held several staff positions in international agencies that include the International Development Research Center in Ottawa, the World Bank in Washington (Africa Technical Division-Infrastructure), and the UN Center for Human Settlements (UNCHS Habitat-Research and Development Division) in Nairobi. During this time, she worked in funding projects in 30 countries of Asia, Africa, and Latin America with a specialization in strengthening institutions of higher learning throughout the less developed countries, instituting policy reform in the field of governance, and funding international social science research.

McCarney is the founding director of the Global Cities Program at the Center for International Studies at the University of Toronto where she teaches political science. She has also served as a member of the Board of Directors of the Canadian Urban Institute, chairing the Executive Committee of the Board on International Programs, and as associate vice president of International Research and Development at the University of Toronto. Her teaching and research in the field of international development concentrates on urban governance, politics, and planning in cities of Asia, Africa, and Latin America as well as local government and global cities in comparative perspective. She has authored or co-authored numerous influential books in the field of global urban growth that include *World Cities and the Environment: Rethinking the Global Agenda* (1993), *The Changing Nature of Local Government in the Developing World* (1996), *Creating Knowledge, Strengthening Nations: The Role of Higher Education* (2005), *Governance on the Ground: Innovations and Discontinuities in Cities of the Developing World* (2008), and *Cities and Governance: Latin America, Asia, and Africa in Comparative Perspective* (2011). She is also the author of numerous articles and papers on these subjects and is presently working on another book tentatively titled *Space, Economy, and Cities: A Case-Based Perspective from India.*

Rose Seisie Molokoane

Rose Molokoane is a champion for the urban poor in South Africa, where she has helped to mobilize slum dwellers and publicize the need to relieve the housing crisis that exists throughout the developing world. She serves as president of the South African Federation of the Urban Poor (FED UP) in Johannesburg, South Africa. The South African Homeless People's Federation has helped more than 150,000 squatters, the vast majority who are women, pool their savings and develop economic enterprises. This has won them sufficient standing to negotiate with the government for a progressive housing policy that has already produced 15,000 new homes and secured more than 1,000 hectares of government land for development. She is also is the chairperson and national savings coordinator of the 80,000-member South African Homeless People's Federation.

A veteran of the anti-apartheid struggle in South Africa, Molokoane, who resides in a modest home in a squatter community in West Pretoria, is internationally recognized among grassroots activists involved in fighting for security of tenure and housing in the developing world. She has spoken at numerous conferences in Cambodia, Thailand, and the Philippines as well as many African nations. She was awarded the United Nations'

Habitat Scroll of Honor in 2005 in recognition for her work to bring land and homes to the poor. In 2007, she was awarded the 2007 Women of the Year Outstanding Achievement Award by the Woman of the Year Foundation in London, England. She presently serves as a board member of Shack Dwellers International (SDI).

Neal Peirce

Neal Peirce is a nationally syndicated journalist who has written extensively about the economics and politics of urban growth in metropolitan United States. He helped to found the *National Journal* and served as a contributing editor in addition to serving as editor of *Congressional Quarterly* in the 1960s and 1970s. He has authored and co-authored numerous books including *The Book of America: Inside Fifty States Today* (1984) and *Citistates: How Urban America Can Prosper in a Competitive World* (1993). Since 1987, 24 *Peirce Reports* that assess the future of metropolitan regions have been sponsored by and appeared in such newspapers as *The Arizona Republic, Seattle Times, Dallas Morning News, Philadelphia Inquirer, Raleigh News & Observer,* and *St. Louis Post-Dispatch*. More recently, Peirce completed a survey of the New England states in 2006. He also served on the National Civic League's executive committee from the early 1970s to 1995. He is one of the founders of the National Academy of Public Administration's Alliance for Redesigning Government.

Recognized widely for his expertise on urban issues, Peirce has appeared on television programs that include *Meet the Press* and *The Today Show*. He is also a lecturer who has been featured on National Public Radio and local media stations across the United States. He presently serves as chairman of the Citistates Group, a network of journalists and speakers who believe that successful metropolitan regions are today's key to economic competitiveness and sustainable communities. Peirce was born in Philadelphia, and is a graduate of Princeton University.

Douglas R. Porter

Douglas R. Porter is an academic who is one of the leading authorities on managing urban growth in the United States. His research and prolific writing books have helped to popularize state and local programs, designs, techniques, and issues concerned with improving the quality of urban development. His approach has often spanned traditional disciplines, helping to synthesize insights from urban planning and development with the politics of affordable housing, transportation, growth strategies, transit-oriented development, community involvement, and concepts like smart growth and sustainable development.

In 1992, Porter founded The Growth Management Institute as a nonprofit organization to promote information exchange and research for public, organizational, and private clients. These activities built on 12 years as director of public policy research for the Urban Land Institute and 20 years of experience before that as a planning and development consultant. From 1979 to 1991, Porter directed the public policy research program of the Urban Land Institute.

His recent publications include *Managing Growth in America's Communities* (2nd ed., 2007), *Breaking the Logjam: Civic Engagement by Developers and Planners* (2006), *Developing Around Transit: Strategies and Solutions that Work* (2005), *The Power of Ideas: Five People Who Changed the Urban Landscape* (2006), *Inclusionary Zoning for Affordable Housing* (2004), *Making Smart Growth Work* (2002), and *The Practice of Sustainable Development* (2000).

Porter is a fellow of the American Institute of Planners and has been an Urban Land Institute fellow and chair of the Maryland Transportation Commission. Most recently he has advised Coweta County, Georgia; Maryville and Blount County, Tennessee; and Palm Beach County, Florida, on growth issues. He received a B.S. and M.S. in urban and regional planning from Michigan State University and the University of Illinois.

Eduardo Rojas

A native of Chile, Eduardo Rojas is an urban planner who has been active in urban development-related research and projects in both Latin America and the United States. His work in integrated urban development planning and implementation has been widely studied and he is a leading expert on housing policy, low-income housing, and settlement upgrading projects in Latin America.

Rojas has worked as an urban and regional development consultant in Chile, later at the Organization of American States, and at the Inter-American Development Bank on sustainable development strategy in several South American countries. He has published four books, including *Ciudades para todos: la experiencia reciente de mejoramiento de barrios* and *Old Cities New Assets* (1999) as well as numerous papers in technical journals and published books. He is a regular guest lecturer, speaker, and external reviewer at several universities including Harvard, the University of Pennsylvania, George Washington University, the University of Barcelona, University of Pernambuco, University of Chile, the United Nations' Latin American Institute for Economic and Social Planning (ILPES), and the International Course on Development, Planning, and Public Policy. Rojas holds degrees from Johns Hopkins, the University of Edinburgh, and the Catholic University of Chile.

Baoxing Qiu

Baoxing Qiu has been an important figure in urban development studies and growth policy in China. He is an urban planner by training, and has served as a faculty member at several institutions in China that include the Chinese Academy of Social Science, School of Management of Zhejiang University, Nanjing University, and Nanjing University of Finance and Economy. He has published over ten books and hundreds of academic papers, some of which include *China's Urbanization, Opportunity, and Challenge; Property Ownership System Reform* and *Harmony and Innovation: Problems, Dangers, and Solutions in Dealing with Rapid Urbanization in China.*

Qiu currently serves as the vice minister of the Ministry of Housing and Urban-Rural Development in charge of urban planning, urban infrastructure construction, building energy saving and technology, natural and historical heritage protection, water pollution prevention, and town and village development. He is also president of Chinese Society for Urban Studies and chairman of IWA (International Water Association) China Committee. Qiu has been the major leader in Leqing County, Jinhua City, and mayor of Hangzhou City of Zhejiang Province. He was chairman of the 5th World Water Conference in 2006. He has received the IWA Award for Outstanding Contribution.

Qiu holds degrees from Hangzhou University (now Zhejiang University), the Institute of Economy of Fudan University, and the Architecture and Urban Planning Institute of Tongji University, and holds doctorates in economics from Fudan University and in engineering from Tongji University.

Samuel Staley

Samuel Staley is a nationally prominent advocate of greater reliance on free market principles in urban development policy in the United States. His views have become influential through his position serving as the director of the Urban Futures Program at the Reason Foundation in Los Angeles, California.

Staley has authored or co-authored many books and articles on growth management and urban policy, including *Mobility First: A New Vision for Transportation in a Globally Competitive 21st Century* (2008), *The Road More Traveled: Why The Congestion Crisis Matters More Than You Think, and What We Can Do About It* (2006), *Smarter Growth: Market-based Strategies for Land-use Planning in the 21st Century* (2001), and *Planning Rules and Urban Economic Performance: The Case of Hong Kong* (1994). His work has also appeared in a variety of academic, professional, and popular publications that include the *Journal of the American Planning Association*, the *Economics of Education Review*, the *Wall Street Journal*, and the *Chicago Tribune*.

Staley presently serves as the vice president of Research at the Buckeye Institute for Public Policy Solutions in Dayton, Ohio. He has served on the Planning Commission and Board of Zoning Appeals in Bellbrook, Ohio and teaches economics at the University of Dayton. Staley received a degree in economics and public policy from Colby College, a master's in economics from Wright State University, and a Ph.D. in public policy and management from Ohio State University.

Anna K. Tibaijuka (1950–)

Anna Tibaijuka is an internationally recognized authority on urban policy and women's rights in the developing world, gaining prominence through her service as under-secretary-general and executive director of UN-HABITAT for two terms between 2002 and 2008. She is the first African woman elected by the UN General Assembly to serve as an under-secretary-general of a UN program.

A Tanzanian national born to smallholder farmers in Muleba, Tanzania, Tibaijuka completed a university degree at the Swedish University of Agricultural Science in Uppsala. After returning to Tanzania, she joined the economics faculty at the University of Dar es Salaam where her research resulted in several books and research papers. She also became active in the women's movement, founding the Tanzanian National Women's Council (BAWATA) to serve as an independent organization fighting for women's economic and social rights. In 1996, she founded the Joha Trust to advocate for quality girls' education through the operation of a model secondary school for girls.

In 1998, Tibaijuka joined the UN Conference on Trade and Development, UNCTAD in Geneva as director and special coordinator for the Least Developed, Land-locked, and Island Developing Countries. In 2000, she was promoted to assistant secretary-general and executive director of the UN Center for Human Settlements (UNCHS) in Nairobi, Kenya. Her strategic vision and energy helped to enhance the organization's performance to the point where it was upgraded into the UN Program on Human Settlements (UN-HABITAT) in 2001. Soon after, Tibaijuka was elected by the General Assembly as the first under-secretary-general of this agency. While in this capacity, she also served as a member of the Commission for Africa established by British Prime Minister Tony Blair which resulted in the cancellation of multilateral debt for several African countries by the G8 Summit in 2005. That same year, she was appointed special envoy on Human Settlements Issues in Zimbabwe following massive evictions of the poor in urban areas. Tibaijuka was also instrumental in promoting water, sanitation, and slum upgrading globally and in assisting the African Union's Ministerial Conference on Housing and Urban Development, and similar regional bodies for Latin American and the Caribbean, and the Asia-Pacific.

Tibaijuka is currently a member of the World Health Organization Commission on the Social Determinants of Health, and is also a member of the Advisory Board of the Commission on the Legal Empowerment of the Poor, co-chaired by the former U.S. Secretary of State Madeleine Albright, and the Peruvian economist Hernando de Soto. She is patron of Tanzania Young Entrepreneurs Initiative, and remains active in various professional associations. She has won several awards including honorary doctorate degrees conferred by the University of McGill in Canada, University College London, and Herriot Watt in Scotland. She is a foreign member of the Royal Swedish Academy of Agriculture and Forestry and the International Center for Tropical Agriculture. Tibaijuka is a widow with five children, one of whom is adopted.

Marc A. Weiss

Marc A. Weiss is an advocate for sustainable urban development who has gained prominence through his leadership serving as chairman and CEO of Global Urban Development, an international policy organization.

Weiss has taught in the graduate school of Architecture, Planning, and Preservation at Columbia University, and also held faculty positions at the Massachusetts Institute of Technology, Stanford University, and several other institutions. He served as deputy director of the state of California's Commission on Industrial Innovation, and produced policy reports for the United Nations, the Organization for Economic Cooperation and Development (OECD), the U.S. Agency for International Development (USAID), the Metropolitan Strategic Plan Association of Barcelona, Sweden's Mistra Foundation for Strategic Environmental Research, the National Governors Association, the Brookings Institution, and the World Future Council, as well as conducting professional training for USAID. He has authored *The Rise of the Community Builders* (1987) and collaborated with former HUD Secretary Henry Cisneros on the American Assembly conference and edited volume, *Interwoven Destinies: Cities and the Nation* (1993), and also co-authored *The Economic Resurgence of Washington, DC: Citizens Plan for Prosperity in the 21st Century* (1998).

Weiss was a policy adviser and spokesman for the Clinton presidential campaign and served as special assistant to the secretary of the U.S. Department of Housing and Urban Development (HUD) from 1993 to 1997. From 1997 to 1999, he served as coordinator of the Strategic Economic Development Plan for Washington D.C. Over the past decade, his work with the Climate Prosperity Alliance to promote sustainable economic development and efforts to assist with development strategies in a number of cities in the United States and abroad has been widely acclaimed.

He presently serves as executive editor of *Global Urban Development Magazine*, and chairman of Sustainable Economic Development Strategies LLC. In addition, he is a member of the Steering Committee of the UN Sustainable Development Knowledge Partnership, a member of the steering committees of the UN Habitat World Urban Campaign and its Best Practices and Policies Program. In addition, he is a member of the Steering Committee of the UN Sustainable Development Knowledge Partnership, and a member of the Steering Committees of the UN Habitat World Urban Campaign and Best Practices and Policies Program. Weiss earned a degree in political science from Stanford University, and received a master's and Ph.D. in city and regional planning from the University of California, Berkeley.

6

Data and Documents

Data

The rapid expansion of urban areas is one of the most significant global trends today. Just how rapid is this growth, and what differences can be detected from one part of the developing world to another? The comparative data from the United Nations presented below offers some answers to these questions with information from each of the major regions of the world. The urbanization data for the United States collected by the USDA is presented state by state so that the contrasts between the fast-growing Sunbelt can be contrasted with the slower growth of the rest of the country.

TABLE 6.1
Number and Total Population of New Cities Established Since 1990 UN–HABITAT Global Urban Observatory (2008)

Region and/or country	New small cities (100,000 to 500,000)	New intermediate cities (500,000 to 1 million)	New big cities (1 to 5 million)	Total
	number (population)	number (population)	number (population)	number (population)
Africa	44 (6,335,094)	1 (523,265)	0	45 (6,858,359)
Latin America & Caribbean	171 (27,138,867)	6 (3,930,127)	2 (3,008,885)	179 (34,077,879)
Asia excluding China & India	72 (13,374,321)	5 (3,109,207)	0	77 (16,483,528)
China	78 (26,331,991)	119 (82,966,103)	49 (64,485,448)	246 (173,783,542)
India	145 (21,119,546)	1 (520,301)	1 (1,006,417)	147 (22,646,264)
Total	510 (94,299,819)	132 (91,049,003)	52 (68,500,750)	694 (253,849,572)

Source: UN-HABITAT, *State of the World's Cities 2008/2009*, p. 36.

TABLE 6.2
Population of Slum Areas by Developing Region UN-HABITAT Global Urban Observatory (2008)

Region	Slum percentage 1990	Slum population (millions) 1990	Slum percentage 2001	Slum population (millions) 2001	Slum percentage 2005	Slum population (millions) 2005	Slum annual growth
Northern Africa	37.7%	21.719	28.2%	21.355	25.4%	21.224	−0.15%
Sub-Saharan Africa	72.3%	100.973	71.9%	166.208	71.8%	199.321	4.53%
Latin America & Caribbean	35.4%	110.837	31.9%	127.566	30.8%	134.257	1.28%
Eastern Asia (excl. China)	25.3%	12.831	25.4%	15.568	25.4%	16.702	1.76%
Asian countries of former USSR	30.3%	9.721	29.4%	9.836	29.0	9.879	0.11%
South Asia	63.7%	198.663	59.0%	253.122	57.4%	276.432	2.20%
Southeast Asia	36.8%	48.986	28.0%	56.781	25.3%	59.913	1.34%
Western Asia	26.4%	22.006	25.7%	29.658	25.5%	33.057	2.71%
Oceania	24.5%	0.350	24.1%	0.499	24.0%	0.568	3.24%

State of the World's Cities Report 2006/07, p. 18.

TABLE 6.3
Proportion of Urban Population Living in Slums (2005)

Region	Urban population in thousands (2005)	Percentage of urban population living in slums (2005)	Slum population (2005)
North Africa	82,809	14.5%	810,441,000
Sub-Saharan Africa	264,355	62.2%	164,531,000
Latin America & Caribbean	434,432	27.0%	117,439,000
East Asia	593,301	36.5%	316,436,000
South Asia	468,668	42.9%	201,185,000
Southeast Asia	243,725	27.5%	67,074,000
West Asia	130,368	24.0%	31,254,000
Oceania	2,153	24.1%	519,000
Developing World Total	2,219,811	36.5%	1,717,879,000

Source: UN-HABITAT State of the World's Cities 2008/2009, p. 90.

FIGURE 6.1

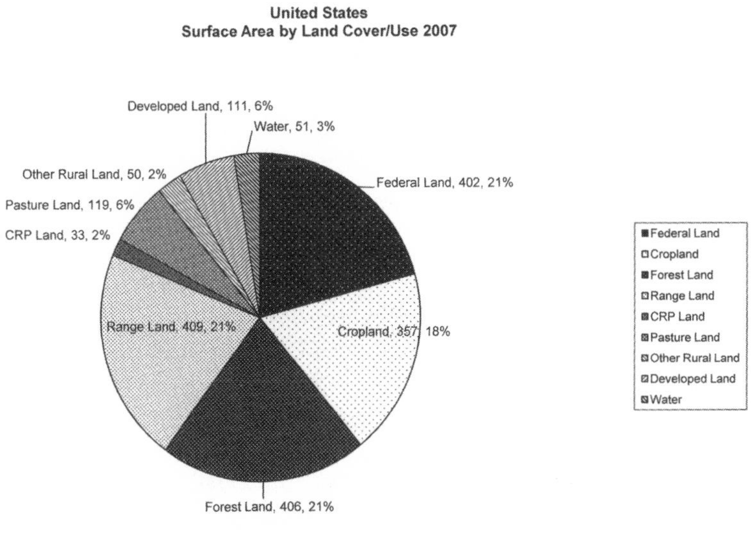

FIGURE 6.2

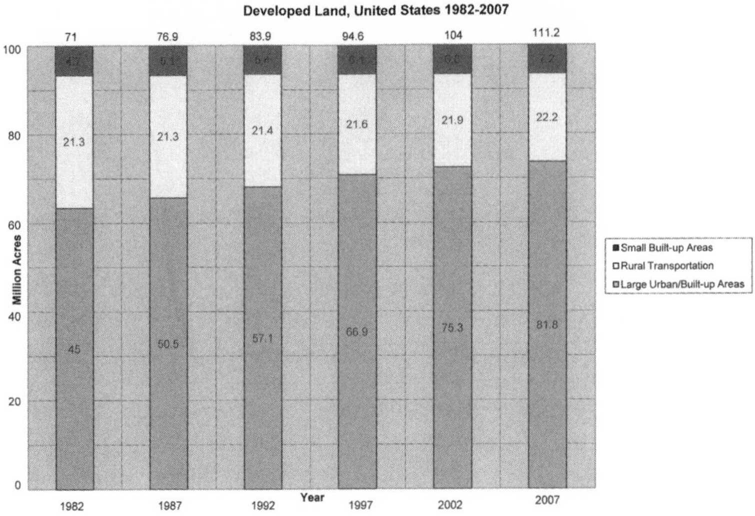

TABLE 6.4
Change in Amount of Developed Non-federal Land in the United States, in Thousands of Acres over 25 years (1982–2007)*

State	Developed land (1982)	Developed land (1992)	Developed land (1997)	Developed land (2007)	Change in Developed land (1982–2007)
Alabama	1,624.1 (+/−113.1)	1,946.4 (+/−129.9)	2,263.6 (+/−140.4)	2,942.9 (+/−203.7)	81.2%
Arizona	1,018.1 (+/−271.0)	1,281.4 (+/−294.8)	1,338.0 (+/−307.1)	2006.2 (+/−462.3)	97.1%
Arkansas	1,232.2 (+/−98.4)	1,338.7 (+/−106.8)	1,528.4 (+/−110.4)	1,809.3 (+/−142.2)	46.8%
California	4,082.8 (+/−342.6)	4,836.9 (+/−371.7)	5,381.9 (+/−370.7)	6,173.8 (+/−403.8)	51.2%
Colorado	1,187.4 (+/−109.5)	1,472.1 (+/−148.9)	1,577.6 (+/−165.2)	1,934.3 (+/−222.5)	62.9%
Connecticut	823.0 (+/−33.4)	916.3 (+/−34.9)	958.8 (+/−33.1)	1,051.6 (+/−41.4)	27.8%
Delaware	158.7 (+/−26.5)	192.5 (+/−29.9)	214.4 (+/−31.7)	280.1 (+/−35.3)	76.5%
Florida	2,771.8 (+/−239.6)	3,677.3 (+/−272.1)	4,368.2 (+/−295.9)	5,515.2 (+/−405.5)	99.0%

Georgia	2,227.1 (+/–116.0)	2,910.5 (+/–139.2)	3,702.2 (+/–158.6)	4,639.9 (+/–220.6)	108.3%
Idaho	562.2 (+/–48.3)	680.0 (+/–59.8)	777.2 (+/–66.8)	907.3 (+/–75.3)	61.4%
Illinois	2,622.5 (+/–115.2)	2,855.2 (+/–125.3)	3,092.9 (+/–125.5)	3,383.3 (+/–166.3)	29.0%
Indiana	1,778.3 (+/–92.1)	1,997.0 (+/–99.2)	2,186.7 (+/–110.8)	2,446.0 (+/–123.8)	27.5%
Iowa	1,634.1 (+/–95.3)	1,689.8 (+/–103.4)	1,765.6 (+/–106.0)	1,892.3 (+/–111.5)	15.8%
Kansas	1,732.4 (+/–69.3)	1,860.0 (+/–70.9)	1,959.2 (+/–70.8)	2,095.7 (+/–94.0)	21.0%
Kentucky	1,124.0 (+/–69.9)	1,470.1 (+/–84.5)	1,703.0 (+/–97.0)	2,093.1 (+/–105.9)	86.2%
Louisiana	1,232.1 (+/–57.2)	1,454.6 (+/–61.9)	1,594.7 (+/–65.8)	1,862.8 (+/–80.0)	51.2%
Maine	506.8 (+/–68.5)	595.6 (+/–77.2)	704.7 (+/–85.9)	851.1 (+/–97.2)	67.9%
Maryland	963.3 (+/–115.6)	1,116.8 (+/–123.8)	1,306.1 (+/–127.5)	1,496.7 (+/–130.0)	55.4%
Massachusetts	1,086.1 (+/–65.6)	1,332.5 (+/–69.0)	1,554.7 (+/–70.7)	1,716.4 (+/–83.3)	58.0%
Michigan	2,839.5 (+/–129.0)	3,320.1 (+/–148.9)	3,700.9 (+/–161.3)	4,227.6 (+/–168.1)	49.0%
Minnesota	1,715.6 (+/–77.0)	1,949.9 (+/–88.7)	2,181.3 (+/–98.7)	2,395.2 (+/–116.7)	39.6%
Mississippi	1,123.3 (+/–95.8)	1,269.3 (+/–96.7)	1,475.4 (+/–106.7)	1,811.9 (+/–142.5)	61.3%
Missouri	2,150.8 (+/–93.4)	2,373.9 (+/–101.9)	2,609.4 (+/–115.5)	2,931.5 (+/–204.8)	36.3%
Montana	820.2 (+/–91.7)	877.7 (+/–96.5)	935.9 (+/–101.2)	1,047.0 (+/–119.5)	27.7%
Nebraska	1,030.7 (+/–104.1)	1,060.6 (+/–111.2)	1,107.2 (+/–112.6)	1,156.5 (+/–108.6)	12.2%
Nevada	237.8 (+/–64.1)	307.5 (+/–69.9)	330.7 (+/–71.8)	582.9 (+/–138.5)	145.1%
New Hampshire	386.9 (+/–45.8)	538.0 (+/–59.2)	603.4 (+/–63.5)	695.6 (+/–63.1)	79.8%
New Jersey	1,178.5 (+/–65.8)	1,453.8 (+/–70.5)	1,653.0 (+/–75.7)	1,849.3 (+/–83.6)	56.9%
New Mexico	707.0 (+/–95.9)	829.1 (+/–116.7)	995.4 (+/–126.7)	1,261.9 (+/–180.9)	78.5%
New York	2,808.9 (+/–123.3)	3,058.9 (+/–132.9)	3,400.3 (+/–142.9)	3,793.9 (+/–160.6)	35.1%
North Carolina	2,317.5 (+/–107.6)	3,191.3 (+/–144.3)	3,673.0 (+/–165.6)	4,796.7 (+/–245.7)	107.0%
North Dakota	902.1 (+/–69.4)	924.7 (+/–70.4)	954.2 (+/–71.7)	973.2 (+/–69.5)	7.9%

(continued)

TABLE 6.4 (CONTINUED)

State	Developed land (1982)	Developed land (1992)	Developed land (1997)	Developed land (2007)	Change in Developed land (1982–2007)
Ohio	2,867.0 (+/–116.8)	3,342.9 (+/–134.4	3,718.5 (+/–147.7)	4,140.3 (+/–164.6)	44.4%
Oklahoma	1,448.7 (+/–89.7)	1,584.2 (+/–96.5)	1,734.0 (+/–108.9)	2,056.8 (+/–128.4)	42.0%
Oregon	967.9 (+/–100.3)	1,134.5 (+/–115.5)	1,241.0 (+/–122.3)	1,389.6 (+/–141.1)	43.6%
Pennsylvania	2,763.8 (+/–103.4)	3,375.3 (+/–130.)	3,911.8 (+/–145.3)	4,360.7 (+/–173.3)	57.8%
Rhode Island	171.6 (+/–12.4)	198.5 (+/–13.8)	205.1 (+/–14.2)	232.2 (+/–17.0)	35.3%
South Carolina	1,359.2 (+/–77.8)	1,749.6 (+/–101.6)	2,117.5 (+/–111.5)	2,672.6 (+/–112.9)	96.7%
South Dakota	811.6 (+/–63.2)	870.6 (+/–89.7)	921.6 (+/–99.3)	962.8 (+/–110.4)	18.6%
Tennessee	1,640 (+/–98.7)	2,157.9 (+/–111.3)	2,606.3 (+/–129.8)	3,038.3 (+/–158.7)	85.3%
Texas	5,073.1 (+/–180.7)	6,102.0 (+/–234.2)	6,770.0 (+/–257.1)	8,515.7 (+/–345.2)	67.9%
Utah	433.7 (+/–89.4)	530.5 (+/–109.4)	601.1 (+/–118.9)	744.6 (+/–139.6)	71.7%
Vermont	261.9 (+/–23.4)	332.2 (+/–26.6)	345.4 (+/–27.3)	393.2 (+/–30.8)	50.1%
Virginia	1,841.9 (+/–108.0)	2,285.3 (+/–115.5)	2,627.7 (+/–111.9)	2,101.2 (+/–127.5)	68.4%
Washington	1,594.7 (+/–147.8)	1,897.2 (+/–162.6)	2,150.5 (+/–176.4)	2,464.5 (+/–192.7)	54.5%
West Virginia	633.2 (+/–44.9)	759.4 (+/–51.5)	958.7 (+/–59.6)	1,151.6 (+/–57.3)	81.9%
Wisconsin	1,974.2 (+/–103.2)	2,213.5 (+/–114.2)	2,400.2 (+/–122.1)	2,724.9 (+/–172.3)	38.1%
Wyoming	535.8 (+/–67.8)	590.3 (+/–71.2)	621.5 (+/–73.7)	681.1 (+/–92.7)	27.1%

* *Note*: The states of Alaska and Hawaii are not covered by this survey.
Source: Summary Report, 2007 National Resources Inventory (December 2009), U.S. Department of Agriculture

Documents

What is being done to address urban growth pressures? The following section offer a sampling of initiatives that are already in place across the world that ranges from Europe to North America, South America, and the Middle East.

In 1992, the Vancouver City Council asked citizens for ideas about Vancouver's future. Over the following three years more than 20,000 people participated in developing a shared vision for the city's future. It is intended that the final product, called City Plan, would cast both a broad vision for the city and serve as a guide to policy decisions, corporate work priorities, budgets, and capital plans.

In 1998, the Munich city council decided on a major urban development strategy called The Munich Perspective. The study of this metropolitan area was authorized to preserve and protect what is widely recognized as a high quality of life. It was hoped that through the process of creating such a document, current and future development would recognize and affirm the ongoing importance of economic prosperity, public spaces, and neighborhood preservation as well integration of new communities. The final product was the result of more than just planning experts and public officials, there were extensive workshops conducted with the public to help determine how the city would want to master its challenges of the future.

In the United States, no state has done more to establish policies and programs designed to shape its future urban development than Oregon. Even after 40 years, the Statewide Planning Program located in this section remains the most revolutionary statewide planning law in the nation. Adopted in 1973, it seeks to better manage growth statewide by coordinating land use planning by the many local, county, and state agencies that share responsibility for impacting on development. Not surprisingly, Oregon's lead city of Portland has also set the standard for innovation in planning at the local level. The charter for its metropolitan government created in 1993 offers a three-country urban region a directly elected body to oversee a variety of important regional services that all impact land-use planning.

The next document represents the more recent focus of statewide planning laws that encompass the so-called "smart-growth" agenda. Rather than shift responsibility to regional- or state-level agencies as Oregon has done, Maryland's 1997 law takes a more indirect approach. It provides both incentives and disincentives to promote greater conservation of land and other resources, and pushes new development into previously developed corridors while preserving relatively pristine rural areas.

What can be done to accommodate the rapid growth of slums and shantytown communities in the cities of the developing world? The Istanbul Declaration on Human Settlements of 1996 was adopted by 171 governments that attended the Habitat II conference in Turkey. It was significant in that it helped to focus global attention on urbanization as one of the most important emerging issues of the twenty-first century. It should be appreciated that this is a broad statement that affirms the commitment of member states to improve the living standards for the teeming millions that are crowding into the fast-growing cities of the developing world.

How can fast-growing cities of the developing world adapt and even flourish in the midst of overcrowded roads, pressing housing needs, and public utilities stretched to the limit? The city of Curitiba is Brazil's showpiece of urban planning, renowned among architects worldwide as a pioneering achievement in metropolitan renovation and innovation. Just as the city's population was beginning to explode in the 1960s, a redesign effort was initiated by aspiring architects who planned to carry the still-small capital of Paraná state into a new era—and to do so without the excessive borrowing. The cost-efficient and environmentally friendly solutions they built into the plan—which has accommodated a population that is almost ten times larger than it was 50 years ago—have since become an international blueprint for sustainable city design.

CityPlan: Directions for Vancouver (1995)

Introduction

In the fall of 1992, Vancouver City Council asked citizens for ideas about Vancouver's future. Over the following three years more than 20,000 people participated in developing a shared vision for Vancouver's future: CityPlan. On June 6, 1995, Vancouver City Council adopted CityPlan: Directions for Vancouver as a broad vision for the city to guide policy decisions, corporate work priorities, budgets, and capital plans.

City of Neighborhoods

Vancouverites want a city of neighborhoods each with its own identity. To make these neighborhoods happen, CityPlan sets directions for neighborhood centers, housing variety, and neighborhood character.

Neighborhood Centers

In all areas of Vancouver, neighborhood centers will provide a "heart" for each neighborhood. Here, people will find shops, jobs, community services, public places, and housing for various ages and incomes. These centers will, for the most part, develop from existing shopping streets and attract people from the surrounding area to shop, work, meet with neighbors and friends, and participate in community activities.

Neighborhood Housing Variety

Neighborhood centers will provide a greater variety of housing in single-family neighborhoods—townhouses, row houses, and apartments—for people at different stages of life and of different incomes. Older people will be able to stay in the community where they've lived most of their lives. More young people and young families will be able to find homes in their familiar neighborhoods. Additional housing will be built around the downtown peninsula within walking distance of the many jobs downtown.

Distinctive Neighborhood Character

Even with more people and more housing, Vancouver will retain much of its traditional look and feel—the trees and greenery, the heritage buildings and areas, the distinctive character of each neighborhood, and the generally low-scale buildings away from the downtown. Change will be focused in the downtown and new neighborhood centers. Around these centers, traditional single-family areas will remain. How the character of each neighborhood develops will reflect the wishes of the people who live there. Working with City Hall, neighborhood residents will have a say in the types of new housing and the look of the neighborhood.

The Challenges

- Defining where and how neighborhood centers develop.
- Agreeing on how much growth and how to distribute this growth in the city. Developing new ways for residents to work with City Hall to shape their neighborhoods.
- Creating the feel of single-family housing in new types of medium density housing.
- Balancing stronger design regulations with the need to reduce red tape and allow innovation.

Sense of Community
Vancouver residents want everyone to feel part of the community, to have access to services, and to live and work safely. To create a sense of community, CityPlan sets directions for accessible, community-based services; promoting safety; addressing housing costs; art and culture; and diverse public spaces.

Accessible, Community-Based Services
CityPlan will help people create a city where community services are developed in consultation with the people who use them. Services will be located in neighborhoods where they are easy to get to and targeted to those who need them most. Health, police, recreation, library, and other City staff will work together as part of community-based service teams

Working Together to Promote Safety
CityPlan will help Vancouver residents create a safer city—not just by reacting to crime, but by preventing crime before it happens. Community-based police officers, neighborhood residents, and social agencies will work together on the social problems that often lead to crime. Neighborhoods and developers will keep safety in mind when creating public spaces and new buildings.

Addressing Housing Costs
CityPlan will help to keep a supply of affordable housing in the city. Subsidized housing measures will continue to provide housing for some low and moderate income households. New City programs will encourage some lower cost market housing so a range of people can continue to afford to live in Vancouver.

Art and Culture in a Creative City
Art and culture will contribute more to the city's identity, neighborhoods' character, and people's learning and self-expression. Vancouver will maintain a strong arts community that encourages local artists and reflects the city's diverse cultural heritage. Arts and cultural activity will increase through partnerships with business, education, and recreation.

New and More Diverse Public Places
CityPlan will lead to the creation of diverse public places. Streets will be designed for people, not just cars. Greenways for walking and biking will connect neighborhoods throughout the city. Parks and open spaces will be developed in areas that need them. Downtown public places will be improved to make the city centre more welcoming.

The Challenges

- Finding innovative ways to fund community services, affordable housing, and parks.
- Forging partnerships between the City, other governments, business, arts, and non-profit groups to provide community services.
- Creating better ways to involve citizens in service delivery.
- Involving residents in the safety of their neighborhoods.
- Defining the City's role in regulating housing costs.
- Securing regional support for Vancouver-based services, arts, and cultural activities.
- Sharing street right-of-ways as public places for walking, socializing, biking, as well as cars.

Healthy Economy, Healthy Environment
Vancouver residents want a livable city with a wide variety of jobs, where our activities are sensitive to the environment. CityPlan sets directions for creating a diverse economy and jobs close to home; ensuring clean air and water; and making transit, walking, and biking a priority.

Diverse Economy and Jobs Close to Home
CityPlan will help create a city with a variety of economic opportunities and more jobs closer to where people live. Downtown Vancouver will continue to be the "region's downtown." Industrial lands will be maintained for new types of industries and businesses—high tech research, repair services, and warehouses located near their customers and workers. More office, service, and retail jobs will be located in neighborhood centers.Vancouver will continue to support job creation in regional town centers to cut down on commuting into the city.

Public Transit, Walking, and Biking as a Priority
CityPlan puts walking, cycling, and transit ahead of cars to cut down on traffic congestion and improve the environment. People will have travel alternatives such as better transit service and streets will be more friendly for biking and walking. Cars will not be as convenient as they once were. More people will live close to shops, services, and jobs in their neighborhoods; this will reduce car trips and congestion.

Clean Air and Water
CityPlan participants put clean air and water as top priorities. People may also be asked to pay user fees for services like water use and garbage collection to encourage conservation and reduce harmful impacts on the environment.

The Challenges

- Attracting suitable businesses to neighborhood centers.
- Reversing the trend of allowing housing and retail developments to replace industry.
- Improving transit services.
- Using cars less.
- Implementing tolls and charges to encourage conservation and transit use.
- Adjusting our lifestyles to reduce, reuse, and recycle to reduce the impact of city life on the environment.

A Vibrant Central Area
Vancouver residents want a downtown that is a welcoming city centre and a place to work, live, and visit.

Downtown Vancouver
Vancouver's central area, surrounded by Burrard Inlet and English Bay, and encircling False Creek, will extend its activity to its waterfronts and have two major office districts—the region's downtown central business district and the medical-civic "uptown" on Broadway. Surrounding the business districts, new residential neighborhoods will provide livable environments for a variety of people. Specialty character and heritage areas, lively retail streets, waterfront walkways, and diverse plazas and open spaces will be welcoming public places for residents, employees, visitors, and tourists. Offices served by transit, people living near work, and pedestrian and bicycle friendly routes will help to minimize the traffic pressures of downtown activity.

The Challenges

- Addressing the social impacts of growth and meeting the social needs of low-income people and families in and near the downtown.
- Keeping traffic impacts in check by encouraging more transit, walking, and biking.
- Enhancing downtown's streets as public places.
- Making CityPlan Happen.

Vancouver residents want a voice in decisions affecting them and their neighborhoods, and they want a city administration that continues to make sound financial decisions.

People Involved in Decision Making
Though City Council will still be the place major decisions are made, CityPlan will lead to more community involvement in decisionmaking.

City staff located in the community will work together and with residents to shape service delivery. Residents will also play a major role in how their neighborhood centers develop and what their neighborhoods look like.

Financial Accountability

Vancouverites want a city that maintains a top notch financial rating and keeps spending under control. To move toward the vision without raising taxes means redirecting the City budget to gradually make CityPlan a reality. This means some parts of CityPlan will take longer to achieve than others.

The City in the Region

Vancouver residents want to do their share to help create a livable region, protect the region's green zone for agriculture and recreation, slow urban sprawl, and cut down on car travel by creating more complete communities. As the largest city in the region, Vancouver will continue to be the engine of the region's economy and play a major role in achieving the "Livable Region Strategic Plan." CityPlan suggests that Vancouver accept a share of the region's housing and job growth and provide for increased transit services. By doing so, Vancouver will help reduce urban sprawl onto farm and greenlands in the Fraser Valley.

Source: City of Vancouver website: http://vancouver.ca/commsvcs/planning/cityplan/dfvs.htm. Used by permission of the City of Vancouver.

The Munich Perspective (1996)

Guidelines and Orientation Projects

How should Munich look like in ten, twenty, or even thirty years? What do we need to do to achieve quality of life and work, now and in the future? What are the influences of economic, political and social changes on life in Munich?

The MUNICH PERSPECTIVE urban planning concept applies exactly on these problems, offering an outlook for the urban economic, social, spatial and regional development. Urban planning is an intrinsically complex process: it depends not just on city council resolutions, but is also affected by many decisions taken by private citizens, companies and associations, as well as the parliaments in Munich, Berlin and Brussels.

Therefore the MUNICH PERSPECTIVE is more of a flexible guide than a rigid plan. Its Guidelines offer definitions for both the direction and ambition of urban planning, while its orientation projects provide specific tools and a "laboratory" for research into new pathways in urban planning and communal urban living.

The MUNICH PERSPECTIVE is bound to two principles. The first is sustainability. Quality of life should not be obtained at the cost of future generations. Instead, improvements to the city's quality should be enduring. The second principle is urbanism—everything that can be regarded as urban in a positive sense, i.e. social and cultural diversity, tolerance, economic opportunities and a creativity, which only can result from high density and mixture.

A public debate about objectives and methods is an essential feature of MUNICH PERSPECTIVE. Teamwork with groups such as youth and senior citizens' groups is just as important as a close cooperation with district committees, chambers of commerce, and other associations; scientific, trade union and church, institutions and clubs, non-profit organizations and local Agenda 21 activists, finally, representatives of the Munich region.

The Guidelines

1. Securing and promoting of employment and economic prosperity

The factors contributing to this are:

- securing of the diversified economic structure in Munich, known as the "Munich Mix";
- promotion of innovative industries and ecologically sustainable economic systems;
- expansion of a business-friendly infrastructure;
- continuation of the image campaign and location marketing for the economic region;
- advancement of the Munich employment and qualification program.

2. Improved regional cooperation–reinforcing the region's competitive credentials

Both a coordinated location policy in the region and regional area management are both crucial to competing effectively as an international business location. The cooperation on the Regional Planning Committee, the Munich Transport Association, with clubs and associations, with cities, local authorities and administrative districts will be enhanced in an efficient, trusting manner.

3. Securing social harmony through communal social policies

Such policies focus principally on:

- acquisition and creation of low cost housing space;
- incorporation of differing gender viewpoints and interests into the urban development process;
- integration of foreign residents;
- access to cultural and educational amenities for all sections of the public;
- encouragement of integration of curative and preventive care, to promote health education in the neighborhoods and among specific target groups and to expand healthy living programs;
- prevention and rehabilitation;
- education policies in tune with the demands of modern living;
- small scale, grassroots, social infrastructure.

4. Neighborhood development to reinforce local identities

Neighborhood development closely involving local residents will be used to:

- enhance quality of life in the neighborhood;
- improve the local job market;
- promote local self-help capabilities and social networks, and also
- strengthen the culture of the urban district.

5. Developing sustainable settlement by upgrading the present urban fabric

The settlement conception devised for Munich envisages an increase in the numbers of city residents as well as the preservation and expansion of landscape and green spaces. It is intended to release the inner city and to enable urban diversity even in suburban districts by strengthening the neighborhood centers.

"Internal development," i.e. construction on new sites released from other uses, takes priority over "external development," which is the settlement on previous agricultural used sites or other vacant spaces. In short, the keywords for future housing development in Munich are: compact/urban/green. Enhanced mobility for all modes of transport—traffic engineering for sustainable urban quality.

6. Preserving the face of Munich–encouraging new architecture

The aim of this is to forge a connection between tradition, contemporary building and design in the city. The "Munich Mix" as a concept is relevant not just to the city's economic structure but also to the lively blend created by the historical townscape and typical new architecture. The residents' identification with their own city takes centre stage. Munich shall remain a beautiful city and preserve and enhance its distinctive character. Instead of representing the lowest common denominator of general taste, its architecture and urban development both can and should provide an impetus for debate and a new, stimulating awareness of the familiar, everyday environment.

7. Enhanced mobility for all modes of transport–traffic engineering for sustainable urban quality

Here, the contributing factors are:

- further expansion of the public transport network;
- extension and improvement of the cycle and footpath network;
- improvement of traffic conditions for commercial and commuter traffic by the creation of freight distribution centers and a city logistics strategy for a more efficient handling of delivery traffic;
- increased use of telematics for better traffic management.

The "New" Guidelines

Following the mandate given by the City Council in 1998, the MUNICH PERSPECTIVE has been complimented with new guidelines on the themes "Securing Inner City Harmony," "New Media," "Ecology," and "Culture." Draft guidelines have been created, and they are now being publicly debated. Once this process has finished, the guidelines will be revised and presented to the City Council for its verdict. Only once the City Council has passed a relevant resolution will they become the MUNICH PERSPECTIVE Guidelines.

8. Securing inner city harmony through communal security, social, education and cultural policies

The inner city harmony and cohesion of Munich society are created and maintained mainly through preventative measures. It is planned that these preventative measures will result from communal social, education, and cultural policies aimed primarily at the particular needs of different segments of the city's population.

Special efforts need to be made in the following areas:

- pro-active, early prevention of social problem situations, such as poverty and homelessness;
- access to education and training.

Cultural projects give the different segments of the city's population space to preserve their distinctive identity and simultaneously to make their culture known to others. Violence committed by men against women and children must be prevented in all areas. Provision of integration-friendly measures must be increased, with the aim of consistently assimilating migrants into the structures within urban districts. Social exclusion and the ghetto-formation must be counteracted at all levels. Provision must be made for individuals to acquire intercultural competence.

One of the main aims of communal security policy is to prevent the creation of areas where the law does not apply, so as, in turn, to maintain law and order in the city. More attention must be paid to future social trends, and action must be taken as early as possible in relation to them.

Cooperation between the security authorities; medical, psychological, and social services; educational and training institutions must be developed and improved. This is because only a holistic strategy, in which prevention, assistance and repression of criminal behavior go together hand-in-glove, is capable of ensuring inner city harmony in the long term.

9. New Media

This term means a lot more than just mobile phones and the Internet. New media transform our lives. Our society is in the process of changing into an information and knowledge society. The looming dimensions of this process can, however, only be assumed. Thus, a major objective has to be to give all city residents the opportunity to participate in the developments occurring in the information society. An essential prerequisite of this has to be the ability to acquire "media competence," in the form of a basic qualification at the city's different educational institutions. Regardless of age, education or earning ability, access to data, communication and interaction (e.g. for exchanging tax or driving license forms) must be open to all city residents. The placing of computers in all the public schools in Munich is clearly a decisive step in this direction.

New media provide a major opportunity to bring city residents and political representatives or the city's administration together in both temporal and organizational terms. The simplification of citizens' interaction with officialdom is an important theme in this context. However, the provision of information and, therefore, the creation of transparency in politics and administration in particular also are important components. Further the encouragement of media economy has a central function.

New media offer a broad range of possibilities and applications that can be used to ensure our city's future.

10. Ecology

The Ecology Guideline (in German) comprehensively brings together for the first time all relevant information concerning soil, water, air, flora and fauna, noise, power and waste. The condition and development trends of the Munich environment are also described. Objectives, strategies and measures are formulated to encourage responsible action, specifically:

- careful use of the natural resources of soil, water, and air,
- preservation of diversity in flora and fauna,
- energy-saving,
- waste prevention,
- noise reduction.

All the environmental themes addressed in the Ecology Guideline have one thing in common: without exception, they have a direct effect on the well-being and quality of life of Munich residents. Thus, they affect each individual.

Source: http://www.muenchen.de/Rathaus/plan/stadtentwicklung/perspektive/pm_en_m/41525/index.html.

Statewide Planning Program-State of Oregon (1973)

The Statewide Planning Goals

Since 1973, Oregon has maintained a strong statewide program for land use planning. The foundation of that program is a set of 19 statewide planning goals. The goals express the state's policies on land use and on related topics, such as citizen involvement, housing, and natural resources.

Most of the goals are accompanied by "guidelines," which are suggestions about how a goal may be applied. As noted in Goal 2, guidelines are not mandatory. The goals have been adopted as administrative rules (Oregon Administrative Rules Chapter 660, Division 15).

Goal 1: Citizen Involvement

To develop a citizen involvement program that insures the opportunity for citizens to be involved in all phases of the planning process. The governing body charged with preparing and adopting a comprehensive plan shall adopt and publicize a program for citizen involvement that clearly defines the procedures by which the general public will be involved in the on-going land-use planning process. The citizen involvement program shall be appropriate to the scale of the planning effort. The program shall provide for continuity of citizen participation and of information that enables citizens to identify and comprehend the issues. Federal, state, and regional agencies, and special-purpose districts shall coordinate their planning efforts with the affected governing bodies and make use of existing local citizen involvement programs established by counties and cities.

Goal 2: Land Use Planning

To establish a land use planning process and policy framework as a basis for all decision and actions related to use of land and to assure an adequate factual base for such decisions and actions. City, county, state, and federal agency and special district plans and actions related to land use shall be consistent with the comprehensive plans of cities and counties and regional plans adopted under ORS Chapter 268.

All land use plans shall include identification of issues and problems, inventories and other factual information for each applicable statewide planning goal, evaluation of alternative courses of action and ultimate policy choices, taking into consideration social, economic, energy and environmental needs. The required information shall be contained in the plan document or in supporting documents. The plans, supporting documents and implementation ordinances shall be filed in a public office or other place easily accessible to the public. The plans shall be the basis for specific implementation measures. These measures shall be consistent with and adequate to carry out the plans. Each plan and related implementation measure shall be coordinated with the plans of affected governmental units.

All land-use plans and implementation ordinances shall be adopted by the governing body after public hearing and shall be reviewed and, as needed, revised on a periodic cycle to take into account changing public policies and circumstances, in accord with a schedule set forth in the plan. Opportunities shall be provided for review and comment by citizens and affected governmental units during preparation, review and revision of plans and implementation ordinances.

Goal 3: Agricultural Lands

To preserve and maintain agricultural lands. Agricultural lands shall be preserved and maintained for farm use, consistent with existing and future needs for agricultural products, forest and open space and with the state's agricultural land use policy expressed in ORS 215.243 and 215.700.

Goal 4: Forest Lands

To conserve forest lands by maintaining the forest land base and to protect the state's forest economy by making possible economically efficient forest practices that assure the continuous growing and harvesting of forest tree species as the leading use on forest land consistent with sound management of soil, air, water, and fish and wildlife resources and to provide for recreational opportunities and agriculture.

Forest lands are those lands acknowledged as forest lands as of the date of adoption of this goal amendment. Where a plan is not acknowledged or a plan amendment involving forest lands is proposed, forest land shall include lands which are suitable for commercial forest uses including adjacent or nearby lands which are necessary to permit forest operations or practices and other forested lands that maintain soil, air, water and fish and wildlife resources.

Goal 5: Open Spaces, Scenic and Historic Areas, and Natural Resources

To protect natural resources and conserve scenic and historic areas and open spaces. Local governments shall adopt programs that will protect natural resources and conserve scenic, historic, and open space resources for present and future generations. These resources promote a healthy environment and natural landscape that contributes to Oregon's livability.

Goal 6: Air, Water and Land Resources Quality

To maintain and improve the quality of the air, water, and land resources of the state. All waste and process discharges from future development, when combined with such discharges from existing developments shall not threaten to violate, or violate applicable state or federal environmental quality statutes, rules, and standards. With respect to the air, water, and land resources of the applicable air sheds and river basins described or included in state environmental quality statutes, rules, standards, and implementation plans, such discharges shall not exceed the carrying capacity of such resources, considering long range needs; degrade such resources; or threaten the availability of such resources.

Goal 7: Areas Subject to Natural Disasters and Hazards

To protect life and property from natural disasters and hazards. Developments subject to damage or that could result in loss of life shall not be planned nor located in known areas of natural disasters and hazards without appropriate safeguards. Plans shall be based on an inventory of known areas of natural disaster and hazards.

Goal 8: Recreational Needs
To satisfy the recreational needs of the citizens of the state and visitors and, where appropriate, to provide for the siting of necessary recreational facilities including destination resorts.

Goal 9: Economic Development
To provide adequate opportunities throughout the state for a variety of economic activities vital to the health, welfare, and prosperity of Oregon's citizens. Comprehensive plans and policies shall contribute to a stable and healthy economy in all regions of the state. Such plans shall be based on inventories of areas suitable for increased economic growth and activity after taking into consideration the health of the current economic base; materials and energy availability and cost; labor market factors; educational and technical training programs; availability of key public facilities; necessary support facilities; current market forces; location relative to markets; availability of renewable and non-renewable resources; availability of land; and pollution control requirements. Comprehensive plans for urban areas shall:

1. Include an analysis of the community's economic patterns, potentialities, strengths, and deficiencies as they relate to state and national trends;
2. Contain policies concerning the economic development opportunities in the community;
3. Provide for at least an adequate supply of sites of suitable sizes, types, locations, and service levels for a variety of industrial and commercial uses consistent with plan policies;
4. Limit uses on or near sites zoned for specific industrial and commercial uses to those which are compatible with proposed uses.

In accordance with ORS 197.180 and Goal 2, state agencies that issue permits affecting land use shall identify in their coordination programs how they will coordinate permit issuance with other state agencies, cities, and counties.

Goal 10: Housing
To provide for the housing needs of citizens of the state. Buildable lands for residential use shall be inventoried and plans shall encourage the availability of adequate numbers of needed housing units at price ranges and rent levels which are commensurate with the financial capabilities of Oregon households and allow for flexibility of housing location, type and density.

Goal 11: Public Facilities and Services
To plan and develop a timely, orderly, and efficient arrangement of public facilities and services to serve as a framework for urban and rural development. Urban and rural development shall be guided and supported by types and levels of urban and rural public facilities and services appropriate for, but limited to, the needs and requirements of the urban, urbanizable, and rural areas to be served. A provision for key facilities shall be included in each plan. Cities or counties shall develop and adopt a public facility plan for areas within an urban growth boundary containing a population greater than 2,500 persons. To meet current and long-range needs, a provision for solid waste disposal sites, including sites for inert waste, shall be included in each plan.

Counties shall develop and adopt community public facility plans regulating facilities and services for certain unincorporated communities outside urban growth boundaries as specified by Commission rules. Local governments shall not allow the establishment or extension of sewer systems outside urban growth boundaries or unincorporated community boundaries, or allow extensions of sewer lines from within urban growth boundaries or unincorporated community boundaries to serve land outside those boundaries, except where the new or extended system is the only practicable alternative to mitigate a public health hazard and will not adversely affect farm or forest land. Local governments shall not rely upon the presence, establishment, or extension of a water or sewer system to allow residential development of land outside urban growth boundaries or unincorporated community boundaries at a density higher than authorized without service from such a system.

In accordance with ORS 197.180 and Goal 2, state agencies that provide funding for transportation, water supply, sewage, and solid waste facilities shall identify in their coordination programs how they will coordinate that funding with other state agencies and with the public facility plans of cities and counties.

Goal 12: Transportation
To provide and encourage a safe, convenient, and economic transportation system. A transportation plan shall:

1. consider all modes of transportation including mass transit, air, water, pipeline, rail, highway, bicycle and pedestrian;
2. be based upon an inventory of local, regional and state transportation needs;
3. consider the differences in social consequences that would result from utilizing differing combinations of transportation modes;
4. avoid principal reliance upon any one mode of transportation;
5. minimize adverse social, economic and environmental impacts and costs;

6. conserve energy;
7. meet the needs of the transportation disadvantaged by improving transportation services;
8. facilitate the flow of goods and services so as to strengthen the local and regional economy; and
9. conform with local and regional comprehensive land use plans. Each plan shall include a provision for transportation as a key facility.

Goal 13: Energy Conservation
To conserve energy. Land and uses developed on the land shall be managed and controlled so as to maximize the conservation of all forms of energy, based upon sound economic principles.

Goal 14: Urbanization
To provide for an orderly and efficient transition from rural to urban land use. Urban growth boundaries shall be established to identify and separate urbanizable land from rural land. Establishment and change of the boundaries shall be based upon considerations of the following factors:

1. Demonstrated need to accommodate long-range urban population growth requirements consistent with LCDC goals;
2. Need for housing, employment opportunities, and livability;
3. Orderly and economic provision for public facilities and services;
4. Maximum efficiency of land uses within and on the fringe of the existing urban area;
5. Environmental, energy, economic and social consequences;
6. Retention of agricultural land as defined, with Class I being the highest priority for retention and Class VI the lowest priority; and,
7. Compatibility of the proposed urban uses with nearby agricultural activities.

The results of the above considerations shall be included in the comprehensive plan. In the case of a change of a boundary, a governing body proposing such change in the boundary separating urbanizable lands from rural land, shall follow the procedures and requirements as set forth in the Land Use Planning goal (Goal 2) for goal exceptions. Any urban growth boundary established prior to January 1, 1975, which includes rural lands that have not been built upon shall be reviewed by the governing body, utilizing the same factors applicable to the establishment or change of urban growth boundaries.

Establishment and change of the boundaries shall be a cooperative process between a city and the county or counties that surround it. Land within the boundaries separating urbanizable land from rural land shall be considered available over time for urban uses. Conversion of urbanizable land to urban uses shall be based on consideration of:

1. Orderly, economic provision for public facilities and services;
2. Availability of sufficient land for the various uses to insure choices in the market place;
3. LCDC goals or the acknowledged comprehensive plan; and,
4. Encouragement of development within urban areas before conversion of urbanizable areas.

In unincorporated communities outside urban growth boundaries counties may approve uses, public Facilities, and services more intensive than allowed on rural lands by Goal 11 and 14, either by exception to those goals, or as provided by Commission rules which ensure such uses do not:

1. adversely affect agricultural and forest operations, and
2. interfere with the efficient functioning of urban growth boundaries.

Goal 15: Willamette River Greenway
To protect, conserve, enhance and maintain the natural, scenic, historical, agricultural, economic, and recreational qualities of lands along the Willamette River as the Willamette River Greenway.

Goal 16: Estuarine Resources
To recognize and protect the unique environmental, economic, and social values of each estuary and associated wetlands; and to protect, maintain, where appropriate develop, and where appropriate restore the long-term environmental, economic, and social values, diversity and benefits of Oregon's estuaries.

Comprehensive management programs to achieve these objectives shall be developed by appropriate local, state, and federal agencies for all estuaries. To assure diversity among the estuaries of the State, by June 15, 1977, LCDC with the cooperation and participation of local governments, special districts, and state and federal agencies shall classify the Oregon estuaries to specify the most intensive level of development or alteration which may be allowed to occur within each estuary. After completion for all estuaries of the inventories and initial planning efforts, including identification of needs and potential conflicts among needs and goals and upon request of any coastal jurisdiction, the Commission will review the overall Oregon Estuary Classification.

Comprehensive plans and activities for each estuary shall provide for appropriate uses (including preservation) with as much diversity as is consistent with the overall Oregon Estuary Classification, as well as with the biological economic, recreational, and aesthetic benefits of the estuary. Estuary plans and activities shall protect the estuarine ecosystem, including its natural biological productivity, habitat, diversity, unique features and water quality. The general priorities (from highest to lowest) for management and use of estuarine resources as implemented through the management unit designation and permissible use requirements listed below shall be:

1. Uses which maintain the integrity of the estuarine ecosystem;
2. Water-dependent uses requiring estuarine location, as consistent with the overall Oregon Estuary Classification;
3. Water-related uses which do not degrade or reduce the natural estuarine resources and values;
4. Nondependent, nonrelated uses which do not alter, reduce, or degrade estuarine resources and values.

Goal 17: Coastal Shorelands

To conserve, protect, where appropriate, develop and where appropriate restore the resources and benefits of all coastal shorelands, recognizing their value for protection and maintenance of water quality, fish and wildlife habitat, water-dependent uses, economic resources and recreation and aesthetics. The management of these shoreland areas shall be compatible with the characteristics of the adjacent coastal waters; and to reduce the hazard to human life and property, and the adverse effects upon water quality and fish and wildlife habitat, resulting from the use and enjoyment of Oregon's coastal shorelands.

Programs to achieve these objectives shall be developed by local, state, and federal agencies having jurisdiction over coastal shorelands. Land use plans, implementing actions and permit reviews shall include consideration of the critical relationships between coastal shorelands and resources of coastal waters, and of the geologic and hydrologic hazards associated with coastal shorelands. Local, state and federal agencies shall within the limit of their authorities maintain the diverse environmental, economic, and social values of coastal shorelands and water quality in coastal waters. Within those limits, they shall also minimize man-induced sedimentation in estuaries, nearshore ocean waters, and coastal lakes. General priorities for the overall use of coastal shorelands (from highest to lowest) shall be to:

1. Promote uses which maintain the integrity of estuaries and coastal waters;
2. Provide for water-dependent uses;

3. Provide for water-related uses;
4. Provide for nondependent, nonrelated uses which retain flexibility of future use and do not prematurely or inalterably commit shorelands to more intensive uses;
5. Provide for development, including nondependent, nonrelated uses, in urban areas compatible with existing or committed uses;
6. Permit nondependent, nonrelated uses which cause a permanent or long-term change in the features of coastal shorelands only upon a demonstration of public need.

Goal 18: Beaches and Dunes
To conserve, protect, where appropriate develop, and where appropriate restore the resources and benefits of coastal beach and dune areas; and to reduce the hazard to human life and property from natural or man-induced actions associated with these areas.

Coastal comprehensive plans and implementing actions shall provide for diverse and appropriate use of beach and dune areas consistent with their ecological, recreational, aesthetic, water resource, and economic values, and consistent with the natural limitations of beaches, dunes, and dune vegetation for development.

Goal 19: Ocean Resources
To conserve the long-term values, benefits, and natural resources of the near shore ocean and the continental shelf. All local, state, and federal plans, policies, projects, and activities which affect the territorial sea shall be developed, managed, and conducted to maintain, and where appropriate, enhance and restore, the long-term benefits derived from the near shore oceanic resources of Oregon. Since renewable ocean resources and uses, such as food production, water quality, navigation, recreation, and aesthetic enjoyment, will provide greater long-term benefits than will nonrenewable resources, such plans and activities shall give clear priority to the proper management and protection of renewable resources.

City and County Planning

Oregon's statewide goals are achieved through local comprehensive planning. State law requires each city and county to have a comprehensive plan and the zoning and land-division ordinances needed to put the plan into effect.

The local comprehensive plans must be consistent with the statewide planning goals. Plans are reviewed for such consistency by the state's Land Conservation and Development Commission (LCDC). When LCDC officially approves a local government's plan, the plan is said to be "acknowledged." It then becomes the controlling document for land use in the area covered by that plan.

Oregon's planning laws apply not only to local governments but also to special districts and state agencies. The laws strongly emphasize coordination—keeping plans and programs consistent with each other, with the goals, and with acknowledged local plans.

A Partnership

Oregon's planning program is a partnership between state and local governments. The state requires cities and counties to plan, and it sets the standards for such planning. Local governments do the planning and administer most of the land-use regulations. The resulting mosaic of state-approved local comprehensive plans covers the entire state.

The state does not write comprehensive plans. It doesn't zone land or administer permits for local planning actions like variances and conditional uses. And unlike some other states, Oregon does not require environmental impact statements.

The Land Conservation and Development Commission
Oregon's statewide planning program is directed by the Land Conservation and Development Commission (LCDC). The commission's seven members are unsalaried volunteers, appointed by the governor and confirmed by the state senate. The term of appointment is four years.

The Department of Land Conservation and Development
LCDC's administrative arm is the Department of Land Conservation and Development (DLCD). DLCD is a small state agency with its main office in Salem. The department has field representatives in Portland, Newport, and Bend.

The Land-Use Board of Appeals
The state has a special "court" (the Land-Use Board of Appeals) that reviews appeals of land use decisions. LUBA has three members, known as "referees." It is based in Salem.

Citizen Involvement
It's no coincidence that Citizen Involvement is the first among Oregon's 19 planning goals. Extensive citizen participation has been the hallmark of the state's planning program from its outset. Every city and county has a Committee for Citizen Involvement (CCI) to monitor and encourage active citizen participation. The state's Citizen Involvement Advisory Committee (CIAC) also encourages such participation in all aspects of planning.

The Local Comprehensive Plan

The local comprehensive plan guides a community's land use, conservation of natural resources, economic development, and public services. Each plan has two main parts. One is a body of data and information called the inventory, background report, or factual base. It describes a community's resources and features. It must address all of the topics specified in the applicable statewide goals. The other part is the policy element. That part of the plan sets forth the community's long-range objectives and the policies by which it intends to achieve them. The policy element of each community's plan is adopted by ordinance and has the force of law.

Local plans may be changed through plan amendments or periodic review. Plan amendments are smaller, unscheduled adjustments to a plan. Periodic reviews are broad evaluations of an entire plan that occur every four to ten years. A plan may be modified extensively after such a review.

Each plan is accompanied by a set of implementing measures. There are many different kinds. The two most common measures are zoning and land-division ordinances. Every city and county in Oregon has adopted such land-use controls.

Source: Oregon Department of Land Conservation and Development. 1996 Edition. Available at http://www.oregon.gov/LCD/goals.shtml.

Charter of the Metropolitan Government of Portland, Oregon (1993)

PREAMBLE

We, the people of the Portland area metropolitan service district, in order to establish an elected, visible, and accountable regional government that is responsive to the citizens of the region and works cooperatively with our local governments; that undertakes, as its most important service, planning and policy making to preserve and enhance the quality of life and the environment for ourselves and future generations; and that provides regional services needed and desired by the citizens in an efficient and effective manner, do ordain this charter for the Portland area metropolitan service district, to be known as Metro.

NAMES AND BOUNDARIES

Section 1. Title of Charter.

The title of this charter is the 1992 Metro Charter.

Section 2. Name of Regional Government.

The Portland area metropolitan service district, referred to in this charter as the "Metropolitan Service District," continues under this charter as a metropolitan service district with the name "Metro."

Section 3. Boundaries.

The Metro area of governance includes all territory within the boundaries of the Metropolitan Service District on the effective date of this charter and any territory later annexed or subjected to Metro governance under state law. This charter refers to that area as the "Metro area." Changes of Metro boundaries are not effective unless approved by ordinance. No change of Metro boundaries requires approval by a local government boundary commission or any other state agency unless required by law. The custodian of Metro records shall keep an accurate description of Metro boundaries and make it available for public inspection.

FUNCTIONS AND POWERS

Section 4. Jurisdiction of Metro.

Metro has jurisdiction over matters of metropolitan concern. Matters of metropolitan concern include the powers granted to and duties imposed on Metro by current and future state law and those matters the council by ordinance determines to be of metropolitan concern. The council shall specify by ordinance the extent to which Metro exercises jurisdiction over matters of metropolitan concern.

Section 5. Regional Planning Functions.
(1) Future Vision.

(a) Adoption. The council shall adopt a Future Vision for the region between January 15, 1995 and July 1, 1995. The Future Vision is a conceptual statement that indicates population levels and settlement patterns that the region can accommodate within the carrying capacity of the land, water and air resources of the region, and its educational and economic resources, and that achieves a desired quality of life. The Future Vision is a long-term, visionary outlook for at least a 50-year period. As used in this section, "region" means the Metro area and adjacent areas.

(b) Matters addressed. The matters addressed by the Future Vision include but are not limited to: (1) use, restoration and preservation of regional land and natural resources for the benefit of present and future generations, (2) how and where to accommodate the population growth for the region while maintaining a desired quality of life for its residents, and (3) how to develop new communities and additions to the existing urban areas in well-planned ways.

(c) Development. The council shall appoint a commission to develop and recommend a proposed Future Vision by a date the council sets. The commission shall be broadly representative of both public and private sectors, including the academic community, in the region. At least one member must reside outside the Metro area. The commission has authority to seek any necessary information and shall consider all relevant information and public comment in developing the proposed Future Vision. The commission serves without compensation.

(d) Review and amendment. The Future Vision may be reviewed and amended as provided by ordinance. The Future Vision shall be completely reviewed and revised at least every fifteen years in the manner specified in subsection (1)(c) of this section.

(e) Effect. The Future Vision is not a regulatory document. It is the intent of this charter that the Future Vision have no effect that would allow court or agency review of it.

(2) Regional Framework Plan.

(a) Adoption. The council shall adopt a regional framework plan by December 31, 1997 with the consultation and advice of the Metro Policy Advisory Committee (MPAC) created under Section 27 of this charter. The council may adopt the regional framework plan in components.

(b) Matters addressed. The regional framework plan shall address: (1) regional transportation and mass transit systems, (2) management and amendment of the urban growth boundary, (3) protection of lands outside the urban growth boundary for natural resource, future urban or other uses, (4) housing densities, (5) urban design and settlement patterns, (6) parks, open spaces and recreational facilities, (7) water sources and storage, (8) coordination, to the extent feasible, of Metro growth management and land use planning policies with those of Clark County, Washington, and (9) planning responsibilities mandated by state law. The regional framework plan shall also address other growth management and land use planning matters which the council, with the consultation and advice of the MPAC, determines are of metropolitan concern and will benefit from regional planning. To encourage regional uniformity, the regional framework plan shall also contain model terminology, standards and procedures for local land use decision making that may be adopted by local governments. As used in this section, "local" refers only to the cities and counties within the jurisdiction of Metro.

(c) Effect. The regional framework plan shall: (1) describe its relationship to the Future Vision, (2) comply with applicable statewide planning goals, (3) be subject to compliance acknowledgment by the Land Conservation and Development Commission or its successor, and (4) be the basis for coordination of framework plan after seeking the consultation and advice of the MPAC.

(d) Implementation. To the maximum extent allowed by law, the council shall adopt ordinances: (1) requiring local comprehensive plans and implementing regulations to comply with the regional framework plan within three years after adoption of the entire regional framework plan. If the regional framework plan is subject to compliance acknowledgment, local plans and implementing regulations shall be required to comply with the regional framework plan within two years of compliance acknowledgment; (2) requiring the council to adjudicate and determine the consistency of local comprehensive plans with the regional framework plan; (3) requiring each city and county within the jurisdiction of Metro to make local land use decisions consistent with the regional framework plan until its comprehensive plan has been determined to be consistent with the regional framework plan. The obligation to apply the regional framework plan to local land-use decisions shall not begin until one year after adoption and compliance acknowledgment of the regional framework plan; and (4) allowing the council to require changes in local land-use standards and procedures if the council determines changes are necessary to remedy a pattern or practice of decision making inconsistent with the regional framework plan.

(3) Priority and Funding of Regional Planning Activities.

The regional planning functions under this section are the primary functions of Metro. The council shall appropriate funds sufficient to assure timely completion of those functions.

Section 6. Other Assigned Functions.

Metro is also authorized to exercise the following functions: (1) Acquisition, development, maintenance, and operation of: (a) a metropolitan zoo, (b) public cultural, trade, convention, exhibition, sports, entertainment, and spectator facilities, (c) facilities for the disposal of solid and liquid wastes, and (d) a system of parks, open spaces and recreational facilities of metropolitan concern; (2) Disposal of solid and liquid wastes; (3) Metropolitan aspects of natural disaster planning and response coordination;.(4) Development and marketing of data; and (5) Any other function required by state law or assigned to the Metropolitan Service District or Metro by the voters.

Section 7. Assumption of Additional Functions.

(1) Assumption Ordinance.

The council shall approve by ordinance the undertaking by Metro of any function not authorized by sections 5 and 6 of this charter. The ordinance shall contain a finding that the function is of metropolitan concern and the reasons it is appropriate for Metro to undertake it.

(2) Assumption of Local Government Service Function.

(a) An ordinance authorizing provision or regulation by Metro of a local government service is not effective unless the ordinance is approved by the voters of Metro or a majority of the members of the MPAC. Voter approval may occur by approval of a referred measure (1) authorizing the function or (2) relating to finances and authorizing financing or identifying funds to be used for exercise of the function. As used in this section, "local government service" is a service provided to constituents by one or more cities, counties or special districts within the jurisdiction of Metro at the time a Metro ordinance on assumption of the service is first introduced.

(b) An ordinance submitted to the MPAC for approval is deemed approved unless disapproved within 60 days after submission.

(c) No approval under this subsection is required for the compensated provision of services by Metro to or on behalf of a local government under an agreement with that government.

(3) Assumption of other service functions.

The council shall seek the advice of the MPAC before adopting an ordinance authorizing provision or regulation by Metro of a service which is not a local government service.

(4) Assumption of functions and operations of mass transit district.

Notwithstanding subsection (2) of this section, Metro may at any time assume the duties, functions, powers and operations of a mass transit district by ordinance. Before adoption of this ordinance the council shall seek the advice of the Joint Policy Advisory Committee on Transportation or its successor. After assuming the functions and operations of a mass transit district, the council shall establish a mass transit commission of not fewer than seven members and determine its duties in administering mass transit functions for Metro. The members of the governing body of the mass transit district at the time of its assumption by Metro are members of the initial Metro mass transit commission for the remainder of their respective terms of office.

(5) Boundary commission functions.

The council shall undertake and complete a study of the Portland Metropolitan Area Local Government Boundary Commission, with advice of the MPAC, by September 1, 1995. The council shall implement the results of the study and shall seek any legislative action needed for implementation.

Section 8. Preservation of Authority to Contract.

All Metro officers shall preserve, to the greatest extent possible, the ability of Metro to contract for all services with persons or entities who are not Metro employees.

Section 9. General Grant of Powers to Carry Out Functions; Construction of Specified Powers.

When carrying out the functions authorized or assumed under this charter: (1) Metro has all powers that the laws of the United States and this state now or in the future could allow Metro just as if this charter specifically set out each of those powers, (2) the powers specified in this charter are not exclusive, (3) any specification of power in this charter is not intended to limit authority, and (4) the powers specified in this charter shall be construed liberally.

FINANCE

Section 10. General Authority.

Except as prohibited by law or restricted by this charter, Metro may impose, levy and collect taxes and may issue revenue bonds, general and special obligation bonds, certificates of participation and other obligations. The authority provided under this section supplements any authority otherwise granted by law.

Section 11. Voter Approval of Certain Taxes.

Any ordinance of the council imposing broadly based taxes of general applicability on the personal income, business income, payroll, property, or sales of goods or services of all, or a number of classes of, persons or entities in the region requires approval of the voters of Metro before taking effect. This approval is not required (1) to continue property taxes imposed by the Metropolitan Service District, (2) for the rate or amount of any payroll tax imposed by a mass transit district as of June 1, 1992, if the functions of that district are assumed by Metro, or (3) for additional payroll tax revenues for mass transit imposed to replace revenues lost by withdrawal of any locality from the service area of the mass transit district after June 1, 1992. For purposes of sections 11, 13, and 14 of this charter, "taxes" do not include any user charge, service fee, franchise fee, charge for the issuance of any franchise, license, permit or approval, or any benefit assessment against property.

Section 12. Voter Approval of General Obligation Bonds.

Issuance of general obligation bonds payable from ad valorem property taxes requires the approval of the voters of Metro.

Section 13. Prior Consultation for Tax Imposition.

Before imposing any new tax for which voter approval is not required, the council shall establish and seek the advice of a tax study committee that includes members appointed from the general population, and from among businesses and the governments of cities, counties, special districts and school districts, of the Metro area.

Section 14. Limitations on Expenditures of Certain Tax Revenues.

(1) General.

Except as provided in this section, for the first fiscal year after this charter takes effect Metro may make no more than $12,500,000 in expenditures on a cash basis from taxes imposed and received by Metro and interest and other earnings on those taxes. This expenditure limitation increases in each subsequent fiscal year by a percentage equal to (a) the rate of increase in the Consumer Price Index, All Items, for Portland-Vancouver (All Urban Consumers) as determined by the appropriate federal agency or (b) the most nearly equivalent index as determined by the council if the index described in (a) is discontinued.

(2) Exclusions from limitation.

This section does not apply to (a) taxes approved by the voters of Metro or the Metropolitan Service District and interest and other earnings on those taxes, (b) payroll taxes specified in section 11 of this charter, and (c) tax increment financing charges on property.

Section 15. Limitations on Amount of User Charges.

Except to the extent receipts in excess of costs from food and beverage sales, parking, and other concessions are dedicated to reducing charges for the provision of goods or services to which the concession directly relates, charges for the provision of goods or services by Metro may not exceed the costs of providing the goods or services. These costs include, but are not limited to, costs of personal services, materials, capital outlay, debt service, operating expenses, overhead expenses, and capital and operational reserves attributable to the good or service.

FORM OF GOVERNMENT

Section 16. Metro Council.

(1) Creation and powers.

The Metro council is created as the governing body of Metro. Except as this charter provides otherwise, and except for initiative and referendum powers reserved to the voters of Metro, all Metro powers are vested in the council.

(2) Composition.

Beginning January 2, 1995, the council consists of seven councilors, each nominated and elected from a single district within the Metro area. Until that date the council consists of the 13 members of the governing body of the Metropolitan Service District whose terms begin or continue in January 1993 and whose districts continue until replaced as provided in this section. The terms of those members expire January 2, 1995.

(3) Apportionment of council districts.

(a) Creation and appointment of apportionment commission. A Metro apportionment commission of seven commissioners is created. To appoint the commission the council shall divide itself into five pairs of councilors and one group of three councilors. Each pair and group of councilors shall be from contiguous districts and appoints one commissioner. The presiding officer appoints one commissioner and the commission chair. At least two commissioners must be appointed from each of the three counties within the Metro area, and each commissioner appointed by a pair or group of councilors shall reside in one of the districts from which the councilors making the appointment are elected or appointed. All appointments to the commission shall be made by February 1, 1993.

(b) Appointment by executive officer. If all appointments to the commission are not made by February 1, 1993, the executive officer shall appoint all commissioners and designate its chair by March 1, 1993. The executive officer shall appoint at least two commissioners from each of the three counties within the Metro area and may not appoint more than one commissioner from a single council district.

(c) Disqualifications from commission membership. No commissioner, or his or her spouse, children, or stepchildren may (1) be a Metro councilor, executive officer or employee, (2) be an elected officer or employee of any city, county, or special district, (3) have an economic interest which is distinct from that of the general public in any policy or legislation adopted by Metro or the Metropolitan Service District within the previous two years or which is being considered for adoption, or (4) be engaged, directly or indirectly, in any business with Metro which is inconsistent with the conscientious performance of the duties of commissioner. No commissioner may be a candidate for the office of councilor or executive officer in the first primary and general elections after adoption of this charter. Any challenge of the qualifications of a commissioner shall be made by May 1, 1993.

(d) Commission vacancies. A vacancy on the commission is filled by action of the authority that appointed the commissioner whose position is vacant.

(e) Filing of apportionment plan. Not later than July 1, 1993, the commission shall adopt and file with the council an apportionment plan dividing the Metro area into seven council districts. Councilors from those districts are first elected in the first statewide primary and general elections after adoption of this charter for a term of office beginning January 2, 1995. The affirmative vote of four commissioners is required to adopt the apportionment plan.

(f) Appointment of apportionment referee. If the commission fails to file an apportionment plan by July 1, 1993, the council shall appoint an apportionment referee by July 15, 1993. The provisions of subsection (3)(c) of this section apply to appointment of the referee. The referee shall prepare and file with the council an apportionment plan within 60 days after his or her appointment.

(g) Effective date of apportionment plan. An apportionment plan filed under this subsection becomes effective on the 30th day after filing unless a voter of Metro petitions for judicial review of the plan as provided by law.

(h) Criteria for districts. As nearly as practicable, all council districts shall be of equal population and each shall be contiguous and geographically compact. The council may by ordinance prescribe additional criteria for districts that are consistent with the requirements of this subsection.

(i) Appropriation of funds. The council shall appropriate sufficient funds to enable the commission and referee to perform their duties under this section.

(j) Abolition of commission. The commission is abolished upon filing the apportionment plan required by this section or on July 2, 1993, whichever is earlier.

(k) Repeal of subsection. Subsection (3) of this section is repealed January 1, 1994. Upon repeal its provisions shall be stricken from this charter and the other subsections of this section renumbered.

(4) Initial terms of office.

The terms of office of the four councilors receiving the highest number of votes among the seven councilors elected in 1994 end January 4, 1999. The terms of office of the other three councilors end January 6, 1997. Thereafter the term of office of councilor is four years.

(5) Council presiding officer.

At its first meeting each year the council shall elect a presiding officer from its councilors.

(6) Council meetings.

The council shall meet regularly in the Metro area at times and places it designates. The council shall prescribe by ordinance the rules to govern conduct of its meetings. Except as this charter provides otherwise, the agreement of a majority of councilors present and constituting a quorum is necessary to decide affirmatively a question before the council.

(7) Quorum.

A majority of councilors in office is a quorum for council business, but fewer councilors may compel absent councilors to attend.

(8) Record of proceedings.

The council shall keep and authenticate a record of council proceedings.

Section 17. Metro Executive Officer.

(1) Creation.

The office of Metro executive officer is created. The executive officer is elected from the Metro area at large for a term of four years. The executive officer serves full time and may not be employed by any other person or entity while serving as executive officer.

(2) Duties.

The primary duty of the executive officer is to enforce Metro ordinances and otherwise to execute the policies of the council. The executive officer shall also: (a) administer Metro except for the council and the auditor, (b) make appointments to Metro offices, boards, commissions, and committees when required to do so by this charter or by ordinance, (c) propose for council adoption measures deemed necessary to enforce or carry out powers and duties of Metro, (d) prepare and submit a recommended annual Metro budget to the council for approval, and (e) keep the council fully advised about Metro operations.

(3) Transition from Metropolitan Service District.

The Metropolitan Service District executive officer in office when this charter takes effect is the Metro executive officer until January 2, 1995 when his or her term expires. The Metro executive officer is elected in the first statewide primary or general election after adoption of this charter for a term beginning January 2, 1995.

(4) Veto.

(a) Except as provided in this subsection, the executive officer may veto the following legislative acts of the council within five business days after enactment: (1) any annual or supplemental Metro budget, (2) any ordinance imposing, or providing an exception from, a tax, and (3) any ordinance imposing a charge for provision of goods, services or property by Metro, franchise fees or any assessment.

(b) The council, not later than 30 days after a veto, may override a veto by the affirmative vote of (1) nine councilors while the council consists of 13 positions and (2) five councilors after the council consists of seven positions as provided by section 16(2) of this charter. (c) A legislative act referred to the voters of Metro by the council is not subject to veto.

Section 18. Metro Auditor.

(1) Creation.

The office of Metro auditor is created. The auditor is elected from the Metro area at large for a term of four years. The auditor serves full time and may not be employed by any other person or entity while serving as auditor.

(2) First election; disqualification for other Metro elected offices.

The auditor is first elected in the first statewide primary or general election after adoption of this charter for a term beginning January 2, 1995. During the term for which elected, and for four years thereafter, the auditor is ineligible to hold the offices of Metro executive officer or Metro councilor.

(3) Duties.

The auditor shall: (a) make continuous investigations of the operations of Metro including financial and performance auditing and review of financial transactions, personnel, equipment, facilities, and all other aspects of those operations, and (b) make reports to the Metro council and executive officer of the results of any investigation with any recommendations for remedial action. Except as provided in this section, the auditor may not be given responsibility to perform any executive function.

Section 19. Term of Office.

The term of office of an officer elected at a primary or general election begins the first Monday of the year following election and continues until a successor assumes the office.

OFFICERS, COMMISSIONS, AND EMPLOYEES

Section 20. Qualifications of Elected Officers.

(1) Councilor.

A councilor shall be a qualified elector under the constitution of this state when his or her term of office begins and shall have resided during the preceding 12 months in the district from which elected or appointed. When the boundaries of that district have been apportioned or reapportioned during that period, residency in that district for purposes of this subsection includes residency in any former district with area in the district from which the councilor is elected or appointed if residency is established in the apportioned or reapportioned district within 60 days after the apportionment or reapportionment is effective.

(2) Executive officer and auditor.

The executive officer and auditor shall each be a qualified elector under the constitution of this state when his or her term of office begins and shall have resided during the preceding 12 months within the boundaries of Metro as they exist when the term of office begins. At the time of election or appointment the auditor shall also hold the designation of certified public accountant or certified internal auditor.

(3) Multiple elected offices.

A Metro elected officer may not be an elected officer of the state, or a city, county, or special district during his or her term of office. As used in this charter, special district does not include school districts.

(4) Judging elections and qualifications.

The council is the judge of the election and qualification of its members.

Section 21. Compensation of Elected Officers.

(1) Council.

The salary of the council presiding officer is two-thirds the salary of a district court judge of this state. The salary of every other councilor is one-third the salary of a district court judge of this state. A councilor may waive a salary.

(2) Executive officer.

The salary of the executive officer is the salary of a district court judge of this state.

(3) Auditor.

The salary of the auditor is eighty percent of the salary of a district court judge of this state.

(4) Reimbursements.

The council may authorize reimbursement of Metro elected and other officers for necessary meals, travel, and other expenses incurred in serving Metro.

Section 22. Oath.

Before assuming office a Metro elected officer shall take an oath or affirm that he or she will faithfully perform the duties of the office and support the constitutions and laws of the United States and this state and the charter and laws of Metro.

Section 23. Vacancies in Office.

(1) Councilor.

The office of councilor becomes vacant upon the incumbent's: (a) death, (b) adjudicated incompetence, (c) recall from office, (d) failure following election or appointment to qualify for the office within 10 days after the time for his or her term of office to begin, (e) absence from all meetings of the council within a 60 day period without the council's consent, (f) ceasing to reside in the district from which elected or appointed, except when district boundaries are reapportioned and a councilor is assigned to a district where the councilor does not reside and the councilor becomes a resident of the reapportioned district within 60 days after the reapportionment is effective, (g) ceasing to be a qualified elector under state law, (h) conviction of a felony or conviction of a federal or state offense punishable by loss of liberty and pertaining to his or her office, (i) resignation from office, or (j) becoming an elected officer of the state or a city, county or special district.

(2) Executive officer and auditor.

The offices of executive officer or auditor become vacant in the circumstances described in subsection (1)(a)–(d) and (g)–(j) of this section, or if the executive officer or auditor ceases to reside in the Metro area. The office of auditor also becomes vacant if the incumbent ceases to hold the designation of certified public accountant or certified internal auditor.

(3) Vacancy after reapportionment.

If a councilor vacancy occurs after the councilor has been assigned to a reapportioned district under section 32 of this charter, the vacancy is in the district to which that councilor was assigned.

(4) Determination of vacancy.

The council is the final judge of the existence of a vacancy.

Section 24. Filling Vacancies.

A majority of councilors holding office shall fill a vacancy by appointment within 90 days after it occurs. The term of office of the appointee runs from the time he or she qualifies for the office after appointment until a successor is duly elected and qualifies for the office. If the vacancy occurs more than 20 days before the first general election after the beginning of the term for that office, the term of office of the appointee runs only until the first council meeting in the year immediately after that election. A person shall be elected for the remainder of the term at the first primary or general election after the beginning of the term.

Section 25. Limitations of Terms of Office.

No person may be elected councilor for more than three consecutive full terms. No person may be elected executive officer for more than two consecutive full terms. The limitations of this section apply only to terms of office beginning on or after January 2, 1995.

Section 26. Appointive Offices and Commissions.

(1) Appointments and confirmation.

The executive officer appoints all employees in the office of the executive officer, all department directors, and all other positions this charter or ordinance requires the executive officer to appoint. Appointments of department directors are subject to council confirmation. The council by ordinance may require confirmation of other positions.

(2) Removal.

Employees in the office of the executive officer and department directors serve at the pleasure of the executive officer. Staff employed by the council serve at the pleasure of the council. The executive officer may remove his or her other appointees as provided by ordinance.

Section 27. Metro Policy Advisory Committee.
(1) Creation and composition.

The Metro Policy Advisory Committee (MPAC) is created. The initial members of the MPAC are:

(a) One member of each of the governing bodies of Washington, Clackamas, and Multnomah Counties appointed by the body from which the member is chosen;

(b) Two members of the governing body of the City of Portland appointed by that governing body;

(c) One member of the governing body of the second largest city in population in Multnomah County appointed by that governing body;

(d) One member of the governing body of the largest city in population in Washington County appointed by that governing body;

(e) One member of the governing body of the largest city in population in Clackamas County appointed by that governing body;

(f) One member of a governing body of a city with territory in the Metro area in Multnomah County other than either the City of Portland or the second largest city in population in Multnomah County, appointed jointly by the governing bodies of cities with territory in the Metro area in Multnomah County other than the City of Portland or the second largest city in population in Multnomah County;

(g) One member of a governing body of a city with territory in the Metro area in Washington County other than the city in Washington County with the largest population, appointed jointly by the governing bodies of cities with territory in the Metro area in Washington County other than the city in Washington County with the largest population;

(h) One member of a governing body of a city with territory in the Metro area in Clackamas County other than the city in Clackamas County with the largest population, appointed jointly by the governing bodies of cities with territory in the Metro area in Clackamas County other than the city in Clackamas County with the largest population;

(i) One member from the governing body of a special district with territory in the Metro area in Multnomah County appointed jointly by the governing bodies of special districts with territory in the Metro area in Multnomah County;

(j) One member from the governing body of a special district with territory in the Metro area in Washington County appointed jointly by the governing bodies of special districts with territory in the Metro area in Washington County;

(k) One member from the governing body of a special district with territory in the Metro area in Clackamas County appointed jointly by the governing bodies of special districts with territory in the Metro area in Clackamas County;

(l) One member of the governing body of Tri-County Metropolitan Transportation District of Oregon appointed by the governing body of that district; and,

(m) Three persons appointed by the executive officer and confirmed by the council. No person appointed under this part of subsection (1) may be an elected officer of or employed by Metro, the state, or a city, county or special district. Each person appointed under this part of subsection (1) shall reside in the Metro area during the person's tenure on the MPAC.

(2) Change of composition.

A vote of both a majority of the MPAC members and a majority of all councilors may change the composition of the MPAC at any time.

(3) Duties.

The MPAC shall perform the duties assigned to it by this charter and any other duties the council prescribes.

(4) Bylaws.

The MPAC shall adopt bylaws governing the conduct and record of its meetings and the terms of its members.

Section 28. Metro Office of Citizen Involvement.

(1) Creation and purpose.

The Metro office of citizen involvement is created to develop and maintain programs and procedures to aid communication between citizens and the council and executive officer.

(2) Citizens' committee in office of citizen involvement.

The council shall establish by ordinance (a) a citizens' committee in the office of citizen involvement and (b) a citizen involvement process. The council shall appropriate sufficient funds to operate the office and committee.

ELECTIONS AND REAPPORTIONMENT

Section 29. State Law.

Except as this charter or a Metro ordinance provides otherwise, a Metro election shall conform to state law applicable to the election.

Section 30. Elections of Metro Officers.

(1) Generally.

Except for certain elections to fill a vacancy in office, the first vote for councilor, executive officer or auditor occurs at an election held at the same time and places in the Metro area as the statewide primary election that year. If one candidate for a Metro office receives a majority of the votes cast at the primary election for all candidates for that office, that candidate is elected. If no candidate receives a majority of the votes cast at the primary election, the candidates receiving the two largest numbers of votes cast for the office are the only names to appear on the general election ballot that year as candidates for that office. The candidate who receives the largest number of votes cast at the general election for that office is elected.

(2) Nonpartisan offices.

All elections of Metro officers are nonpartisan. Election ballots shall list the names of candidates for Metro offices without political party designations.

Section 31. Multiple Candidacies.

No person may be a candidate at a single election for more than one Metro elected office.

Section 32. Reapportionment of Council Districts After Census.

(1) General requirements.

Within three months after an official census indicates that the boundaries of council districts deny equal protection of the law, the council shall change the boundaries to accord equal protection of the law and shall assign councilors to the reapportioned districts. As nearly as practicable, all council districts shall be of equal population and each shall be contiguous and geographically compact. The council may by ordinance specify additional criteria for districts that are consistent with this section.

(2) Failure to reapportion.

If the council fails to establish council district boundaries as provided by this section, the executive officer shall establish the boundaries within 60 days.

Section 33. Recall.

(1) Generally.

An elected officer of Metro may be recalled in the manner and with the effect described by the constitution and laws of this state.

(2) Effect of reapportionment.

Upon the effective date of a council reapportionment under section 32 of this charter, a councilor is subject to recall by the voters of the district to which the councilor is assigned and not by the voters of the district of that councilor existing before the reapportionment.

Section 34. Initiative and Referendum.

The voters of Metro reserve to themselves the powers of initiative and referendum. The council may provide for the exercise of those powers in a manner consistent with law.

Section 35. Amendment and Revision of Charter.

The council may refer, and voters of Metro may initiate, amendments to this charter. A proposed charter amendment may embrace only one subject and matters properly connected with it. The council shall provide by ordinance for a procedure to revise this charter.

ORDINANCES

Section 36. Ordaining Clause.

The ordaining clause of an ordinance adopted by the council is: "The Metro Council ordains as follows":. The ordaining clause of an initiated or referred ordinance is: "The People of Metro ordain as follows":.

Section 37. Adoption by Council.

(1) General requirements.

The council shall adopt all legislation of Metro by ordinance. Except as this charter otherwise provides, the council may not adopt any ordinance at a meeting unless: (a) the ordinance is introduced at a previous meeting of the council, (b) the title of the ordinance is included in a written agenda of the meeting at which the ordinance is adopted, (c) the agenda of that meeting is publicized not less than three business days nor more than ten days before the meeting, and (d) copies of the ordinance are available for public inspection at least three business days before that meeting. The text of an ordinance may be amended, but not substantially revised, at the meeting at which it is adopted.

(2) Immediate adoption.

The provisions of this section do not apply to an ordinance adopted by unanimous consent of the council and containing findings on the need for immediate adoption.

(3) Vote required.

Adoption of an ordinance requires the affirmative votes of (a) seven councilors while the council consists of 13 positions, and (b) four councilors after the council consists of seven positions as provided by section 16(2) of this charter.

Section 38. Endorsement.

The person presiding over the council when an ordinance is adopted shall endorse the ordinance unless the council prescribes a different procedure by general ordinance.

Section 39. Effective Date of Ordinances.

(1) Generally.

An ordinance takes effect 90 days after its adoption unless the ordinance states a different effective date. An ordinance may state an earlier effective date if (a) an earlier date is necessary for the health, safety, or welfare of the Metro area, (b) the reasons why this is so are stated in an emergency clause of the ordinance, and (c) the ordinance is approved by the affirmative vote of two-thirds of all councilors. An ordinance imposing or changing a tax or charge, changing the boundaries of Metro, or assuming a function may not contain an emergency clause.

(2) Vetoed and referred ordinances.

If the executive officer vetoes an ordinance and the council overrides the veto, the date of adoption is the date on which the veto is overridden. If the council refers an ordinance to the voters of Metro, the ordinance effective date is the 30th day after its approval by a majority of the voters voting on the measure unless the ordinance specifies a later date. If a referendum petition is filed with the filing officer not later than the 90th day after adoption of an ordinance, the ordinance effective date is suspended. An ordinance is not subject to the referendum after it is effective. An ordinance referred by a referendum petition (a) does not take effect if a majority of the voters voting on the measure reject it and (b) takes effect, unless the ordinance specifies a later date, on the date the results of the election are certified if a majority of the council.

Section 40. Content of Ordinances.

Each ordinance may embrace only one subject and all matters properly connected with it. The council shall plainly word each ordinance and avoid technical terms as far as practicable.

Section 41. Public Improvements and Special Assessments.

General ordinances govern the procedures for making, altering, vacating or abandoning a public improvement and for fixing, levying, and collecting special assessments against real property for public improvements or services. State law governs these procedures to the extent not governed by general ordinances.

MISCELLANEOUS PROVISIONS

Section 42. Transition Provisions.

All legislation, orders, rules, and regulations of the Metropolitan Service District in force when this charter takes effect remain in force after that time to the extent consistent with this charter and until amended or repealed by the council. All rights, claims, causes of action, duties, contracts, and legal and administrative proceedings of the Metropolitan Service District that exist when this charter takes effect continue and are unimpaired by the charter. Each is in the charge of the officer or agency designated by this charter or by its authority to have charge of it. The unexpired terms of elected officers of the Metropolitan Service District continue as provided by this charter. Upon the effective date of this charter, the assets and liabilities of the Metropolitan Service District are the assets and liabilities of Metro.

Section 43. Effective Date.

This charter takes effect January 1, 1993.

Section 44. Severability.

The terms of this charter are severable. If a part of this charter is held invalid, that invalidity does not affect any other part of this charter unless required by the logical relation between the parts.

Section 45. State Legislation.

By adopting this charter the voters of Metro direct the council to seek, and request the Legislative Assembly of this state to enact, any legislation needed to make all parts of this charter operative.

Source: http://www.oregonmetro.gov/index.cfm/go/by.web/id=629

Smart Growth and Neighborhood Conservation Initiatives–State of Maryland (1997)

An Overview

In 1996, Governor Parris N. Glendening announced his priority commitment to develop and secure passage of a wide-ranging package of legislation to strengthen the state's ability to direct growth and to enhance our older developed areas. The goal was to develop a coordinated strategy to better prepare for the growth of over one million people in the next twenty years and to preserve Maryland's desired quality of life for tomorrow's generations.

Over several months, the Governor and key staff reached out to hundreds of interested groups and citizens. Meetings and forums were held in all 23 counties and Baltimore City; letters and phone calls seeking input and ideas were generated. By the end of the year, over 100 legislative and administrative suggestions were submitted. This effort resulted in a package of five bills and one budget item submitted to the General Assembly for its consideration. Within four months, the General Assembly approved the following:

- *Smart Growth Areas Act*: A law limiting most State infrastructure funding related to development to existing communities or to those places designated by State or local governments for growth.
- *Rural Legacy*: A grant program to create greenbelts to protect geographically-large rural areas from sprawl through purchase of easements and development rights.
- *Brownfield–Voluntary Cleanup and Revitalization Incentive Program*: Three programs to facilitate clean-up of contaminated areas and commercial/industrial development on those sites.
- *Job Creation Tax Credit*: Income tax credits to businesses which create new jobs within designated areas to promote development.
- *Live Near Your Work Demonstration Program*: State, employer and local government matching cash grants to home buyers who purchase homes near their workplace.

Collectively, these initiatives employ the power of planning and the purse to improve older urban areas, encourage infill and compact new development and preserve rural areas. Other incentives, especially administrative initiatives, are under consideration. An overview of the 1997 Smart Growth Initiatives follows:

Smart Growth Areas

Smart Growth Areas or "Priority Funding Areas" reflect Maryland's policy to support, and where necessary, revitalize existing communities. These are areas where there already is significant financial investment in existing infrastructure. This policy fosters economic vitality and improves the quality of life by maintaining and improving infrastructure and services in existing communities.

The 1997 Smart Growth Areas Act builds on the foundation created by the set of Visions for Maryland's Future adopted as State policy in the 1992 Growth Act. That Act requires local governments to revise and periodically update their Comprehensive Plans to reflect these Visions.

The 1997 Smart Growth Areas Act capitalizes on the influence of State expenditures on economic growth and development. This legislation directs State spending to "Priority Funding Areas." Priority Funding Areas area existing communities and other logically designated areas, consistent with the 1992 Visions, where State and local governments want to encourage and support economic development and new growth. Focusing State spending in these areas will provide the most efficient and effective use of taxpayer dollars, avoid higher taxes which would be necessary to fund infrastructure for sprawl development, and reduce the pressure for sprawl into agricultural and other natural resource areas.

The Smart Growth legislation automatically designates several areas which form the traditional core of the State's urban development locations targeted for economic development, as Priority Funding Areas: municipalities, Baltimore City, areas inside the Baltimore and Washington beltways, neighborhoods which have been designated by the Maryland Department of Housing and Community Development for revitalization, Enterprise Zones, and Heritage Areas within county designated growth areas.

This legislation authorizes counties to designate additional Priority Funding Areas which meet established minimum criteria. Priority Funding Areas designated by counties must be based on an analysis which determines the capacity of land area available for development, and the land area which be necessary to satisfy demand for development. With this analysis in hand, counties may designate areas as Priority Funding Areas if they meet specified use, water and sewer service, and residential density requirements. Counties may designate existing communities and areas where industrial or other economic development are desired. In addition, counties may designate areas planned for new residential development. Areas eligible for county designation are:

- Areas with industrial zoning (Areas with new industrial zoning after January 1, 1997, must be in a county-designated growth area and be served by a sewer system.);
- Areas with employment as the principal use which are served by, or planned for, a sewer system (Areas zoned after January 1, 1997, must be in a county-designated growth area.);
- Existing communities (as of January 1, 1997) within county-designated growth areas which are served by a sewer or water system and which have an average density of 2 units per acre;
- Rural villages designated in local Comprehensive Plans before July 1, 1998; and
- Other areas within county-designated growth areas that:
  - reflect a long-term policy for promoting an orderly expansion of growth and an efficient use of land and public services,
  - are planned to be served by water and sewer systems, and
  - have a permitted density of 3.5 or more units per acre for new residential development.

Counties are not required to designate Priority Funding Areas or to designate all of the eligible areas. In addition, county designation of Priority Funding Areas does not restrict the location of private sector or county employment. County-designated Priority Funding Areas simply are areas the county wants to be eligible for State funded growth projects. One goal of directing State projects to Priority Funding Areas is to make these areas more attractive for residents, potential residents and private sector development and redevelopment.

Beginning October 1, 1998, the State must direct funding for "growth-related" projects to Priority Funding Areas. "Growth-related" projects defined in the legislation include most State programs which encourage or support growth and development such as highways, sewer and water construction, economic development assistance, and State leases or construction of new office facilities. State funding in communities with only water service (without a sewer system) and in rural villages is restricted to projects which maintain the character of the community. The projects must not increase the growth capacity of the village or community.

The Smart Growth bill does recognize that there are times when the State will need to fund projects that are outside Priority Funding Areas and makes provision for determining and approving those exceptions on a case-specific basis.

Rural Legacy

The 1997 Rural Legacy initiative establishes a grant program to protect targeted rural greenbelts from sprawl through the purchase of easements and development rights in "Rural Legacy Areas." The mission of the program is to protect "Rural Legacy Areas" —regions rich in a multiple of agriculture, forestry, natural and cultural resources that, if conserved, will promote resource-based economies, protect green belts and greenways and maintain the fabric of rural life. The Rural Legacy Program provides the focus and funding necessary to protect large contiguous tracts of land and other strategic areas from sprawl development, and enhance natural resource, agricultural, forestry and environmental protection through cooperative efforts among State and local governments and land trusts. Protection is provided through the acquisition of easements and fee estates from willing landowners and the supporting activities of Rural Legacy sponsors and local governments.

Local governments and private land trusts are being encouraged to identify Rural Legacy Areas and to competitively apply for funds to complement existing land conservation efforts or create new ones. This Program is in addition to—not in place of—existing programs such as the Agricultural Land Preservation Program and Program Open Space.

For fiscal year 1998 through 2002, $71.3 million has been authorized. If funding is continued at this level after five years, the State could protect up to 200,000 acres of resource lands by the year 2011.

The program is administered by the Rural Legacy Board. Board members are the Secretary of Natural Resources, the Secretary of Agriculture, and the Director of the Maryland Office of Planning. An eleven-member advisory committee is comprised of government officials, agricultural and forestry and mineral industry representatives, environmental and conservation organization representatives, developers and a private land owner.

The Voluntary Cleanup and Brownfields Programs

Many unused or abandoned properties that are contaminated, or even perceived to be contaminated, are not attractive to commercial and industrial developers because of the uncertainty about future liability. Because of these liability concerns, developers and businesses often choose to locate on "greenfields"—pristine farms and open spaces—without needed infrastructure, such as roads and utilities. This contributes to the loss of farms and open spaces, increases the amount of taxpayer dollars spent on funding new infrastructure and impedes neighborhood revitalization efforts.

This package of three bills aims to make development on these former industrial sites more feasible and desirable—and a reality.

Voluntary Cleanup

The Voluntary Cleanup Program, administered by the Department of the Environment, reforms the process used to clean up eligible properties that are or are perceived to be contaminated by hazardous waste. In addition to providing a streamlined cleanup process, the legislation changes the liability scheme for certain prospective owners of eligible properties in the Program to encourage the transfer of properties. These changes provide more "certainty" regarding environmental requirements to both responsible persons and future owners of a property, thereby allowing parties to more accurately predict costs and time lines associated with a cleanup and increasing the likelihood of cleanup and redevelopment.

Brownfields Programs

The Department of Business and Economic Development's Brownfields Revitalization Incentive Program provides economic incentives to certain properties proposed to be purchased by someone who has not previously owned the site and who has not been responsible for the contamination of the site. The property must be a former industrial or commercial site located in a densely populated urban area and substantially underutilized. Furthermore, an existing site which poses a threat to the public health and the environment qualifies for economic incentives, provided that in all of the above cases the jurisdiction where it is located has adopted local ordinances granting a Brownfield Property Tax Credit.

Brownfield Site Assessment

The Maryland Department of the Environment is continuing its Brownfield Assessment Initiative, using federal funding to conduct site assessments at no cost to property owners on certain brownfield sites. To be eligible for the program, sites must be vacant or underutilized. Remediation must be feasible. Finally, sites must allow for redevelopment which will create jobs and improve the local tax base. The assessments conducted by MDE include complete Phase I and Partial Phase II assessments. To date, assessments have been conducted at 24 sites; 29 new assessments are planned.

Job Creation Tax Credit

The Job Creation Tax Credit Act, passed in 1996, was expanded to encourage mid-sized and smaller businesses to invest in Smart Growth Areas around the State. Small businesses comprise almost 80 percent of Maryland business and generate the majority of new job growth in the State.

This new initiative will encourage small business development and job growth in areas accessible to available labor pools and will encourage more efficient use of the State's existing infrastructure. It promotes job creation by providing income tax credits to "targeted growth sector" businesses which create at least 25 jobs in Priority Funding Areas or 60 jobs outside those areas.

The jobs must be full-time, permanent, and pay at least 150 percent of the minimum wage. Positions filled after December, 1996, must be newly created in a single Maryland location. As of July 1, 1997, the Sate had issued 43 certifications (associated with 10,300 new jobs, paying an average of $36,000) and received 39 additional letters of intent (associated with 4,600 jobs) statewide.

Live Near Your Work

The Live Near Your Work initiative provides a package of incentives, support services, and partnerships with local governments, financial institutions and private market employers to encourage employees to buy homes near their work. The Maryland Department of Housing and Community Development is administering this pilot program. This initiative will stabilize the neighborhoods surrounding the State's major employers by stimulating home ownership in targeted communities. In addition to providing resources for programs sponsored by public and private institutions, the State is participating as a major employer.

Three hundred thousand dollars have been appropriated for fiscal year 1998 for this program. The State hopes to continue to expand this pilot program in future years to other employers and jurisdictions. Through the program, a participating employer contributes $1,000 for every employee. The $1,000 is matched by $1,000 from the state and $1,000 from the local government. The employee also contributes $1,000 as part of the down-payment or closing costs of the house. Currently, 24 employer partners have opted to take part in the program. They include small and large businesses and institutions in Baltimore City, Baltimore County, College Park, Denton, Hagerstown, Salisbury, and Silver Spring. More businesses have expressed interest and undoubtedly will participate.

Source: Maryland Office of Planning, 1998 Annual Report

Istanbul Declaration on Human Settlements (1996)

1. We, the Heads of State or Government and the official delegations of countries assembled at the United Nations Conference on Human Settlements (Habitat II) in Istanbul, Turkey from 3 to 14 June 1996, take this opportunity to endorse the universal goals of ensuring adequate shelter for all and making human settlements safer, healthier and more liveable, equitable, sustainable and productive. Our deliberations on the

two major themes of the Conference—adequate shelter for all and sustainable human settlements development in an urbanizing world—have been inspired by the Charter of the United Nations and are aimed at reaffirming existing and forging new partnerships for action at the international, national and local levels to improve our living environment. We commit ourselves to the objectives, principles and recommendations contained in the Habitat Agenda and pledge our mutual support for its implementation.

2. We have considered, with a sense of urgency, the continuing deterioration of conditions of shelter and human settlements. At the same time, we recognize cities and towns as centers of civilization, generating economic development and social, cultural, spiritual and scientific advancement. We must take advantage of the opportunities presented by our settlements and preserve their diversity to promote solidarity among all our peoples.

3. We reaffirm our commitment to better standards of living in larger freedom for all humankind. We recall the first United Nations Conference on Human Settlements, held at Vancouver, Canada, the celebration of the International Year of Shelter for the Homeless and the Global Strategy for Shelter to the Year 2000, all of which have contributed to increased global awareness of the problems of human settlements and called for action to achieve adequate shelter for all. Recent United Nations world conferences, including, in particular, the United Nations Conference on Environment and Development, have given us a comprehensive agenda for the equitable attainment of peace, justice and democracy built on economic development, social development and environmental protection as interdependent and mutually reinforcing components of sustainable development. We have sought to integrate the outcomes of these conferences into the Habitat Agenda.

4. To improve the quality of life within human settlements, we must combat the deterioration of conditions that in most cases, particularly in developing countries, have reached crisis proportions. To this end, we must address comprehensively, inter alia, unsustainable consumption and production patterns, particularly in industrialized countries; unsustainable population changes, including changes in structure and distribution, giving priority consideration to the tendency towards excessive population concentration; homelessness; increasing poverty; unemployment; social exclusion; family instability; inadequate resources; lack of basic infrastructure and services; lack of adequate planning; growing insecurity and violence; environmental degradation; and increased vulnerability to disasters.

5. The challenges of human settlements are global, but countries and regions also face specific problems which need specific solutions. We

recognize the need to intensify our efforts and cooperation to improve living conditions in the cities, towns and villages throughout the world, particularly in developing countries, where the situation is especially grave, and in countries with economies in transition. In this connection, we acknowledge that globalization of the world economy presents opportunities and challenges for the development process, as well as risks and uncertainties, and that achievement of the goals of the Habitat Agenda would be facilitated by, inter alia, positive actions on the issues of financing of development, external debt, international trade and transfer of technology. Our cities must be places where human beings lead fulfilling lives in dignity, good health, safety, happiness and hope.

6. Rural and urban development are interdependent. In addition to improving the urban habitat, we must also work to extend adequate infrastructure, public services and employment opportunities to rural areas in order to enhance their attractiveness, develop an integrated network of settlements and minimize rural-to-urban migration. Small- and medium-sized towns need special focus.

7. As human beings are at the centre of our concern for sustainable development, they are the basis for our actions as in implementing the Habitat Agenda. We recognize the particular needs of women, children and youth for safe, healthy and secure living conditions. We shall intensify our efforts to eradicate poverty and discrimination, to promote and protect all human rights and fundamental freedoms for all, and to provide for basic needs, such as education, nutrition and life-span health care services, and, especially, adequate shelter for all. To this end, we commit ourselves to improving the living conditions in human settlements in ways that are consonant with local needs and realities, and we acknowledge the need to address the global, economic, social and environmental trends to ensure the creation of better living environments for all people. We shall also ensure the full and equal participation of all women and men, and the effective participation of youth, in political, economic and social life. We shall promote full accessibility for people with disabilities, as well as gender equality in policies, programmes and projects for shelter and sustainable human settlements development. We make these commitments with particular reference to the more than one billion people living in absolute poverty and to the members of vulnerable and disadvantaged groups identified in the Habitat Agenda.

8. We reaffirm our commitment to the full and progressive realization of the right to adequate housing as provided for in international instruments. To that end, we shall seek the active participation of our public, private and non-governmental partners at all levels to ensure legal security of tenure, protection from discrimination and equal access to affordable, adequate housing for all persons and their families.

9. We shall work to expand the supply of affordable housing by enabling markets to perform efficiently and in a socially and environmentally responsible manner, enhancing access to land and credit and assisting those who are unable to participate in housing markets.

10. In order to sustain our global environment and improve the quality of living in our human settlements, we commit ourselves to sustainable patterns of production, consumption, transportation and settlements development; pollution prevention; respect for the carrying capacity of ecosystems; and the preservation of opportunities for future generations. In this connection, we shall cooperate in a spirit of global partnership to conserve, protect and restore the health and integrity of the Earth's ecosystem. In view of different contributions to global environmental degradation, we reaffirm the principle that countries have common but differentiated responsibilities. We also recognize that we must take these actions in a manner consistent with the precautionary principle approach, which shall be widely applied according to the capabilities of countries. We shall also promote healthy living environments, especially through the provision of adequate quantities of safe water and effective management of waste.

11. We shall promote the conservation, rehabilitation and maintenance of buildings, monuments, open spaces, landscapes and settlement patterns of historical, cultural, architectural, natural, religious and spiritual value.

12. We adopt the enabling strategy and the principles of partnership and participation as the most democratic and effective approach for the realization of our commitments. Recognizing local authorities as our closest partners, and as essential, in the implementation of the Habitat Agenda, we must, within the legal framework of each country, promote decentralization through democratic local authorities and work to strengthen their financial and institutional capacities in accordance with the conditions of countries, while ensuring their transparency, accountability and responsiveness to the needs of people, which are key requirements for Governments at all levels. We shall also increase our cooperation with parliamentarians, the private sector, labor unions and non-governmental and other civil society organizations with due respect for their autonomy. We shall also enhance the role of women and encourage socially and environmentally responsible corporate investment by the private sector. Local action should be guided and stimulated through local programs based on Agenda 21, the Habitat Agenda, or any other equivalent program, as well as drawing upon the experience of worldwide cooperation initiated in Istanbul by the World Assembly of Cities and Local Authorities, without prejudice to national policies, objectives, priorities and programs. The enabling strategy

includes a responsibility for Governments to implement special measures for members of disadvantaged and vulnerable groups when appropriate.

13. As the implementation of the Habitat Agenda will require adequate funding, we must mobilize financial resources at the national and international levels, including new and additional resources from all sources—multilateral and bilateral, public and private. In this connection, we must facilitate capacity-building and promote the transfer of appropriate technology and know-how. Furthermore, we reiterate the commitments set out in recent United Nations conferences, especially those in Agenda 21 on funding and technology transfer.

14. We believe that the full and effective implementation of the Habitat Agenda will require the strengthening of the role and functions of the United Nations Centre for Human Settlements (Habitat), taking into account the need for the Centre to focus on well-defined and thoroughly developed objectives and strategic issues. To this end, we pledge our support for the successful implementation of the Habitat Agenda and its global plan of action. Regarding the implementation of the Habitat Agenda, we fully recognize the contribution of the regional and national action plans prepared for this Conference.

15. This Conference in Istanbul marks a new era of cooperation, an era of a culture of solidarity. As we move into the twenty-first century, we offer a positive vision of sustainable human settlements, a sense of hope for our common future and an exhortation to join a truly worthwhile and engaging challenge, that of building together a world where everyone can live in a safe home with the promise of a decent life of dignity, good health, safety, happiness, and hope.

Curitiba Experience

The bus system of Curitiba, Brazil, exemplifies a model Bus Rapid Transit system, and plays a large part in making this a livable city. The buses run frequently—some as often as every 90 seconds—and reliably, commuters ride them in great numbers, and the stations are convenient, well-designed, comfortable, and attractive. Curitiba has one of the most heavily used, yet low-cost, transit systems in the world. It offers many of the features of a subway system—vehicle movements unimpeded by traffic signals and congestion, fare collection prior to boarding, quick passenger loading and unloading—but it is above ground and visible. Even with one automobile for every three people, one of the highest automobile ownership rates in Brazil, and with a significantly higher per capita income than the national average, around 70 percent of Curitiba's commuters use transit daily to travel to work. Greater

Curitiba with its 2.2 million inhabitants enjoys congestion-free streets and pollution-free air.

3.1 Evolution of the Bus System

The bus system did not develop overnight, nor was it the result of transit development isolated from other aspects of city planning. It exists because thirty years ago Curitiba's forward-thinking and cost-conscious planners developed a Master Plan integrating public transportation with all elements of the urban system. They initiated a transportation system that focused on meeting the transportation needs of the population—rather than focusing on those using private automobiles—and then consistently followed through over the years with staged implementation of their plan. They avoided large scale and expensive projects in favor of hundreds of modest initiatives.

A previous comprehensive plan for Curitiba, developed in 1943, had envisioned exponential growth of automobile traffic and wide boulevards radiating from the central core of the city to accommodate the traffic. Rights of way for the boulevards were acquired, but many other parts of the plan never materialized. With the adoption of the new Master Plan in 1965, the projected layout of the city changed dramatically. The Master Plan sprang from a competition among urban planners prompted by fears of city officials that Curitiba's rapid growth, if unchanneled, would lead to the congested, pedestrian-unfriendly streets and unchecked development that characterized their neighbor city, São Paulo, and many other Brazilian cities to the north.

As a result of the Master Plan, Curitiba would no longer grow in all directions from the core, but would grow along designated corridors in a linear form, spurred by zoning and land use policies promoting high density industrial and residential development along the corridors. Downtown Curitiba would no longer be the primary destination of travel, but a hub and terminus. Mass transit would replace the car as the primary means of transport within the city, and the high density development along the corridors would produce a high volume of transit ridership. The wide boulevards established in the earlier plan would provide the cross section required for exclusive bus lanes in which express bus service would operate.

3.2 The Bus System

Curitiba's bus system evolved in stages over the years as phases of the Master Plan were implemented to arrive at its current form. It is composed of a hierarchical system of services. Small minibuses routed through residential neighborhoods feed passengers to conventional buses on circumferential routes around the central city and on interdistrict routes. The backbone of the bus system is composed of the express buses operating on five main arteries leading into the center of the city much as spokes on a wheel lead to its hub. This backbone service, aptly described as Bus Rapid Transit, is characterized by several features that enable Curitiba's bus service to approach the speed, efficiency, and reliability of a subway system:

- integrated planning
- exclusive bus lanes
- signal priority for buses
- pre-boarding fare collection
- level bus boarding from raised platforms in tube stations
- free transfers between lines (single entry)
- large capacity articulated and bi-articulated wide-door buses
- overlapping system of bus services

Each artery is composed of a "trinary" road system, consisting of three parallel routes, a block apart. The middle route is a wide avenue with "Express" bus service running down dedicated high-capacity express busways in the center two lanes, offering frequent stop service using standard, articulated and bi-articulated buses carrying up to 270 passengers apiece. The outer lanes are for local access and parking. Back in the 1960s the building of a light rail system in these avenues had been considered, but proved to be too expensive. The two outer routes are one-way streets with mixed vehicle traffic lanes next to exclusive bus lanes running "direct" high-speed bus service with limited stops. Both the express and direct services use signal priority at intersections.

Passengers board and alight via a special tube on Curitiba's central transit routes so that boarding is not delayed by fare collection.

Buses running in the dedicated and exclusive lanes stop at tube stations. These are modern design cylindrical-shaped, clear-walled stations with turnstiles, steps, and wheelchair lifts. Passengers pay their bus fares as they enter the stations, and wait for buses on raised station platforms. Instead of steps, buses are designed with extra wide doors and ramps which extend when the doors open to fill the gap between the bus and the station platform. The tube stations serve the dual purpose of providing passengers with shelter from the elements, and facilitating the efficient simultaneous loading and unloading of passengers, including wheelchairs. A typical dwell time of only 15 to 19 seconds is the result of fare payment prior to boarding the bus and same-level boarding from the platform to the bus.

Passengers pay a single fare equivalent to about 40 cents (U.S.) for travel throughout the system, with unlimited transfers between buses. Transfers are accomplished at terminals where the different services intersect. Transfers occur within the prepaid portions of the terminals so transfer tickets are not needed. In these areas are located public telephones, post offices, newspaper stands, and small retail facilities to serve customers changing buses.

Ten private bus companies provide all public transportation services in Curitiba, with guidance and parameters established by the city administration. The bus companies are paid by the distances they travel rather than by the passengers they carry, allowing a balanced distribution of bus routes and eliminating the former destructive competition that clogged the main roads and left other parts of the city unserved. All ten bus companies earn an operating profit.

The city pays the companies for the buses, about 1 percent of the bus value per month. After ten years, the city takes control of the buses and uses them for transportation to parks or as mobile schools. The average bus is only three years old, largely because of the recent infusion of newly designed buses, including the articulated and bi-articulated buses, into the system.

3.3 Integration of Transit with Land-Use Planning

Curitiba's Master Plan integrated transportation with land use planning, with the latter as the driving force, and called for a cultural, social and economic transformation of the city. It limited central area growth, while encouraging commercial growth along the transport arteries radiating out from the city center. The city's central area was partly closed to vehicular traffic, and pedestrian streets were created. The linear development along the arteries reduced the traditional importance of the downtown area as the primary focus of day-to-day transport activity, thereby minimizing congestion and the typical morning flow of traffic into the central city and the afternoon outflow. As a result, during any rush hour in Curitiba, there are heavy commuter movements in both directions along the public transportation arteries.

The Master Plan also provided economic support for urban development along the arteries through the establishment of industrial and commercial zones and mixed-use zoning, and encouraged local community self-sufficiency by providing each city district with its own adequate education, health care, recreation, and park areas. By 1992, almost 40 percent of Curitiba's population resided within three blocks of the major transit arteries.

Other policies have contributed to the success of the transit system, in the areas of zoning, housing development, parking and employer-paid transit subsidies. Land within two blocks of the transit arteries has been zoned for mixed commercial-residential uses. Higher densities are permitted for office space, since it traditionally generates more transit ridership per square foot than residential space. Beyond these two blocks, zoned residential densities taper with distance from transitways. Land near transit arteries is encouraged to be developed with community-assisted housing. The Institute of Urban Research and Planning of Curitiba (IPPUC), established in the 1960s to oversee implementation of the Master Plan, must approve locations of new shopping centers. They discourage American style auto-oriented shopping centers by channeling new retail growth to transit corridors. Very limited and time-restricted public parking is available in the downtown area, and private parking is very expensive. Finally, most employers offer transportation subsidies to workers, especially low-skilled and low-paid employees, making them the primary purchasers of tokens.

3.4 Staged Development of the Bus System

As the population increased during the period from 1970 through the present, Curitiba's bus system evolved incrementally. It required expansion of service routes, frequencies, and capacities, and improvements in fare payment, scheduling, and facility design to facilitate the passenger transferring process. Innovative low-cost and low-tech options for new services and features were chosen over more expensive alternatives at each stage. Planners did not hesitate to abandon choices that did not work in favor of more effective solutions.

At several points throughout the bus system development, the option of constructing a rail network was considered. Initially, buses were chosen over rail because they were far more adaptable and cheaper for a developing city such as Curitiba. In the mid-1980s the ridership had grown enough to support a rail network, but capital costs were prohibitive. Instead, the high capacity, high speed service known as "direct" service was eventually introduced on the one-way exclusive bus lanes that parallel the main corridors one block away. This service, including the tube stations, cost about $200,000 per kilometer to build, and was far cheaper, faster and less disruptive than the estimated $20 million per kilometer for a light rail system.

Not to be underestimated in the evolution of the transit system is the influence of the current governor of the State of Parana, Jaime Lerner. Lerner left his position as president of the IPPUC to become a three-time Mayor of Curitiba, and then governor. With a stake in the development of the Master Plan, he was its champion throughout the years, providing guidance, a firm governmental commitment to transit, and leadership. His steady promotion of the plan enabled it to withstand any tendencies for local politics to alter its course.

3.5 Results of Bus Rapid Transit

The popularity of Curitiba's Bus Rapid Transit system has effected a modal shift from automobile travel to bus travel, in spite of Curitibanos' high income and high rate of car ownership relative to the rest of Brazil. Based on 1991 traveler survey results, it was estimated that service improvements resulting from the introduction of Bus Rapid Transit had attracted enough automobile users to public transportation to cause a reduction of about 27 million auto trips per year, saving about 27 million liters of fuel annually. In particular, 28 percent of direct bus service users previously traveled by car. Compared to eight other Brazilian cities its size, Curitiba uses about 30 percent less fuel per capita, because of its heavy transit usage. The low rate of ambient air pollution in Curitiba, one of the lowest in Brazil, is attributed to the public transportation system's accounting for around 55 percent of private trips in the city.

Residential patterns changed to afford bus access on the major arteries to a larger proportion of the population. Between 1970 and 1978, when the three main arteries were built, the population of Curitiba as a whole grew by 73 percent, while the population along the arteries grew by 120 percent. Today about 1,100 buses make 12,500 trips per day, serving more than 1.3 million passengers per day, 50 times more than 20 years ago. Eighty percent of the travelers use either the express or direct bus service, while only 20 percent use the conventional feeder services. Plans for extending the rapid bus network will reduce the need for conventional services. In addition to enjoying speedy and reliable service, Curitibanos spend only about 10 percent of their income on travel, which is low relative to the rest of Brazil.

Source: USDOT, Federal Transit Administration (2006) http://www.fta.dot.gov/assistance/technology/research_4391.html

7

Directory of Organizations

The number of public and private organizations devoted to the issue of urban growth and development has mushroomed over the last twenty years. At the global level, a variety of different nongovernmental institutes work with the United Nations and governmental development agencies to collect data on cities, analyze problems, and offer policy recommendations. In the United States, most organizations fall into more narrow categories related to specific urban policy areas as well as environmental and agricultural issues.

Global Urban Growth

Brazilian Foundation for Sustainable Development
http://www.fbds.org.br

The Brazilian Institute for Municipal, Administration (IBAM) was created in Rio de Janeiro in 1952. IBAM is a not-for-profit nongovernmental organization, with the objective of sponsoring research into and search for the solutions to municipal and urban problems in the area of regional and national development. The Institute is recognized as a public utility institution by the federal government and the governor of the state of Rio de Janeiro. It is also recognized as a philanthropic institution by the National Council of Social Services. IBAM's mission is promoting the municipality as an autonomous sphere of government, strengthening its capacity to formulate policies, render more efficient services, and encourage local development, with the objective of a democratic society that values citizenship.

Publications: research papers and reports, some available in English online.

Center for Policy Research
http://www.cprindia.org

The Center for Policy Research (CPR) is an independent and nonpartisan research institute and think tank based in India. Its main objectives are to provide research and creative solutions that address pressing intellectual and policy issues facing India today, among which is a concern for meeting the current pressures of urbanization. It is one of the 27 national social science research institutes recognized by the Indian Council of Social Science Research (ICSSR) and makes use of a multidisciplinary approach that blends scholarship with practical expertise. The Center provides advisory services to governments, public bodies, or any other institutions including international agencies on matters having a bearing on the performance and optimum use of national resources for social and economic development.

Publications: journals, reports, policy briefs, sponsored research papers and books.

Cities Alliance
http://www.citiesalliance.org/ca

The Cities Alliance was launched in May 1999 by the World Bank and United Nations Centre for Human Settlements (UN-Habitat). The Cities Alliance is a multidonor coalition of cities and their development partners and was conceived to improve the efficiency and impact of urban development cooperation in two key areas: making unprecedented improvements in the living conditions of the urban poor by developing citywide and nationwide slum-upgrading programs; and supporting city-based consensus-building processes by which local stakeholders define their vision for their city and establish city development strategies with clear priorities for action and investments. The Alliance fosters new tools, practical approaches, and knowledge sharing in these two areas, so as to create a new coherence of effort to help realize the rich promise of what well-managed cities can achieve. The organization provides a wide range of documents, reports, papers, presentations, articles, project profiles, and multimedia resources related to slum upgrading and city development strategies on its website.

Publications: Annual Report, e-newsletter *@Cities Alliance*, CIVIS, and other publications related to slum upgrading and city development strategies available online.

Cities Development Initiative for Asia
http://cdia.asia

The Cities Development Initiative for Asia (CDIA) is a regional partnership supported by the Asian Development Bank (ADB) and the governments of Germany, Sweden, and Spain. Founded in 2007, its purpose is to assist medium-sized Asian cities to bridge the gap between their development plans and the implementation of their infrastructure investments. CDIA uses a demand-driven approach to support the identification and development of urban investment projects in the framework of existing city development plans that emphasize urban environmental improvement, poverty reduction, climate change mitigation or adaptation, and good urban governance. To facilitate these initiatives, CDIA provides a range of international and domestic expertise to cities that can include support for the preparation of pre-feasibility studies for high priority infrastructure investment projects as one of several elements. The management team is based in Manila, Philippines.

Publications: *Managing Asian Cities Report*, CDIA Newsletter, tools, and learning materials.

City Mayors Foundation
http://www.citymayors.com

The City Mayors Foundation is an international think tank consisting of professionals working together to promote strong and prosperous cities as well as good local government. Established by practicing professionals in 2003, City Mayors encourages urban leaders around the world to "develop innovative and sustainable solutions to long-standing urban problems such as housing, transport, education and employment." City Mayors also debates ways to meet the latest environmental, technological, and social challenges, which affect the well-being of citizens. The Foundation has no association with any city or organization and is run on strictly noncommercial, nonprofit lines.

Publications: news articles and city data available online.

Comparative Urban Studies Project
http://www.wilsoncenter.org

Founded in 1992, the Comparative Urban Studies Project (CUSP) at the Woodrow Wilson International Center for Scholars utilizes a multidisciplinary and comparative framework to explore the growing significance of issues impacting urban areas around the world. The Center brings together a network of urban scholars, practitioners, community leaders, and policymakers who share a commitment to improving knowledge about sustainable urban development and better understand the challenges and opportunities brought by urbanization.

Publications: a variety of research publications, policy briefs and conference reports are available online at the organization's website.e-Geopolis
http://www.e-geopolis.eu

This website operates as a clearinghouse for seven different French-language institutes that study population and urbanization around the world. These organizations include SEDET (Sociétés En Développement Etudes Transdisciplinaires), IFP (French Institute of Pondichery), CEPED (Centre Population Et Developpement), THéMA (Théoriser et Modeliser pour Aménager), iRVSIG (i Revers la Société de l'Information Géographique rvg), ANR (Agence Nationale de la Recherche), AFD (Agence Française de Développement), CNRS (Centre National de la recherche Scientifique), and UPLD (Université Paris-Diderot).

Publications: a variety of different databases, research reports, and other resources offered in several languages (including English).

Environment and Development Action in the Third World
http://www.enda.sn/english/index.htm

Environment and Development Action in the Third World (ENDA-TM) is an international nonprofit organization based in Dakar, Senegal. Founded in 1972, its executive secretariat coordinates the actions of 21 teams operating in developing countries throughout Africa, Asia, and Latin America, each of which works with grassroots groups to develop alternative models of urban development, basic social services, and reaching women and child workers.

Publications: reports on sponsored projects available online.

Global Urban Development
http://www.globalurban.org

Global Urban Development (GUD) brings together leaders in urban affairs from around the world that include scholars, professionals, business executives, public officials, civic and religious leaders, and community activists representing the complete spectrum of nongovernmental organizations. The organization sponsors meetings in many cities around the world to discuss how best to address worldwide urban challenges from pollution, poverty, and property rights, to economic growth, social justice, human rights, and civic harmony. A key function of GUD is to be directly involved in action-oriented projects as advisors to businesses, governments, communities, and international agencies on global urban problem solving. It is guided by a mission to "design and propose creative solutions that are market-oriented, equity-based, pro-environment, inclusive, productive, and democratic." The organization is guided by smart growth, sustainable development, new urbanism, metropolitan economic strategy, and a wide range of additional strategic initiatives. The GUD organization maintains 11 offices worldwide: Barcelona, Beijing, Curitiba, Hong Kong, Istanbul, London, Prague, San Francisco Bay Area, Singapore, Sydney, and Washington, DC.

Publications: Global Urban Development magazine, large archive of documents, articles, and publications available online.

Global Urban Studies Program at Michigan State University
http://gusp.msu.edu

The Global Urban Studies Program began in 2006 at Michigan State University with the purpose of encouraging new scholarship on important urban issues around the world. Researchers undertake projects on a variety of topics that include urban poverty, housing and welfare policy, redevelopment, transportation, education, and the role of culture, arts and public services.

Publications: Journal of Urban Affairs, research reports and papers.

Globalization and World Cities Research Network
http://www.lboro.ac.uk/gawc

Based in the Geography Department at Loughborough University, this research network focuses upon the growth and development of relations between world cities. The group seeks to address the subject of relations between cities, which has been neglected by researchers. It encourages members to submit data bases on inter-city relations to facilitate more research on this topic.

Publications: GaWC Research Bulletins available online.

Institute for Housing and Urban Development Studies
http://www.ihs.nl

Situated in the School of Economics (ESE) and the Faculty of Social Sciences (FSS) of the Erasmus University Rotterdam, The Netherlands, The Institute for Housing and Urban Development Studies (IHS) has offered post graduate education, training, advisory services, and applied research on urban development since 1958. IHS was selected as the winner for the 2007 UN-HABITAT Scroll of Honor Award for its training programs in housing, urban management, and urban environmental management and planning. A major emphasis of the institute is assisting countries, cities, and institutions to find suitable approaches to housing and sustainable urban development, and strengthen their capacity to implement them.

Publications: research is disseminated free online through a variety of different publications that include working papers, project reports, and thesis series.

Institute for Research on World-Systems
http://irows.ucr.edu

The Institute for Research on World-Systems (IROWS) organizes collaborative research among social and physical scientists on long-term, large-scale social change and its ecological, geographical, and epidemiological causes and effects. Located at the University of California at Riverside, IROWS pursues comparative research on the rise and fall of civilizations, long-term processes of globalization, urbanization, and climate change.

Publications: IRWS Annual Reports, working papers available online.

International Council for Local Environmental Initiatives
http://iclei.org

The International Council for Local Environmental Initiatives (ICLEI) was founded in 1990 as a worldwide movement to bring together local and regional officials who share a strong common commitment to achieving sustainable development. Today, over 1,220 local governments, regional, and national organizations from 70 different countries are members of ICLEI. It provides technical consulting, training, and information services to build capacity, share knowledge, and support local government in the implementation of sustainable development at the local level. The main premise is that locally designed initiatives can provide an effective and cost-efficient way to achieve local, national, and global sustainability objectives. In 2002, ICLEI established a major initiative to build "Sustainable Communities and Cities" through efforts that would assist local governments in achieving just, secure, resilient, and viable economies and healthy environments.

Publications: policy practice manuals, newsletters, regional updates on activities, case studies, training guides, and fact sheets are available online.

International Institute for Environment and Development
http://www.iied.org

The International Institute for Environment and Development (IIED) was launched in 1971 as an independent international research organization that seeks to promote more equitable and sustainable development at the local level. While IIED has been a prominent actor in international conferences and environmental summits, its primary mission is to forge alliance with marginalized individuals and organizations that represent them in developing countries. It is active in Africa, Asia, the Caribbean, Central and South America, the Middle East, and the Pacific, working with some of the world's most vulnerable people to ensure they have a say in the policy arenas that most closely affect them—from village councils to international conventions. The institute also advises governments, business, and international development agencies on matters related to climate change, governance, human settlements, natural resources, and sustainable markets.

Publications: IIED Briefings, Sustainable Development Opinion Papers, numerous book and research reports available online for purchase or free download.

International Society of City and Regional Planners
http://www.isocarp.org

The International Society of City and Regional Planners (ISOCARP) is an association of professional planners that was founded in 1965 to enhance the exchange of ideas and opportunities from members of this discipline across the world. The organization is recognized as a partner with the United Nations and the Council of Europe and seeks to use its resources and membership to improve cities through the development and dissemination of better planning practices as well as training of professionals and research. Although its primary focus is Europe, the society aims at becoming a more global organization and is particularly looking for a bigger role in the promotion of planning in the rapidly urbanizing areas of Asia, Latin America, and Africa. The main tools of ISOCARP are the yearly congresses, symposia, workshops, and publications.

Publications: ISOCARP Review, Congress and Activity Reports, professional papers and reports.

International Union of Local Authorities
http://www.irc.nl

The International Union of Local Authorities (IULA) was established in 1913 in the Netherlands with the intention to promote democratic local self-government, and it began with a focus on newly founded European cities. After the Second World War, it expanded its work to impact communities worldwide. The organization believes that close contact between different local municipalities of the world will result in both cross-cultural exchanges and mutual benefits. It was particularly active in opening the lines of communication between the burgeoning municipalities of the early postcolonial era and more established cities elsewhere. In this tradition, the group now attempts to organize and oversee relationships between municipalities all over the world in both industrialized and developing countries. Key areas of cooperation and exchange are local governance, sanitation, hygiene promotion, innovative communication, water supply, gender and equality, participatory development, and capacity management.

Publications: a wide variety of books, pamphlets, and papers on key water and sanitation topics, and *Thematic Overview Papers (TOPs)*, which combine recent experiences, expert opinions, and foreseeable trends with links to the most informative publications, websites, and research information.

Global Cities Program, Munk School of International Affairs, University of Toronto
http://www.globalcities.ca

The Global Cities Program uses information technology in distance learning, sponsors a speaker series, and develops workshop linkages for the exchange of ideas and comparative research on urban growth and development around the globe. The program targets comparative research in five areas: global economic linkages, governance, entrepreneurialism, global connectivity, and inclusiveness and the public realm.

Publications: books and research papers.

The Mega-Cities Project
http://megacitiesproject.org/index.php

The Mega-Cities Project is a transnational nonprofit network of leaders from grassroots groups, nonprofits, government, business, academia, and media dedicated to sharing innovative solutions to the problems their cities face in common. The special focus of projects is on the intersection of poverty and environment with special attention to voice and livelihood for marginalized groups. The mission of Mega-Cities is to "shorten the time lag between ideas and implementation through experiential learning, collective creation of new knowledge and preparing the next generation of urban leaders." Since 1987, local teams in 21 cities have identified and document hundreds of existing but often un-recognized solutions; brokered the transfer of 40 of these across national, regional, and neighborhood boundaries; invent a leadership–partnership development strategy; designed a three-continent undergraduate travel/study course, "Cities for the 21st Century"; and conducted a Global Leaders Survey which will be replicated periodically to track changes. The organization's approach to sharing, awarding, and scaling-up local solutions has been adopted by UN-Habitat as Urban Best Practices and has been instrumental in fostering an asset-based view of the urbanization of the world's population.

Publications: reports on sponsored projects are available free online.

New Geography
http://www.newgeography.com

The NewGeography.com website offers a clearinghouse of resources for analyzing and discussing urban places, city growth, and development. It offers a variety of articles and commentary on how people and their communities can best adapt to rapidly changing conditions, and as such, offers extensive opportunities for online networking and discussion on economic development, metropolitan demographics, and community leadership. The focus of this resource is primarily on the United States, but also contains substantial resources related to urban problems in the rest of the world as well as global-level concerns.

Overseas Development Institute
http://www.odi.org.uk

The Overseas Development Institute (ODI) is an independent think tank on international development and humanitarian issues based in Great Britain. The institute's mission is "to inspire and inform policy and practice which lead to the reduction of poverty, the alleviation of suffering and the achievement of sustainable livelihoods in developing countries." ODI works across a wide range of international development and humanitarian themes in countries. Among its concerns are an exploration of urbanization, challenges of rapid growth, migration, policies, and public investment that might enable urban areas to become not only engines of growth and reduce poverty.

Publications: Development Policy Review Journal, opinion and working papers, policy briefings, video blogs and podcasts; clearinghouse for publications and resources available on the Internet on topics generated as part of ODI projects working on issues in international development.

Planetizen
http://www.planetizen.com

Planetizen is a public-interest information exchange provided by Urban Insight for the urban planning, design, and development community. It is a one-stop source for urban planning news, commentary, interviews, event coverage, book reviews, announcements, jobs, consultant listings, training, and more. Planetizen covers a wide number of planning, design, and development issues, from transportation to global warming, architecture to infrastructure, housing and community development to historic preservation. It is dedicated to providing a forum for people across the political and ideological spectrum, ensuring a healthy debate on these and other important issues from across the United States and around the world.

Publication: Planetizen Email Newswire.

Population Reference Bureau
http://www.prb.org

The Population Reference Bureau is committed to enhancing research and focusing public attention on global population, health, and the environment. Their mission focuses on four "core themes" that include reproductive health and fertility; children and families; population and the environment; and future trends in population growth that relate to aging, inequality and poverty, migration and urbanization, and gender. The website provides country pages that allow for access to essential information on population, health, and the environment for over 200 countries along with selected PRB reports or articles, and links to key sources of information, including the most relevant searchable databases on international development. Funding for these pages has been provided by the U. S. Agency for International Development.

Publications: website offers full text of all PRB publications that include *Population Bulletins*, PowerPoint slideshows for educators, and abundant data and analysis.

Tellus Institute
http://www.tellus.org

The Tellus Institute was established in 1976 as an interdisciplinary not-for-profit research and policy organization in Boston, Massachusetts. Over the years, the Institute has conducted over 3,500 projects throughout the world in resource and environmental management strategies, and has been a pioneer in the field of sustainable development. Tellus has worked at the global, regional, national, local, and enterprise level to fashion strategies, policies that span environmental, social, and economic dimensions of development. Key foci have included energy, water, sustainable communities, corporate social responsibility, and climate change in projects that have been funded by private nonprofit foundations, government agencies, multilateral organizations, civil society organizations, and business. Since 2005, the Institute has been committed to achieving a "transition to a sustainable, just, and livable global civilization."

Publications: publications on scenarios, energy, water, solid waste, corporate responsibility, and sustainable development available online.

Urban Institute
http://www.urban.org

Growing interest in the problems facing U.S. urban areas in the early 1960s led to a presidential commission that recommended chartering an independent nonpartisan center to conduct research and make recommendations to policy makers about the nations' cities. The Urban Institute was founded in 1968 to fulfill this mission. Today, the organization consists of ten policy institutes that analyze a variety of different urban policies, offer evaluation of programs, and promote improved social, civic, and economic well-being. Over the years, the Institute's work has expanded beyond the United States to include work in over 28 countries. The UI's Center on International Development and Governance (IDG) sponsors research and develops projects promoting economic and democratic development in developing countries.

Publications: books, reports, data sets, *Issues in Focus*, press releases available online.UN-HABITAT
http://www.unhabitat.org/

The UN Human Settlements Program, known as UN-HABITAT, was created by the UN General Assembly to promote socially and environmentally sustainable towns and cities with the goal of providing adequate shelter for all. UN-HABITAT programs are designed to help policymakers and local communities become better informed about the urban issues they face, and to help them find workable, lasting solutions. The organization's mandate is outlined in the Vancouver Declaration on Human Settlements, Habitat Agenda, Istanbul Declaration on Human Settlements, the Declaration on Cities and Other Human Settlements in the New Millennium, and Resolution 56/206. UN-HABITAT's work is also linked to the UN Millennium Declaration, particularly the goals of member States to improve the lives of at least 100 million slum dwellers by the year 2020, Target 11, Millennium Development Goal No. 7, and Target 10 which calls for the reduction by half of the number without sustainable access to safe drinking water.
Publications: UN-HABITAT publishes hundreds of books, reports, and other materials related to urban development, land and housing, environment, water sanitation and infrastructure, urban economics and finance, social inclusion, and risk and disaster

management. These publications are available for direct purchase and, in many cases, also available for free download from the website.

World Association of Major Metropolises
http://metropolis.org

The World Association of Major Metropolises was founded in 1985 to serve as an international forum for exploring issues and concerns common to all big cities and metropolitan regions. Its website seeks to "build a global alliance between metropolitan governments and their associates to promote urban sustainability" by promoting a cross-sectoral approaches between the different aspects of urban sustainability: environmental, economic, social, and cultural. Prominent among its concerns are issues of rapid urbanization and livability of cities: what makes cities livable to their inhabitants and attractive to investors; and what governments are doing (or should do) to protect, promote, and enhance the livability of cities. The organization holds a world congress every three years, and seeks to promote technical assistance, training, and cooperation among the world's cities.

Publications: Metropolis newsletter, annual report on metropolitan regions, and other information available online.

World Bank
http://www.worldbank.org

The World Bank offers a source of financial and technical assistance to developing countries around the world. Their mission is to fight poverty and to help people help themselves and their environment by providing resources, sharing knowledge, building capacity, and forging partnerships in the public and private sectors. The World Bank was central to the establishment of the Millennium Development Goals which partners with the United Nations under an ambitious agenda to eliminate global poverty and promote sustainable development. The goals are unprecedented in that they provide clear targets and yardsticks for measuring results for all countries that are participating. The Bank is actually made up of two institutions owned by 187 member countries: the International Bank for Reconstruction and Development (IBRD) and the International Development Association (IDA).

Urbanization and urban development have always figured prominently in the projects and research the World Bank has sponsored.

Publications: The World Bank website provides access to over 80,000 free, downloadable documents, including operational documents (project documents, analytical and advisory work, and evaluations), formal and informal research papers, and most Bank publications. The annual *World Development Report* contains valuable research and analysis on urban conditions around the world.

World Resources Institute
http://www.wri.org

The World Resources Institute is a global environmental think tank launched in 1982 that works with governments, private companies, and civil society organizations to help develop solutions to urgent environmental challenges. Its programs work in four areas that include protect the global climate system from further harm due to emissions of greenhouse gases and climate change, empower people and strengthen governing institutions to foster environmentally sound and socially equitable decision-making, harness markets and enterprise to expand economic opportunity and protect the environment, and reverse rapid degradation of ecosystems and assure their capacity to provide humans with needed goods and services.

Publications: research reports, harts, maps, data sets available online.

World Policy Institute
http://www.worldpolicy.org

Founded in New York City in 1961 as the Fund for Education Concerning World Peace through World Law, this nonpartisan organization became the World Policy Institute in 1982 to reflect a shift from a primarily educational focus to incorporating a strong policy emphasis. The World Policy Institute "develops and champions innovative policies that require a progressive and global point of view" that emphasizes "cooperative policy solutions to achieve an inclusive and sustainable global market economy, engaged global civic participation and effective governance, and collaborative approaches to national and global security." Through its fellows program, sponsored events, collaborative policy development, media activities, and its *World Policy Journal*, the institute seeks to provide a forum for solution-focused policy analysis and public debate on issues including migration, climate change, technology, economic development, human rights, and counterterrorism.

Publications: World Policy Journal, newsletter, and blogs available online.

Worldwatch Institute
http://www.worldwatch.org

The Worldwatch Institute was founded in 1974 by economist Lester Brown as a source for independent research and analysis of global environmental concerns. Over time, Worldwatch has become recognized around the world as an important source for accessible, fact-based analysis of critical global issues that include urbanization and sustainable urban growth. Today, the Institute develops solutions to environmental and growth-related problems that emphasize "a blend of government leadership, private sector enterprise, and citizen action that can make a sustainable future a reality." Programs are concerned with energy and climate change, food and agriculture, and a seeking ways for economies, cultures, and societies to balance development with their ecosystems.

Publications: annual *State of the World Report, Worldwatch Reports*, Vital Signs online, newsletters and briefs, and a large library of books published by the institute available for purchase online.

U.S. National Advocacy Organizations

American Land Rights Association
http://www.landrights.org

The American Land Rights Association began in 1978 as a grassroots organization known as the National Park Inholders Association. Initially, its mission was originally to protect private property owners from unwanted land takings by the National

Park Service. In 1995, the organization changed its name to the American Land Rights Association to reflect its new role as a national clearinghouse and coalition builder for individuals and sympathetic citizen's groups that are seeking to oppose restrictive land-use designations. Its purpose is to "oppose selfish, single-use, restrictive land-use designations that damage local economies." It is not anti-park, but argues that parks and wilderness areas "should be established where they do not damage the socio-economic fabric of rural America." The organization provides a substantial archive of online resources designed to facilitate grassroots groups, provides consulting services, speakers bureau, congressional alert system, maintains a federal land-users database, and a Land Rights Network fax list.

Publications: clearinghouse of articles, links, and press release *Action Alerts.*

American Farmland Trust
http://www.farmland.org
The American Farmland Trust provides information and advocacy to farmers and allied organizations that are dedicated to stopping the loss of productive farmland to urban development. The organization acts as a resource for promoting survival strategies for small farms, assists farmers in adopting farming practices that lead to a healthier environment, and helps facilitate the establishment of land trusts to protect farmlands. The organization has articulated a strong call for growth management to protect farmlands in a report titled *Living on the Edge: The Costs and Risks of Scatter Development*, published in 1998.

Publications: variety of educational materials including books, technical reports, and fact sheets available for purchase.

American Planning Association
http://www.planning.org

The American Planning Association and its professional institute, the American Institute of Certified Planners, are organized to advance the art and science of planning and foster awareness of the importance of local, regional, state, and national level planning among elected officials and the general public. Among the many issues addressed by the organization, it has sponsored a great deal of research and conferences featuring the theme of urban sprawl, and acted as an advocacy organization in policy development at both state and federal levels. In offers a wide variety of publications and resource materials though its Planners Bookstore.

Publications: many books, research reports, manuals, audio and video resources, software, along with the peer-reviewed quarterly *Journal of the American Planning Association*, and *Planning*, a monthly magazine, and a newsletter titled *The Commissioner.*

American Road & Transportation Builders' Association
http://www.artba.org

The American Road and Transportation Builders Association is a national organization founded in 1902 to serve as the voice of the transportation construction industry. It works to represent the interests of this industry in Washington, DC before all branches of the federal government, while also providing its members with information on the policymaking process to facilitate grassroots advocacy. It works closely with other interest groups that include the American Highway Users Alliance, National Asphalt Pavement Association, and the Road Information Program to advocate for greater federal spending for public transportation and consumer choice in transportation policy alternatives.

Publications: generate research reports on road construction, press releases, and member resources that include the *Monthly U.S. Transportation Construction Market Report.*

Association of Metropolitan Planning Organizations
http://www.ampo.org

The Association of Metropolitan Planning Organizations (AMPO) is a nonprofit, membership organization established in 1994 to serve the needs and interests of metropolitan planning organizations across the United States. Federal highway and transit statutes require, as a condition for spending federal highway or transit funds in urbanized areas, the designation of MPOs, which have responsibility for planning, programming, and coordination of federal highway and transit investments. AMPO offers technical assistance and training, conferences and workshops, print and electronic communications, research, a forum for transportation policy development and coalition building, and a variety of other services.

Publications: studies, research reports.

Brookings Institution
http://www.brook.edu/es/urban/urban.htm

The Brookings Institution was founded in 1916 as an independent organization devoted to nonpartisan research, education, and publication in economics, government, foreign policy, and the social sciences. The Center on Urban and Metropolitan Policy seeks to advance research and understanding to "help build strong neighborhoods, cities, and metropolitan regions." It advocates regional solutions to urban problems, a strong role for private sector actors in development, and solutions that come from communities themselves.

Publications: a wide range of books and research papers.

Center for Neighborhood Technology
http://www.cnt.org

The Center for Neighborhood Technology was founded in 1978 to help create self-sufficient neighborhood economies in Chicago. Expanding its scope in 1990, its mission is to promote "public policies, new resources and accountable authority which support sustainable, just and vital urban communities." It seeks to help build prosperous, sustainable communities by linking economic and community development with ecological improvement in communities around the country. The Center is involved in public policy advocacy, market development, and community planning. Its Neighborhood Early Warning System is a database and electronic bulletin board as a means to increase community access to local government information in the Chicago area.

Publications: numerous reports and books.

Center for the Defense of Free Enterprise
http://www.cdfe.org

The Center for the Defense of Free Enterprise was founded in 1976 as a nonpartisan, nonprofit foundation to protect individual rights in the face of restrictions imposed upon the free enterprise system by government. Its members share a concern about "the rollback of 200 years of individual rights and the multitude of restrictions being imposed on America's free enterprise system by big government—and the lack of understanding of this problem by the American people." It serves the purpose of publishing and disseminating information regarding the principles of free enterprise system, fosters research and study of issues related to economics and governmental regulation, maintains a legal defense fund, sponsors speakers and conferences, funds youth scholarships, and makes available its publications through the Free Enterprise Press. The Center also maintains close contacts with a variety of business organizations, grass roots groups, and legislative leaders.

Publications: numerous books published through the Free Enterprise Press.

Citistates Group
http://www.citistates.com

The Citistates Group is a national network of journalists, speakers, and consultants who are committed to fostering greater public awareness about the advantages of metropolitan regional cooperation. They are united by the belief "that successful metropolitan regions are critical to economic competitiveness and sustainable communities." They provide information resources, guest speakers, and sponsors conferences that will encourage greater awareness of the need for the many local governments that comprise large metropolitan centers to cooperate with one another to their mutual advantage. They also provide consulting services to facilitate visioning, strategic planning, and leadership training in metropolitan (citistate) regions.

Publications: numerous *Citistates Reports* conducted on metro regions.

Competitive Enterprise Institute
http://www.cei.org

The Competitive Enterprise Institute was created in 1984 with a dedication to the principles of free enterprise and limited government. It members believe that U.S. consumers are best served not by government regulation, but by being allowed to make their own choices in a free market place. Its Center for Private Conservation is dedicated to advancing knowledge and information in support of advancing environmental goals through private efforts rather than governmental controls. They sponsor and publish policy-based research, advocate their views through press releases, and provide a variety of information resources to supporters.

Publications: studies on a variety of economic subjects, and online newsletters titled *CEI Planet*, *CEI Weekly*, and *Cooler Heads Digest*.

Congress for New Urbanism
http://www.cnu.org

The Congress for New Urbanism was founded in 1993 to act as an advocate for "the restructuring of public policy and development practices to support the restoration of existing urban centers and towns within coherent metropolitan regions . . . [and] stand for the reconfiguration of sprawling suburbs into communities of real neighborhoods and diverse districts, the conservation of natural environments, and the preservation of our built legacy." The organization takes its name from the Congresses it sponsors, which are annual gatherings that provide architects, planners, developers, elected officials and community representatives the opportunity to discuss issues related to urban development and revitalization. Currently, nine task forces focus work on specific issues of importance to urban development, seeking to incorporate the insights of New Urbanist thinking into practical proposals. The central office makes available a wide variety of printed resources to disseminate to the public.

Publications: variety of different resources that include an Image Bank, Project Database, reports, and Directory of New Urbanists.

Demographia
http://www.demographia.com

Demographia is an online clearinghouse for research and information on urban growth and development in the United States and the global scale. It is a project of Wendell Cox, a public policy consultant specializing in urban policy, transportation, and demographics. The website offers a wealth of data on many topics related to urban areas and urban growth. Cox represents a philosophy about urban planning and policy that is "pro-choice with respect to urban development" and reflects an orientation in which "people should have the freedom to live and work where and how they like."

Publications: extensive data sets, news, and commentary by the author available online.

Environmental Law Institute
http://www.eli.org

Founded in 1969, the Environmental Law Institute (ELI) calls for "a healthy environment, prosperous economies, and vibrant communities founded on the rule of law." ELI works with government officials, environmental and business leaders, academics, members of the environmental bar, and journalists to promote more informed debate on important environmental issues. Among its concerns are prevailing patterns of land development in the United States that often contribute to the high cost of public services, the decline of cities and older suburbs, and the rapid conversion of farmland and forest and range lands to inefficient and costly developed uses. They advocate smart-growth policies that provide choices and protect livelihoods for people while safeguarding the environment.

Publications: publishes books, research reports, and several periodicals that include the *Environmental Law Reporter*, the *Environmental Forum*, and *National Wetlands Newsletter.*

International Economic Development Council
http://www.iedconline.org

The International Economic Development Council (IEDC) is a nonprofit membership organization dedicated to helping economic developers do their job more effectively and raising the profile of the profession. When we succeed, our members create more high-quality jobs, develop more vibrant communities, and generally improve the quality of life in their regions.

Publications: a large number of IEDC reports, white papers and manuals, along with quarterly *Economic Development Journal,* biweekly *Economic Development Now* and *Economic Development America,* a quarterly magazine published through a partnership among the Economic Development Administration and the National Association of Regional Councils.

Heartland Institute
www.heartland.org

The Heartland Institute is a national nonprofit research and education organization founded in Chicago in 1984. It is a nonpartisan independent institute whose mission is to discover, develop, and promote free-market solutions to social and economic problems. With regard to urban growth, such solutions include market-based approaches to environmental protection, privatization of public services, and deregulation in areas where property rights and markets do a better job than government bureaucracies. The Heartland Institute remains skeptical of the benefits of smart-growth initiatives.

Publications: books, policy briefs, and newsletters.

International City/County Management Association
http://www.icma.org

The International City/County Management Association has served as a professional and educational organization for appointed administrators, managers, and other professional staff who serve local governments around the United States since 1914. The organization was the prime sponsor of the Smart Growth Network, and also has sought to provide education and assistance to local governments in dealing with sprawl-related policy challenges, including environmental programs, brownfields, and urban redevelopment planning. The organization provides technical assistance, training, and a wide variety of publications for local government professionals and students.

Publications: publishes many books as well as handbooks such as *Best Development Practices: A Primer for Smart Growth*, reports, data sets, CDs, classroom and teaching resources, and three free online newsletters that include *Academic Matters*, *Local Government Matters*, and *Performance Matters*.

Land Tenure Center, University of Wisconsin
http://www.nelson.wisc.edu/ltc

Established in 1962, the University of Wisconsin's Nelson Institute for Environmental Studies and Land Tenure Center develops project management for short- and long-term activities, sponsors conferences and panels, and facilitates researchers around the world on natural resource tenure, agrarian reform, and related institutional aspects of rural development and natural resource management. It also oversees a doctorate program in Development Studies. While the initial focus was on overseas concerns, the Center expanded in 1993 to include a program covering land-use issues in North America, including urban sprawl. The Center approaches land policy issues from a multidisciplinary perspective, and manages an extensive library collection and series of databases on land-related issues. It is funded in part by the U.S. Agency for International Development, and is affiliated with the College of Agricultural and Life Sciences at the University of Wisconsin-Madison.

Publications: on-line resources include *Land Tenure Center Briefs* along with a wide variety of documents, sponsored research papers, and working papers.

Land Trust Alliance
http://www.lta.org

The Land Trust Alliance promotes voluntary land conservation around the nation. It seeks to strengthen the land trust movement by providing leadership, information, skills, and resources to those interested in conserving land through the formation of land trusts. It maintains three field offices that provide a variety of programs to help land trusts operate in a more effective manner through technical assistance, coordination, grant funding, and legal services across the United States.

Publications: quarterly magazine *Saving Land*, the on-line LTC Learning Center offers access to a large amount of information about land trusts, fact sheets, and other resources also available online.

Lincoln Institute of Land Policy
http://www.lincolninst.edu

The Lincoln Institute of Land Policy was established in 1974 to both encourage both the study and teaching of land policy, including land economics and taxation in the United States and in foreign countries. Its mission is to explore the fundamental forces affecting land use and development: government strategies for managing change, community and individual rights and responsibilities, taxation and regulation, markets, patterns of human settlement and production, and transportation systems. To accomplish these goals, it offers professional development courses, sponsors national and international conferences, funds research and curriculum development projects, and publishes a wide variety of resources.

Publications: multimedia resources, books, policy focus reports, working papers, abstracts, and a quarterly publication *Land Lines*.

Local Government Commission
http://www.lgc.org

The Local Government Commission is a nonpartisan membership organization composed of elected officials, city and county staff, and others who are "committed to developing and implementing local solutions to problems of state and national significance." Through its Center for Livable Communities, it provides a forum and technical assistance to enhance the ability of local governments and community leaders to "be proactive in their land use and transportation planning, and adopt programs and policies that lead to more livable and resource-efficient land-use patterns." These tasks are accomplished through the organization of conferences and training workshops, the dissemination of publications and other resources, and the maintenance of a Land Use Library.

Publications: informational guidebooks, *Livable Places Update* monthly newsletter, slideshows, and videos.

National Association of Counties
http://www.naco.org

The National Association of Counties was created in 1935 to ensure that the nation's 3,066 counties are given a voice in state and national affairs. It is a full-service organization that provides extensive advocacy services for its membership, including legislative, research, and technical assistance. The organization recently formed a Joint Center for Sustainable Communities, which is committed to "curbing sprawl, promoting brownfields redevelopment, and encouraging smart growth through greater multi-jurisdictional cooperation." It represents a partnership with the U.S. Conference of Mayors and the National Association of Counties, and is dedicated to helping devise solutions to the complicated set of issues caused by inadequate regional planning and uncontrolled sprawl.

Publications: guidebooks, research publications, electronic databases on counties.

National Association of Home Builders
http://www.nahb.com

The National Association of Home Builders represents people who work in the home building industry around the United States. The organization primarily exists as an advocacy organization for the industry, and is "committed to pursuing reasonable and market-driven Smart Growth strategies that will meet the nation's housing needs, expand homeownership opportunities, help revitalize the nation's cities and inner suburbs, and build attractive and livable neighborhoods." As such, it has been an active participant in policy debates and legislative deliberation surrounding urban development planning. It seeks to achieve its aims by sponsoring conventions and home expos, conducting research on issues related to the homebuilding industry through its Research Center, and disseminating this information to members, elected officials at all levels, and the general public

Publications: electronic data bases, fact sheets, public surveys, e-newsletter *HouseKeys.*

National Association of Realtors
http://www.realtor.org/government_affairs/smart_growth

The National Association of Realtors was founded in 1908 and strives to be the collective force influencing and shaping the real estate industry. It seeks to be the leading advocate of the right to own, use, and transfer real property; the acknowledged leader in developing standards for efficient, effective, and ethical real estate business practices. NAR's "Smart Growth" program provides a variety of resources and tools to help members build communities based on smart-growth principles.

Publications: field guides, technical assistance toolkits, surveys, *Smart Growth e-news*, and *On Common Ground* published twice each year.

National Association of Regional Councils
http://www.narc.org

The National Association of Regional Councils (NARC) represents the interests of regional councils of government, regional planning and development districts, and a variety of other nongovernmental interests that seek to foster urban cooperation and build regional communities. The organization assists community leaders and citizens in developing regional strategies and solutions to sprawl-related issues that cut across local political boundaries. Its activities include policy advocacy, sponsoring "regional summits" among affiliates, acting as an information resource on regional issues, and encouraging research through its Institute for the Regional Community. NARC is closely affiliated with the Association of Metropolitan Planning Organizations.

Publications: reports, articles, and *e-regions* electronic newsletter.

National Center for Appropriate Technology (Smart Communities Network)
http://ncat.org

The National Center for Appropriate Technology has been serving economically disadvantaged people since 1976 by providing information and access to appropriate technologies that can help improve their lives. Its Smart Communities Network promotes sustainable development by promoting economic development approaches that also benefit the local environment and quality of life. The organization challenges traditional approaches to planning and development that create rather than solve societal and environmental problems. Where traditional approaches can lead to congestion, sprawl, pollution, and resource overconsumption, sustainable development offers real, lasting solutions that will strengthen our future. Sustainable development provides a framework under which communities can use resources efficiently, create efficient infrastructures, protect and enhance quality of life, and create new businesses to strengthen their economies.

National Center for Public Policy Research
http://www.nationalcenter.org

The National Center for Public Policy Research is a communications and research foundation dedicated to providing free market solutions as they apply to a variety of public policy issues, including land-use regulation. Founded in 1982, this organization believes that private property owners are the best stewards of our land and environment, and that a free market, individual liberty, and personal responsibility therefore provide the best focus for public policy action, not burdensome government regulation. Its Center for Environmental and Regulatory Affairs focuses in part on smart-growth-related issues.

Publications: national policy analysis reports, press releases.

National Center for Smart Growth Research and Education
http://www.smartgrowth.umd.edu

The National Center for Smart Growth Research and Education was founded in 2000 with support from the University of Maryland as a nonpartisan center for research and leadership training on smart growth and related land-use issues. Although initially focused on Maryland in 2000, it has expanded its reach to include metropolitan regions around the nation, and in Asia and Europe. The mission of the Center is to bring the diverse resources of the University of Maryland and a network of national experts to bear on issues related to land use and the environment, transportation and public health, housing and community development, and international urban development. The Center accomplishes this through a commitment to independent, objective, interdisciplinary research, outreach, and education. Upon request, the Center also offers smart-growth leadership training to federal, state, and local government officials as well as to private sector decision-makers.

Publications: sponsored research in refereed academic journals.

National Conference of State Legislatures
http://www.ncsl.org

The National Conference of State Legislatures is a bipartisan organization that seeks to improve the quality and effectiveness of state legislatures, foster communication and cooperation among legislators, and ensure that states retain a strong and cohesive voice in the federal system. As such, the organization acts as an information source and advocacy organization for the elected legislators and staffs of state, commonwealth, and territorial governments of the United States. With an increasing number of states adopting "smart-growth" measures and federal funds now targeting these goals, it has sponsored research in growth management and land conservation issues through its Environment and Natural Resources division.

Publications: books, monthly *State Legislatures* magazine, *LegisBriefs* weekly newsletter, multimedia resources, guidebooks, and reports.

National League of Cities
http://www.nlc.org

The National League of Cities was established in 1924 by state municipal leagues around the county that shared a commitment to reform. Today, it represents 49 leagues, 1,500 member cities, and more than 18,000 cities and towns through its membership. Its mission is to strengthen and promote cities as center of opportunity, leadership, and governance. Through this organization, mayors and council members join together to establish unified policy positions, advocate these policies, and share information that strengthens municipal government throughout the nation.

Publications: Nation's Cities Weekly, National Municipal Policy, City Practice briefs, municipal action guides, press releases, and research reports.

National Trust for Historic Preservation
http://www.preservationnation.org

Chartered by the U.S. Congress in 1949, the National Trust for Historic Preservation is committed to ensuring that historic buildings, neighborhoods, and landscapes are preserved and protected from urban development pressures. The organization has taken a strong stance in favor of growth management planning as a means to limit sprawl and shift investment back to neglected, deteriorating central cities and historic downtown areas. It maintains six regional offices, directly oversees the administration of twenty historic sites, and works with local governments and community groups nationwide to facilitate the acquisition and preservation of historic structures and landscapes from urban development. It acts as a national information resource, sponsors conferences, funds research as well as preservation projects, and engages in public policy advocacy in legislative as well as legal affairs. It also gives out a variety of honor awards to recognize organizations and individuals who are committed to historic preservation.

Publications: electronic databases, books, reports, *Preservation,* a bimonthly magazine, and online news.

Northeast-Midwest Institute
http://nemw.org

The Northeast-Midwest Institute is a private nonprofit, nonpartisan research organization that promotes economic vitality, environmental quality, as well as regional equity for the 18 northeastern and midwestern states: Connecticut, Delaware, Illinois, Indiana, Iowa, Maine, Maryland, Massachusetts, Michigan, Minnesota, New Hampshire, New Jersey, New York, Ohio, Pennsylvania, Rhode Island, Vermont, and Wisconsin. Its focus on urban and land-related issues is part of a larger concern to promote economic vitality for the region. The Institute explores strategies for federal economic development initiatives, analyzes legislation, tracks trends, and distributes information to educate and inform Congressional staff, federal policy makers, and state officials. Institute efforts have addressed a range of federal policies, including the Community Development Block Grant program, the Manufacturing Extension Partnership, community infrastructure, brownfields redevelopment, housing, business development, and industrial energy efficiency.

Publications: reports, economic data, news releases.

Pacific Research Institute for Public Policy
http://www.pacificresearch.org

The Pacific Research Institute for Public Policy was founded in 1979 to "to champion freedom, opportunity, and personal responsibility for all individuals by advancing free-market policy solutions." As such, the Institute is a strong advocate of policies that emphasize private initiative and limited government. With regard to urban growth-related policy questions, the institute rejects the need for any national, state, and local land-use policies that restrict individual choices and limit market forces in the cause of combating urban sprawl.

Publications: books, research reports, archive of articles, newsletter, and PRI blogs.

Reason Public Policy Institute
http://www.reason.org

The Reason Public Policy Institute was created in 1968 to sponsor and publicize academic research and writing that "advances a free society by developing, applying, and promoting libertarian principles, including individual liberty, free markets, and the rule of law." Its nonpartisan research promotes choice, competition, and a market economy as the core foundation for all policies related to urban growth management. The Institute has sponsored numerous research projects on issues related to infrastructure and transportation, urban land use and economic development, and environmental quality. Its urban growth and land-use promotes voluntary, private-sector, and market-oriented solutions.

Publications: Reason magazine, research reports, policy studies, and e-newsletters.

Scenic America
http://www.scenic.org

Scenic America is a nonprofit advocacy organization that is dedicated to "preserving and enhancing the visual character of America's communities and countryside." Scenic America is active at federal, state, and local levels in pursuit of its goal of protecting the scenic heritage of U.S. natural landscapes from the "blizzard of monstrous billboards, badly sited telecommunications towers, a tangle of overhead lines, and a hodgepodge of visual clutter." As such, the organization is deeply involved in debates over urban growth in its efforts to reduce billboard blight, promote strict community planning and design guidelines, preserve open space and scenic resource conservation, and work to produce transportation plans that is in harmony with physical settings and preserves scenic, aesthetic, historic and environmental resources. The organization provides resources and tools to activists seeking to advance these goals across the United States.

Publications: books, reports available for purchase online.

Sierra Club
http://www.sierraclub.org

The Sierra Club was launched in 1892 to protect wilderness areas, promote responsible use of natural resources, and restore the quality of natural and human environments. Since 1986, the Sierra Club has been involved in sponsoring research and advocacy related to urban growth. Its report titled *The Dark Side of the American Dream: The Costs and Consequences of Suburban Sprawl* helped to frame the national debate when it was released in 1998. More recently, the Sierra Club has moved away from "urban sprawl" toward a focus on advocating clean and efficient vehicles, green energy, and transportation planning that expands the U.S. public transit and passenger rail system.

Publications: Sierra magazine books and reports available online.

Smart Communities Network
http://www.smartcommunities.ncat.org

The National Center for Appropriate Technology maintains this website, which serves as a clearinghouse of resources which help to inform the public about community-level initiatives that are accomplishing the goal of sustainable development. The organization defines sustainable development as "a strategy by which communities seek economic development approaches that also benefit the local environment and quality of life, in which traditional approaches to planning and development are creating, rather than solving, societal and environmental problems."

Smart Growth America
http://www.smartgrowthamerica.org

Smart Growth America is a coalition of national, state, and local organizations seeking to work with developers, elected officials, and communities to achieve "smart growth" by fostering better planned towns, cities, and metro areas. The organization is committed to the idea that all Americans deserve the "right to live in healthy communities in homes that are both affordable and close to jobs and activities." Other quality of life concerns addressed through their work include fewer hours in traffic and more opportunities to enjoy recreation and natural areas, and clean air and water. The coalition unites many national organizations that advocate on behalf of historic preservation, the environment, farmland and open space preservation, neighborhood revitalization, and other urban issues. Smart Growth America serves as a policy resource that works with leaders at all levels of government to show which policy options are best for different communities and can help communities go from idea to implementation.

Publications: reports, blogs accessible online.

Smart Growth Network
http://www.smartgrowth.org

The Smart Growth Network was begun in 1998 under the sponsorship of the U.S. Environmental Protection Agency's Urban and Economic Development Division. The Network was formed to provide a more comprehensive response to concerns about sprawling urban development patterns that were detracting from the quality of life in U.S. cities and suburbs as well as degrading the natural environment. Its partners include environmental groups, historic preservation organizations, professional organizations, developers, real estate interests; local and state government entities that share a common commitment to raising public awareness of how growth can improve community quality of life and promoting smart-growth best practices. The goals of this alliance are to develop and share innovative policies, tools, and ideas that will advance opportunities for smart growth.

Publications: a variety of guide books, articles, fact sheets, and newsletters offered through member organizations within the network.-
Sprawl-Busters
http://www.sprawl-busters.com

Sprawl-Busters was begun by Al Norman, who was part of a citizen-based grassroots organization that successfully prevented national retailer Wal-Mart from locating a store in the small community of Greenfield, Massachusetts in 1993. His organization exists to disseminate information and offer consultant services to assist local community coalitions seeking to block against megastores and other undesirable large-scale developments.

Sustainable Cities Institute
http://www.sustainablecitiesinstitute.org

A project of The Home Depot Foundation, the Sustainable Cities Institute works to support efforts across the United States to promote environmental stewardship and proactive solutions to helping create environmentally healthy communities. As such, the Institute is committed to "a long-term, integrated and systematic approach to developing and achieving a healthy community by jointly addressing economic, environmental, and social issues." The SCI website offers an online toolbox that is built in partnership with its users, who post, comment, and contribute to the website. Topics addressed online include Economic Development, Water, Materials Management, and Land Use and Transportation. The City Program is composed of a panel of sustainable development experts who serve as a resource to cities in developing and implementing sustainable community development plans.

Publications: planning center and a library, forums, webinars, a calendar, City Profiles, and an interactive "Sustainable City" map.

Thoreau Institute
http://www.ti.org

The Thoreau Institute was founded by Randal O'Toole in 1975 to offer a critical perspective of mainstream planning and prevailing conceptions regarding urban management and smart growth. It regards such efforts as inherently flawed, producing disastrous counter-productive results, and altogether "promotes the repeal of federal and state planning laws and the closure of state and local planning departments." Critiques and alternative free market policies are offered on a variety of different land-use issues such as public lands, parks, transportation, and urban planning. In 2006, updates and information were shifted to the Institute's blog titled *The Antiplanner.*

Publications: archive of articles and reports.

Trust for Public Land
http://www.tpl.org

The Trust for Public Land (TPL) was created in 1972 by a group of lawyers, real estate professionals, and finance experts who wanted to bring a modern business approaches to the goal of conserving valuable natural landscapes in areas threatened by urban development. It has helped to create many local land preservation trusts, and served as a pioneer in developing new land preservation techniques that have resulted in over 4,250 park and conservation projects across the United States. TPL is a national leader and innovator in city park creation, state and local conservation funding, and the use of GIS for conservation planning, and offers a variety of services to landowners, community groups, and government agencies in order to further the creation of urban parks, gardens, greenways, and rivers, conserve land for protection and recreational uses, and safeguard historic landmarks and landscapes.

Publications: Land & People magazine, books, reports, and e-newsletters.

Urban Land Institute
http://www.uli.org

The Urban Land Institute (ULI) dates back to 1936 to study and interpret real estate trends and to examine principles through which private enterprise could effectively develop real estate and act as a statistical clearinghouse for the dissemination of real estate data. Today, it has over 40,000 members in 95 countries and continues to serve as "an open exchange of ideas, information, and experience among local, national, and international industry leaders and policy makers dedicated to creating better places." ULI initiates research that anticipates emerging land-use trends and issues, as well as proposing creative solutions based on that research. ULI documents best practices and publishes materials to assist the real estate developers and community planners.

Publications: Urban Land magazine, books, and research reports.

U.S. Department of Housing and Urban Development Office of Sustainable Housing and Communities
hud.gov/sustainability

The mission of the Office of Sustainable Housing and Communities is to create strong, sustainable communities by connecting housing to jobs, fostering local innovation, and helping to build a clean energy economy. In order to better connect housing to jobs, the office coordinates federal housing and transportation investments with local land-use decisions in order to reduce transportation costs for families, improve housing affordability, save energy, and increase access to housing and employment opportunities. By ensuring that housing is located near job centers and affordable, accessible transportation, it is intended that these policies we will nurture healthier, more inclusive communities that provide opportunities for people of all ages, incomes, races, and ethnicities to live, work, and learn together.

U.S. Department of the Interior
http://www.doi.gov

The Department of the Interior is the nation's leading public lands management agency. It also has responsibilities that include wildlife protection, natural resources conservation, and promoting research. The department is committed to facilitating local and state efforts to mitigate the detrimental impact of urban growth through the provision of data, mapping, and planning assistance, especially as it applies to recreation, wildlife habitat, and historic preservation. Its Land and Wildlife Conservation Fund provides matching grants to states and local governments for the acquisition and development of public outdoor recreation areas and facilities.

U.S. Department of Transportation
http://www.fhwa.dot.gov/tcsp

The Transportation, Community, and System Preservation (TCSP) Program is a comprehensive initiative involving both research and grant funding to investigate the relationships between transportation, community, and system preservation plans and practices and identify private sector-based initiatives to improve such relationships. States, metropolitan planning organizations, local governments, and tribal governments are eligible for discretionary grants to carry out eligible projects to integrate transportation, community, and system preservation plans and practices that: improve the efficiency of the transportation system of the United States, reduce environmental impacts of transportation, reduce the need for costly future public infrastructure investments, ensure efficient access to jobs, services, and centers of trade. It encourages communities to study development patterns and identify strategies to encourage private sector development patterns and investments that support these goals.

U.S. Environmental Protection Agency
http://www.epa.gov/smartgrowth

The Environmental Protection Agency (EPA) has incorporated the "smart-growth" agenda into its larger mission of protecting the health and well-being of Americans and their natural environment. It is committed to helping communities grow in ways that expand economic opportunity, protect public health and the environment, and create and enhance the places that people love. Working in partnership with the Departments of Transportation and Housing and Urban Development, it provides research, tools, partnerships, case studies, grants, and technical assistance to help local communities improve access to affordable housing, more transportation options, and lower transportation costs while protecting the environment.

U.S. Department of Agriculture
http://www.nrcs.usda.gov

The Natural Resources Conservation Service (NRCS) is the branch of Agriculture Department that works with local communities and landowners to adopt conservation planning that preserves and protects productive lands and healthy ecosystems. The NRCS also oversees the federal Farmland Protection Program that enables individuals and groups to purchase conservation easements with the assistance of local, state, and federal funds. The federal government provides up to a 50 percent share of the fair market value for land acquired under this program. The "National Resources Inventory" is a valuable statistical survey of land use and natural resource conditions in the 48 continental states that offers a truly national perspective on urban growth-related concerns in the United States.

U.S. State and Regional Urban Growth Agencies and Advocacy Organizations

Arizona Preserve Initiative
http://www.land.state.az.us/programs/operations/api.htm

The Arizona Preserve Initiative (API) was passed by the Arizona State Legislature as HB 2555 and signed into law in 1996. It is designed to encourage the preservation of select parcels of state trust land in and around urban areas for open space to benefit future generations. The law lays out a process by which Trust land can be leased for up to 50 years or sold for conservation purposes. Leases and sales must both occur at a public auction.

Cascade Policy Institute
http://www.cascadepolicy.org

The Cascade Policy Institute is a nonprofit, nonpartisan public policy research and educational organization founded in 1991 that focuses on state and local issues in the state of Oregon. Cascade's mission is "to develop and promote public policy alternatives that foster individual liberty, personal responsibility and economic opportunity." Its agenda includes a strong emphasis on land-use planning, offering a critical perspective that opposes statewide planning in favor of the interests of property owners, unregulated markets, and decentralized decision-making.

EcoCity Cleveland
http://www.ecocitycleveland.org/smartgrowth/smartgrowthpage.html

EcoCity Cleveland is a nonprofit environmental planning organization founded in 1992 to promote more carefully designed cities and urban growth that is in balance with nature in Northeast Ohio. In the region's core cities, they advocate environmentally-friendly redevelopment that improves quality of life and makes cities more sustainable while seeking to preserve the countryside to promote sensitive development that preserves open space and the ecological integrity in surrounding rural areas. At a broader level, EcoCity Cleveland hopes to promote the metropolitan region as a key unit of analysis, "helping citizens and policy-makers adopt a more thoughtful regional perspective—a 'bioregional' perspective that transcends the political fragmentation."

Envision Utah
http://envisionutah.org

Envision Utah has its origins in 1988 when a diverse group of community leaders from the Salt Lake City region began to work on ways to attract new businesses and jobs in the state during an economic downturn. Within a decade, the purpose of the organization expanded to include consensus-building on a variety of issues such as affordable housing, neighborhood and community issues, urban-growth related concerns, environmental protection, and transportation among other issues. In 1997, Envision Utah launched a public effort aimed to "keep Utah beautiful, prosperous, and neighborly for future generations" by serving as a "neutral facilitator" among diverse constituencies that eventually resulted in the Quality Growth Strategy. This provides a framework for "voluntary, locally-implemented, market-based solutions" to the state's communities as part of a "vision to protect Utah's environment, economic strength, and quality of life" in the Greater Wasatch Area through coordination in planning.

Greater Ohio
http://www.greaterohio.org

The Greater Ohio Policy Center was founded to promote policies that accomplish the both strong economic growth and improve state residents' quality of life through sustainable land use and growth practices. The organization uses research, public education, and grassroots advocacy to "advance policies and programs that revitalize Ohio's urban cores and regions, strengthen regional cooperation and protect Ohio's open space, natural resources and farmland."

Green Environmental Coalition
http://www.greenlink.org

The Green Environmental Coalition was founded in 1991 in Yellow Springs, Ohio when a number of neighborhood groups concerned about a hazardous waste facility realized their common interest. Since that time, it has continued to work for greater environmental accountability in the private business sector, while also encompassing other issues related to clean water, toxic chemicals, and urban sprawl.

Greenbelt Alliance
http://www.greenbelt.org

The Greenbelt Alliance (GA) is a land conservation organization active in the San Francisco Bay area since 1958. The organization was originally created to protect parks and recreational areas, but eventually expanded its scope to a larger commitment to preserving additional spaces such as ranch lands, agricultural lands, and wildlife preserves. In recent years, the GA has become the leading advocate for regional "smart-growth" planning that concentrates growth in the center of a city to avoid sprawl. Its "Grow Smart Bay Area" plan envisions "prosperous and livable communities, providing better housing and transportation opportunities while protecting farmland, open space, and the environment."

Livable Communities Coalition
http://www.livablecommunitiescoalition.org

The Livable Communities Coalition was formed in 2005 through the initiative of the Metro Atlanta Chamber of Commerce's Quality Growth Task Force. It was intended that this body would seek out new ways to accommodate regional growth that would protect the environment, improve the quality of life, and strengthen area businesses. The coalition is headed by a Board of Trustees, and consists of diverse network of representatives from local governments, the state legislature, universities, businesses, civic, and environmental groups "who all share a determination to work together to achieve quality growth for the Atlanta region." The Livable Communities Coalition provides a wide range of services that help communities accelerate smart growth at a modest cost to local governments and citizen groups. This includes audits of existing land-use policies and zoning codes; planning exercises and other public participation events; assessments of growth opportunities, and technical assistance.

Massachusetts Smart Growth Alliance
http://www.ma-smartgrowth.org

Massachusetts Smart Growth Alliance works to improve the state's development policies in order to "build welcoming communities with a high quality of life." Founded in 2003, its objectives include the promotion of healthy and diverse communities, the protection of critical environmental resources and working landscapes, the creation of housing and transportation choices, and equitable community development and urban reinvestment. The Alliance seeks to achieve its mission by advancing legislation, promoting a favorable regulatory environment, and advocating for state planning, funding, and construction decisions in line with sustainable development principles. Furthermore, the Alliance seeks to identify best practices as well as tackle implementation challenges by strengthening place-based initiatives in strategic locations.

Metropolitan Council (Minneapolis–St. Paul)
http://www.metrocouncil.org

The Metropolitan Council (MC) is a regional government agency created by the Minnesota Legislature in 1967. It serves Minneapolis, St. Paul, and 180 other communities spread across Anoka, Carver, Dakota, Hennepin, Ramsey, Scott, and Washington counties with a total land area of 2,975 square miles and a population of 2.85 million. The Council establishes policies for the region's urban growth as they relate to transportation, aviation, water resources, and parks and open space, and directly administers regional bus and rail systems, transit services for people with disabilities, and wastewater collection and treatment. In addition, the MC works with local communities to plan for future growth, forecast population and household growth, assess affordable housing needs, and plan for future acquisitions and funding for parks and trails. The 17-member Metropolitan Council board has 16 members who each represent distinct geographic districts and one chair who serves at-large. Its operations are funded by a mix of local property taxes, user fees, and state and federal money.

Montana Coalition for Smart Growth
http://www.mtsmartgrowth.org

The Montana Smart Growth Coalition brought together some 40 diverse organizations across the state in 1999 to seek to "protect and enhance Montana's unique quality of life, big sky, waters, and wildlife while helping our communities grow more sustainably and affordably." The organization conducts reports on transportation and land-use related issues, holds conferences, and provides communities with information and planning resources to "take control over their own future." They also serve as an advocate in state government for smarter growth policies that "do not promote inefficient sprawling development patterns that pass the real costs of growth off to taxpayers, neighbors, and senior water rights holders." The coalition argues that "smart growth means making the market work efficiently and correctly by making smarter development in and around existing cities and towns faster, easier, and more profitable."

New Jersey Future
http://njfuture.org

New Jersey Future (NJF) was founded in 1987 by corporate, civic, and environmental leaders across the state who shared a commitment to advancing more coordinated land-use and growth policies. Today, this nonprofit nonpartisan organization is the leading voice on policies for curbing sprawl and spurring community redevelopment in New Jersey. Its activities have included serving as a leading advocate for State Development and Redevelopment Plan, New Jersey's smart-growth blueprint for revitalizing communities and protecting natural resources. In addition, NJF has pushed for the adoption of new local and state laws for protecting the environment and encouraging smarter growth, including the Highlands Water Protection Act and Transfer of Development Rights.

One Thousand Friends Organizations

In 1975, and organization called "1,000 Friends of Oregon" was founded to represent citizens who were committed to supporting Governor Tom McCall's initiative to institute mandatory growth management planning across the state. Since that time, several other states and local communities have created "1,000 Friends" movements of their own. While each is unique and separate, all follow a similar pattern of bringing together a diverse coalition of businesses, elected officials, interest groups, and citizens who are united by a commitment to educating and empowering citizens about the dangers of sprawl and the need for state and regional land-use planning. The list presently includes:

1,000 Friends of Connecticut
http://www.1000friends-ct.org

1,000 Friends of Florida
http://www.1000friendsofflorida.org

1,000 Friends of Fresno
http://www.1000friendsoffresno.org

1,000 Friends of Iowa
http://1000friendsofiowa.org

1,000 Friends of Hawaii
http://www.hawaiis1000friends.org

1,000 Friends of Maryland
http://www.friendsofmd.org

Envision Minnesota (formerly 1,000 Friends of Minnesota)
http://www.envisionmn.org

1,000 Friends of Oregon
http://www.friends.org

10,000 Friends of Pennsylvania
http://10000friends.org

1,000 Friends of Wisconsin
http://www.1kfriends.org

1,000 Friends of Waco
http://www.1000friendsofwaco.com

Futurewise (formerly 1,000 Friends of Washington)
http://futurewise.org

Sierra Nevada Alliance
http://www.sierranevadaalliance.org

Founded in 1993, the Sierra Nevada Alliance unites together citizens and some 70 different organizations that share a common concern to protect and restore the natural resources of the Sierra Nevada Mountain region. In addition to wildlife and habitat protection, the alliance vigorously encourages actions and local planning processes to increase the sustainability of rural communities through on-the-ground projects, model programs, publications, events, and workshops. Its "Sustainable Sierra Land Use Campaign" further helps communities to develop land-use plans that "protect Sierra water, wildlands, agriculture and rural communities by building the capacity of local groups working to advance smart growth in their communities."

Smart Coast
http://smartcoast.org/smartcoast/html/home.html

Smart Coast began in 2002 as the Healthy Coastal Communities Initiative (HCCI). From 2002–2004 HCCI operated as a project of the Mobile Bay National Estuary Program carried out in coordination with the Dauphin Island Sea Lab Coastal Policy Center, the Mississippi Alabama Sea Grant Consortium, and the Alabama Department of Conservation and Natural Resources' State Lands Division, Coastal Section. During this time, HCCI completed a number of studies on coastal growth and development. In March 2004, HCCI joined with Envision Coastal Alabama and many other partners to host a Smart Coastal Growth Conference that was held in Mobile. Smart Coast was formed in 2005 to serve as the nonprofit whose mission is to continue the work of bringing the region together to dialogue about growth and development and how our region can design healthier communities.

Smart Growth Coalition of Cincinnati and Northern Kentucky
http://sgcoalition.org

The Smart Growth Coalition is a nonprofit created in the year 2000 to bring together a diverse group of planners, architects, civic groups, professional organizations, and concerned individuals who are seeking to promote "a positive vision for improving the quality of life" in the tri-state metropolitan area that includes Cincinnati and adjacent regions of the northern Kentucky and eastern Indiana. The organization seeks to cultivate public interest in smart-growth alternatives to sprawling development through education and community outreach.

Smart Growth for Louisiana
http://smartgrowthla.org

Smart Growth for Louisiana is a nonprofit group based in New Orleans that was founded in 1998 to advocate for more balanced urban development that is sensitive to the need for environmental preservation. The organization believes that "uncontrolled and unplanned growth inflicts irreparable harms on our communities" and seeks to use its resources to encourage more carefully planned development and growth management.

Smart Growth Vermont
http://www.smartgrowthvermont.org

In the mid-1990s, several leading environmentalists saw an urgent need for an organization that would bring together diverse, and at times opposing, interests to discuss how Vermont could have a strong economy and housing options while protecting the farm and forests that define the state's landscape. The Vermont Forum on Sprawl was founded in 1997 as a project of the Orton Family Foundation dedicated to raising public awareness about the financial and cultural costs of sprawl, providing alternative development models and promoting state policies that protect and nurture our downtowns and village centers. In 2007, the organization was renamed Smart Growth Vermont.

Urban Choice Coalition
http://www.urbanchoice.org

The Urban Choice Coalition was founded in 1998 by a coalition of business, labor, and civic leaders in St. Louis, Missouri who were opposed to the idea of imposing urban growth boundaries and other state-level restrictions on local communities in St. Charles County. The initial goal of this organization was to "educate and inform so as to dispel myths that the success of suburban communities in the St. Louis region was at the expense of the urban core and so as to show that growth in the suburban counties was well planned and sustainable." The organization offers resources to other groups that are seeking to combat urban growth management policies that impinge on local-level land-use control.

8

Resources

There are many books and articles on urbanization and the challenges associated with rapid urban growth and urban sprawl. Most works explore the subject of urban growth in a case study context, often in the historical context of a single city like Tokyo, New York, Mumbai, or Cairo. Other works focus on urban growth challenges as a nationwide phenomenon, with the United States well represented in the urban policy literature along with Western Europe. The decline of industrial cities, transportation analyses, and sprawling patterns of urban development take up the lion's share of this research. Less work has been done on the former Communist countries of Eastern Europe and the Soviet Union, and only recently have a large number of researchers been turning to the diverse cities of the developing world for insights into this phenomenon. Since large-scale urbanization took root in Latin America several decades ago, it has received the most attention, while China and India are attracting a lot of recent research interest owing to the urban transformations under way in each society. Missing from the bookshelf are works on Africa, the Middle East, and the rest of Asia, which are only beginning to be recognized as places where urban-related growth pressures are evident. To date, there are a number of excellent general works on the conditions surrounding slums and urban poverty.

The following review of current resources will introduce the reader to a sampling of the types of publications that are available, with attention to those works that have attracted the most attention from the scholarly community as well as general readers. An effort to read even a few of these works should provide an overview of urbanization and related policy challenges as a general phenomenon of modern societies, while also giving consideration to important variations in culture, historical background, economic, political and social development in different regions of the world.

Print

General

Books

Barnett, Jonathan. *Redesigning Cities*. Washington, DC: American Planning Association Press, 2008.

This text reminds us that cities do grow by design rather than happenstance. Exploring the essential elements of good urban planning, this book helps the reader understand how one can design places that either detract or enhance the quality of life of residents through a consideration of community, equity, and sustainability. The author explains how design can also work to reshape already established urban areas for the better—whether through improving suburbs or revitalizing declining neighborhoods where earlier development decisions went wrong. For planners and laymen alike, this book details specific techniques, materials, and technologies that can help planners, public officials, concerned citizens, and others involved in development improve their communities.

Brunn, Stanley D., Maureen Hays-Mitchell, and Donald J. Ziegler, eds. *Cities of the World: World Regional Development*. Lanham, MD: Rowman & Littlefield, 2008.

Written in textbook format, this comprehensive book is one of the few works available today that offers a truly world view of urbanization. The authors divide up the world into 11 major culture realms, each of which is explored from the standpoint of history, economy, and culture and society. Case studies are used throughout to offer representative examples of key themes. Introductory and concluding chapters frame the regional discussion by summarizing world urban history and by looking to the future of urban development. Richly illustrated with maps, graphs, tables, photos, and satellite images, as well as recommended readings, websites, and UN data on major cities.

Burdett, Ricky and Deyan Sudjic, eds. *The Endless City*. London: Phaidon Press, 2008.

This book offers a comparative study of the structural growth of six international cities (New York, Shanghai, London, Mexico City, Johannesburg, and Berlin). The presentation of each city is accomplished using an urban planning and design perspective, and shows how differences in culture and past historical experience can bring different outcomes, especially in such unusual cases as the legacy of apartheid in Johannesburg. This book is highly recommended as a helpful introduction to the challenges of contemporary urban planning.

Gonzales, George A. *Urban Sprawl, Global Warming, and the Empire of Capital*. Albany, NY: SUNY Press, 2009.

This book offers penetrating analysis that links the political and economic behavior of elites to urban growth patterns that have spawned greater dependence on automobiles. Both an exercise in historical research as well as political economy, the book goes on to assess the role that urban sprawl has played in contributing to massive carbon dioxide emissions and global climate change. None of this would have occurred without the political and economic influence of corporations and wealthy individuals who continue to benefit from U.S. access to abundant supplies of fossil fuels. Analysis focuses on the real estate industry, oil companies, and the favorable relationship these pro-sprawl interests have with Washington policymakers.

Jenks, Mike, Daniel Kozak, and Pattaranan Takkanon, eds. *World Cities and Urban Form: Fragmented, Polycentric, Sustainable?* London: Routledge, 2008.

This book presents new research and theory at the regional scale showing the forms metropolitan regions might take to achieve sustainability. At the city scale, the book presents case studies based on the latest research and practice from Europe, Asia, and North America, showing how both planning and flagship design can propel cities into world class status, and also improve sustainability. The contributors explore the tension between polycentric and potentially sustainable development, and urban fragmentation in a physical context, but also in a wider cultural, social, and economic context.

Krauss, Frauke, ed. ***Megacities: Our Global Urban Future.*** **New York: Springer, 2011.**

Current trends suggest that the mass movement of people into cities will result in as many as sixty "megacities"—urban areas with more than five million inhabitants—emerging by the year 2015. This book offers a multidisciplinary analysis of social, economic, and political developments associated with the rise of megacities. Contributors analyze the impact of urbanization at this scale on environmental change and natural resources, seeking to trace out policies in the management of these urban areas that can achieve a greater degree of sustainability. Topics explored by each author range from health management in Indian megacities, to planning in New York and transportation solutions for Bangkok.

Ling, Ooi Giok, and Belinda Yuen, eds. ***World Cities: Achieving Liveability and Vibrancy.*** **Singapore: World Scientific, 2009.**

How does a city promote ongoing economic growth and vitality in a globalizing world? This edited volume explores the major challenges that cities face in such key areas as governance, social inclusiveness, infrastructural development, financial solvency as well as environmental and ecological sustainability. Illustrated by numerous case studies drawn from the experience of cities in North America, Europe, and the Asia-Pacific, this collection offers a wide range of perspectives and ideas from academics, professionals, and policymakers from several different countries.

Newman, Peter, Timothy Beatley, and Heather Boyer. ***Resilient Cities: Responding to Peak Oil and Climate Change.*** **Washington, DC: Island Press, 2009.**

Urban growth is taking place in cities that have largely inefficient transportation systems, poorly designed buildings, and many other features that waste carbon-based fuels. In the face of increasing pressure of a limited quantity of energy resources and rising levels of greenhouse gases, is there any way cities can be redesigned? Or, are the world's cities headed for inevitable collapse? The authors of this book make the argument that more intelligent planning and visionary leadership can help cities meet the impending crises. They look at existing initiatives in cities around the world and find reason to hope. Their analysis is followed by four possible outcomes for cities that range from a dreary future collapse based on "carbon-consuming urbanism," to vibrant, resilient, new urban centers that practice a new ethic of "sustainable urbanism."

Peirce, Neal R. and Curtis W. Johnson with Farley M. Peters. *Century of the City: No Time To Lose*. New York: Rockefeller Foundation, 2009.

This book is an impassioned call for action that resulted from a month-long Global Urban Summit hosted by the Rockefeller Foundation in Bellagio, Italy in 2007. The group was charged with the task of identifying the challenges faced by rapidly urbanizing twenty-first century cities in both the Northern and Southern Hemisphere. The focus is on taking multidisciplinary approaches to the growth-related issues faced by cities.

Pomeroy, George and Gerald Webster, eds. *Global Perspectives On Urbanization*. Lanham, MD: University Press of America, 2005.

This edited work offers a variety of perspectives on urbanization from the United States and several countries around the world. Drawing from research in both developed and developing world contexts, each contributor offers empirically grounded analysis of historical perspectives on phases of urbanization, case studies of poverty in large cities, the divide between central city and suburb, and implications for planning for growth management. Several states and localities of the United States are featured, as are studies drawn from Romania, India, Mexico, and Canada. Maps show population trends and factors that distinguish between rich and poor.

United States and Canada

Books

Barnett, Jonathan, ed. *Smart Growth in a Changing World*. Chicago: American Planning Association Press, 2007.

In spite of high standard of living and seemingly endless supply of natural resources, the authors of this book contend that the United States is in the midst of a crisis of energy consumption and environmental degradation. As population grows and cities sprawl ever outward into high quality farmland and vanishing forestlands, the costs of current development policies will ultimately take a toll on our quality of life. In eloquent and fact-enriched prose, these authors chronicle in detail the way sprawl is unbalancing the natural environment, undermining the quality of life for urban residents, and increasing dependence on imported oil resources. In contrast, other nations are investing in smart growth: high-speed rail; regional rapid transit; compact, mixed-use development; and natural resources conservation. This book highlights policies that will help to build a more sustainable future.

Bruegmann, Robert. ***Sprawl: A Compact History.*** **Chicago: University of Chicago Press, 2006.**

The author traces the history of urban development in the United States over the past 100 years, demonstrating that urban sprawl occurs naturally in those societies that have the financial means escape the congestion and high costs of city life. He acknowledges that the effects on cities are not always positive, but the main point of the book is an argument that many of the criticisms of suburban sprawl are exaggerated, ignoring the benefits of privacy, mobility, and choice associated with this form of urban development.

De Grove, John M. ***Planning Policy and Politics: Smart Growth in the States.*** **Boston: Lincoln Institute of Land Policy, 2005.**

Can state governments lead the way to smarter growth? The author is a leading authority on state-level growth management policies designed to counter the effects of urban sprawl. This volume updates previous ground-breaking work by tracing the ongoing evolution of smart-growth systems in nine states that have led the way in combating sprawl. These include Oregon, Florida, New Jersey, Maine, Rhode Island, Vermont, Georgia, Maryland, and Washington. Each state chapter helps the reader to understand how these policies developed, who is behind current efforts to alter or advance such policies, and what direction state-level growth management policy is moving in the future.

Duany, Andres, Elizabeth Plater-Zyberk, and Jeff Speck. ***Suburban Nation: The Rise of Sprawl and the Decline of the American Dream.*** **New York: North Point Press, 2001.**

This book remains a classic in the urban growth management literature for its hard-hitting critique of unimaginative and unsustainable modern urban growth patterns. The authors, who themselves are leading practitioners in the field who have personally designed neighborhoods and community revitalization plans, boldly challenge the logic behind planning and building conventions that have produced environmentally unsustainable subdivisions, shopping centers, and office parks which serve to destroy important bonds that otherwise might exist among neighbors. This is as much a book about renewing citizenship and community as it is about urban design. It offers a new vision for planners and architects that would engage them in an effort to foster neighborhood-friendly designs in which homes, schools, commercial and municipal buildings are better integrated in pedestrian-accessible, safe, and friendly settings.

Dunham-Jones, Ellen, and June Williamson. *Retrofitting Suburbia: Urban Design Solutions for Redesigning Suburbs*. New York: John Wiley & Sons, 2008.

This book fills an important gap in the literature of urban growth and design by exploring the ways in which existing suburban developments in the United States can be redesigned to better meet the needs of the community. Serving as a guidebook for architects, planners, urban designers, and builders, it offers concrete ideas and abundant illustrations to show how and why it makes sense to pursue these plans as a way to accommodate new growth while serving the changing demographic, technological, and economic conditions of the U.S. city.

Elliott, Donald L. *A Better Way to Zone: Ten Principles to Create More Livable Cities*. Washington, DC: Island Press, 2008.

An attorney and experienced city planner argues that standard land-use zoning in the United States often discourages the very development that bigger cities need to recover and flourish. After reviewing the constitutional and legal framework of zoning, the author demonstrates how such complex laws formulated decades ago no longer fit the needs of the modern twenty-first century city. Elliott identifies ten principles for change that will produce more livable cities, and make zoning simpler to understand and use. He also proposes five practical steps to get started on the road to zoning reform. *A Better Way to Zone* provides a way forward that is not tied to a particular predetermined picture of how cities should look, but is instead based on how cities should operate to serve the needs of citizens more successfully.

Flint, Anthony. ***This Land: The Battle Over Sprawl and the Future of America.*** **Baltimore: Johns Hopkins University Press, 2006.**

The author is a veteran journalist who has covered planning, development, and housing-related issues in several large U.S. cities. From his perspective as an outsider looking in, we learn the story of how the modern U.S. landscape was shaped over time through the conflicts among rival interests and ultimately the convergence of prevailing political, economic, and cultural forces. It helps the reader understand how and why the anti-sprawl movement, New Urbanism, smart growth, and green building all developed to challenge the assumptions of landowners, free-market libertarians, homebuilders, road pavers, financial institutions, and even the lawn-care industry. After helping the reader understand how we have gotten to this point, the author then ponders whether Americans are ready to embrace a new approach to development based on different principles than what has guided us in the past.

Hanlon, Bernadette, John R. Short, and Thomas J. Vicino. ***Cities and Suburbs: New Realities in the U.S.,*** **New York: Routledge, 2009.**

This is a comprehensive and systematic review of the ways in which cities and suburbs have been evolving in the United States. It explores the history of cities and suburbs, their changing relationships with each other, growing diversity, and environmental concerns. Using demographic data and a socio-spatial perspective, the authors also look at the extent and nature of urban decline and the possibilities for renewal. Case studies offer a closer look at suburban successes and failures, and the book concludes with reflections on metropolitan policy and planning for the twenty-first century.

Hayden, Delores. ***Building Suburbia: Green Fields and Urban Growth, 1820–2000,*** **New York: Vintage Books, 2004.**

The author provides a history of almost two centuries of urban growth in the United States. From the perspective of both an urban historian and an architect, she helps the reader understand how the tastes and preferences of ordinary people, designers, builders, and politicians have shaped the diverse suburbs of the

United States. The book explores environmental controversies and complex issues related to race, gender, and class.

Heuton, Robert. *Urban Sprawl and Cityscapes*. New York: VDM Verlag, 2008.

This book looks into policy choices that are available to municipalities seeking to control the side effects of urban sprawl such as congested roads, and the expansion of costly infrastructure such as schools and utilities. Using a comparative analysis of Detroit, Michigan and Windsor, Ontario help to answer questions about what kinds of regional and local-level public policies have been most successful in controlling urban growth. The author concludes that the most important variable in managing urban growth is the existence of a local sense of community as well as the emergence of common interests around growth management. Advocates for declining inner city communities must also be a part of the process.

Hudnut, William H., Tom Murphy, Ed McMahon, Michael Beyard, John McIlwain, Robert Dunphy, and Steve Blank. *Changing Metropolitan America: Planning for a Sustainable Future*. Washington, DC: Urban Land Institute, 2008.

The co-authors, all of whom are leading voices in urban planning and design, provide a broad overview of the ways the large metropolitan areas of the United States are changing and impacting our quality of life. This book also makes recommendations for reducing sprawl and dependence on cars, encouraging sustainability, investing in infrastructure, and related issues such as workforce housing availability, commercial redevelopment, and land-use planning. The authors' analysis incorporates a wide range of factors that include changing demographics, trends in housing, energy alternatives, transportation efficiency, and new forms of governance.

Inman, Robert P., ed. *Making Cities Work*. Princeton, NJ: Princeton University, 2009.

This collection of essays brings together some of the leading academic voices on U.S. cities with aim of identifying ways to sustain prosperous, livable cities in fast-evolving globalizing world. Cities that are managed well provide jobs, good schools, safe and clean neighborhoods, effective transportation, and welcoming spaces for all residents. Drawing on extensive research, the contributors explore optimal ways to manage the modern city and propose potential solutions to today's most pressing urban problems. Topics include the urban economy, transportation, housing and open space, immigration, race, the impacts of poverty on children, education, crime, and financing and managing services.

Kehde, Karl. ***Smarter Land Use: How to Enhance Proposed Projects to Get Better Neighborhoods, Less Sprawl, and Fewer Lawsuits.*** **Northampton, MA: Land Use Forum Network, 2002.**

The policy debates and discussions about smart growth and the costs of urban sprawl can be rather esoteric and inaccessible to the average person. This is a practical guidebook for landowners, real estate developers, and government officials written in a straightforward fashion that intended to help get the process going at the local level. The book combines easy-to-understand language with diagrams, pictures, and lots of illustrations that take the reader through every step of the process. Highly recommended.

Kelly, Eric D. ***Managing Community Growth.*** **2nd ed. New York: Praeger, 2004.**

The urban planning profession offers considerable research and expertise in growth management, and yet its insights are largely unknown to most Americans. Planning typically takes the form of local boards responding to initiatives coming from private developers. As a consequence, communities lose sight of important quality of life concerns, do little to attract business, and neglect considerations about conservation and open space preservation. Does it have to be this way, or do communities have other options? This book brings insights from state and local experiences with growth management, and helps nonspecialist practitioners assess what tools will work best in their community. Highly recommended for volunteers who sit on planning, zoning, and conservation boards and commissions.

Knox, Paul L. 2008. ***Metroburbia, USA.*** **Piscataway, NJ: Rutgers University Press, 2008.**

Decades of economic prosperity in the United States have had a big impact on the built landscape as Americans have sought larger and larger homes on the fringes of metropolitan areas. The consequence is "metroburbia"; vast, sprawling regions that have fragmented mixtures of employment and residential settings that combine urban and suburban characteristics. Covering changes in home design, real estate, the work of developers, and the changing wishes of consumers, the author helps explain how contemporary landscapes are combination of consumer demand mediated by design professionals and institutions of governance. Contemporary conflicts and controversies figure into this analysis as well.

Lang, Robert E., and Jennifer Lefurgy. *Boomburbs: The Rise of America's Accidental Cities* Washington, DC: Brookings Institution, 2007.

This study of 25 U.S. fastest-growing incorporated cities with populations over 100,000 are all suburbs situated within larger metropolitan areas. Cities like Anaheim, California; Coral Springs, Florida; Naperville, Illinois; North Las Vegas, Nevada; and Plano, Texas are labeled "boomburbs" have doubled, tripled, even quadrupled in size between census reports. Some, like Mesa, Arizona are actually now larger than cities like Minneapolis and Miami. The large and sprawling urban areas are "accidental cities" that actually involve the merger of planned communities that have grown into one another. Few anticipated becoming big cities and unintentionally arrived at their status. Although boomburbs possess many elements common to full-fledged cities (diverse housing, retailing, offices, high-profile industries, and entertainment), they all lack large downtowns. This book will help the reader understand how these "drive-by cities" are evolving in ways that are both similar and dissimilar to traditional urban places.

Lucy, William H., and David L. Phillips. *Tomorrow's Cities, Tomorrow's Suburbs*. Chicago: American Planning Association Press, 2006.

Two planning scholars explore urban trends in the United States through an extensive analysis of data from the 2000 U.S. Census. Examining such factors as income disparities, housing age and size, racial segregation, immigration, and poverty, they offer a new perspective that challenges popular misperceptions about inner cities, suburbs. This includes startling data that challenge the "cul-de-sac safety myth." They contend that the quality of life in older neighborhoods in the cities can be improved, while looming crises affecting life in surrounding suburbs are more intractable and likely to continue. This book offers an optimistic perspective on U.S. metro areas, pointing out ways that the current decline of cities can be reversed through the combined efforts of local groups, planners, elected officials, and citizens.

Marshall, Alex. ***How Cities Work: Suburbs, Sprawl, and the Roads Not Taken.*** **Austin, TX: University of Texas, 2001.**

The author argues that rising public concern over traffic congestion, environmental problems, declining schools, and poverty are increasingly being linked to poorly planned land development patterns. Growing awareness of the many consequences of sprawl has led to calls for "smart growth" and stimulated architects and planners to consider the principles of New Urbanism. In this book, we are reminded that ultimately, the responsibility for making and maintaining good communities is dependent on public leadership, not acquiescence to private caprice.

Morris, Douglas. ***It's a Sprawl World After All.*** **Vancouver: New Society, 2005.**

This book holds nothing back in its dark critique of the growth of suburbs, which the author believes have twisted the U.S. dream into a nightmare. The proliferation of fragmented housing developments, automobile-dependent transportation, big-box shopping centers, and decline in traditional neighborhoods is all linked to increases in violence and the corresponding breakdown in society with the post WWII era. Without appropriately constructed communities to bring people together that once existed in the United States, sprawl has left people isolated, alienated, and afraid of the strangers that surround them. Suburbia has isolated society into a lot of strangers burdened by isolation, loneliness, and depression, and promoted the emergence of a culture of incivility characterized by extreme individualism and a callous disregard for others. In response, the author calls for urgent attention to managing development by emulating the smart-growth examples of European cities.

Owen, David. ***Green Metropolis: Why Living Smaller, Living Closer, and Driving Less Are the Keys to Sustainability.*** **New York: Riverhead Books, 2009.**

The author challenges conventional thinking about urban sprawl and smart-growth planning by arguing that the most environmentally sound community in the United States is New York City. Rather than an ecological nightmare of concrete, massive garbage, diesel fumes, and traffic jams, the author finds compact urban centers are actually more energy-efficient and less wasteful than other urban and rural places. This book is deeply critical of the anti-urban bias of U.S. environmentalism as well as added criticism of wasteful, sprawl-producing development patterns associated with the real estate and homebuilding industry.

Porter, Douglas R. ***Managing Growth in America's Communities*****, 2nd ed. Washington, DC: Island Press, 2007.**

In this revised edition, readers will learn the principles that guide professional planners, appreciate the controversies associated with managing growth, and discover what has actually worked in practice. The author, who is one of the nation's leading authorities on managing community growth, provides examples from dozens of communities across the country, as well as state and regional approaches. The book explores new and innovative ways in which communities in the United States are adapting smart-growth principles, green building designs, and environmental conservation into their planning and includes examples from towns and cities across the country.

Rusk, David. ***Inside Game/Outside Game: Winning Strategies for Saving Urban America*****. Washington, DC: Brookings Institution Press, 2001.**

In this book, Rusk follows up on his earlier work with policy strategies he recommends for declining cities that cannot seem to break out of poverty. Acknowledging the dilemma of sprawling suburban growth sitting around poverty-stricken city neighborhoods, the author calls for solutions based on an "outside game" strategy that pulls together entire metropolitan regions. Key elements for his recommendations include regional growth management, fair-share affordable housing programs, as well as regional tax base sharing. Most important in his recommendations is a mandatory mixed-income housing policy for all new residential construction. His analysis cites cases where such measures have been implemented through a variety of political alliances that include business associations, faith-based coalitions, and state-level political support. Illustrations are drawn from case studies in Portland, Oregon; Montgomery County, Maryland; Dayton, Ohio; and Minneapolis-St. Paul, Minnesota.

Shaw, Jane S., and Ronald D. Utt, eds. ***A Guide to Smart Growth: Shattering Myths, Providing Solutions.*** **Washington, DC: Heritage Foundation, 2000.**

Not everyone is a supporter of smart growth. This edited collection of essays questions much of the conventional logic presented by advocates of smart growth. The contributors object to explanations for the causes of sprawl as well as the policy implications of proposals such as growth boundaries, subsidized mass transit, higher-density development, and the like. Full chapters are devoted to issues such as zoning law reform and traffic congestion. The book also offers a re-evaluation of the supposed success of smart-growth initiatives in Portland, Oregon and Atlanta, Georgia, illustrating where these policies have gone awry, and what needs to be done to correct them.

Squires, Gregory D., ed, ***Urban Sprawl: Causes, Consequences, and Policy Responses.*** **Washington, DC: Urban Institute Press, 2002.**

This is collection of scholarly essays that explore virtually every dimension of urban sprawl in the United States. Subjects include analysis of the major causes and consequences of urban sprawl. Readers will learn about the detrimental environmental impacts of sprawl, as well as its links to inner city poverty, racial inequality, and impacts on poor children and families. Other contributors offer a close look at a variety of different policy initiatives that include Maryland's "smart-growth" program, Portland's urban growth boundary, and tax-based revenue sharing in the Twin Cities and Chicago metropolitan areas. Case studies on Washington and Atlanta provide illustrations of how urban sprawl has specifically impacted these two fast-growing metro regions.

Soule, David C., ***Urban Sprawl: A Comprehensive Reference Guide.*** **New York: Greenwood, 2005.**

Urban sprawl is not only an issue of land use, but also a legal, political, and social concern that impacts schools, the environment, and race relations. This book provides a series of articles from leading voices in the field, offering many different perspectives about the challenges of urban sprawl and dynamics surrounding different policy options. Complete with a glossary, resources, and contact information for smart-growth alliances, this book is designed to be a resource for those seeking to get involved.

Wasik, John F. *The Cul-de-Sac Syndrome: Turning Around the Unsustainable American Dream* New York: Bloomberg Press, 2009.

The author takes a critical look at the costs and consequences associated with the suburban lifestyle. This includes a variety of unsustainable and unhealthy side-effects that impact our economy, cultural development, health, and physical environment. These observations are firmly grounded in research, interviews with thought leaders, and the latest studies and statistics. The trenchant analysis of this book helps to debunk the many myths of suburban living, while exploring innovative solutions being developed in cities and suburbs across the country.

Articles and Reports

American Farmland Trust. *Farming on the Edge*. Washington, DC: American Farmland Trust, 1997.

This report offers a summary of the views and positions of the U.S.'s leading farm preservation organization. It vividly demonstrates how urban sprawl development is leading to the loss of irreplaceable fertile agricultural lands as well as threatening an entire sector of the U.S. economy. The 20 most threatened agricultural regions in the nation are identified and analyzed. The report includes information on the GIS methodology used to analyze land patterns, extensive discussion of issues surrounding farmland loss, as well as research and policy recommendations.

Basu, Pratyusha, and Jayajit Chakraborty. "The other side of sprawl: a county-level analysis of farm loss in Florida." *Southeastern Geographer* 48 (2; August 2008): 219–236.

What is the impact of ex-urban sprawl on rural communities in the United States.? This article focuses on the nature and extent of farm losses in the rapidly urbanizing state of Florida, and the impact this is having on declining social and economic conditions.

Bauer, David, et al. ***Building Better Communities: A Toolkit for Quality Growth.*** **Washington, DC: The Quality Growth Coalition, 1999.**

What is the best way to deal with worsening road congestion, pollution, and loss of open space associated with urban sprawl? Should the U.S.'s longstanding habit of continually expanding its highway and road system be dramatically changed? Sponsored by a coalition of groups that include the American Highway Users Alliance and the American Road and Transportation Builders Association, this monograph offers what its writers describe as "common sense solutions that will work" to balance these concerns with the ongoing need to expand and improve the national transportation system, promote economic growth, and honor the rights of citizens to be free to choose their own means of travel. It provides background information, case studies, and policy recommendations that offer alternatives to the "smart-growth" agenda.

Beaumont, Constance. ***Challenging Sprawl: Organizational Responses To A National Problem.*** **Washington: National Trust for Historic Preservation, 1999.**

Debates over urban development were once dominated by environmental groups arguing with real estate developers. This is no longer the case though, according to the author of this report. She documents the many different voices of the growing movement against sprawl, demonstrating that the new consensus over development represented by the "smart-growth" movement includes not only environmental groups, but also business executives, religious leaders, politicians from both major political parties, academics, and governmental officials from all levels.

Behan, Kevin, Hanna Maoh, and Pavlos Kanaroglou. "Smart growth strategies, transportation and urban sprawl: simulated futures for Hamilton, Ontario." ***Canadian Geographer*** **52 (3; Fall 2008): 291–308.**

This article acknowledges the detrimental impacts of decentralized sprawling urban development in the metro area of Hamilton, Ontario, and examines the possible beneficial outcomes if this region would adopt smart-growth policies. In particular, strategies to increase population densities in the urban core are analyzed with an aim to measure changes in vehicular emissions, traffic congestion, and energy consumption.

Brookings Institution. ***State of Metropolitan America: On the Front Lines of Demographic Transformation*, 2010.**

This comprehensive study chronicles the continued growth and outward expansion of U.S. urban areas and the impact this is having on racial and ethnic diversification, aging, educational attainment, and income patterns. The authors put these patterns together and identify a new configuration of metro areas that follow seven different models of growth. These range from the "Next Frontier" which exceed national averages in all five categories, to the "New Heartland" that contains rapid growth but little ethnic and racial diversification. Other patterns show less promising levels of growth, and reveal deeper problems that present great challenges for leaders in these metro areas in the future.

Bruegmann, Robert. "How sprawl got a bad name." ***The American Enterprise*** **17 (5; June 2006): 16–22.**

What explains heightened concern over the threat of urban sprawl in the United States? The author argues that there is overwhelming evidence that urban sprawl has been beneficial for many people, citing evidence that the vast majority of Americans indicate satisfaction with where they live, whether it is a city or the suburbs. So what explains the power of today's anti–sprawl crusade? He makes the case that during economically prosperous times, a "revolution of expectations" rises that leads to panics such as this one.

Cox, Wendell. ***The President's New Sprawl Initiative: A Program in Search of a Problem*. Heritage Foundation Backgrounder #1263, 1999.**

This report from the ideologically conservative Heritage Foundation offers one of the most comprehensive rebuttals to date of both President Bill Clinton's "Livable Communities Initiative" and the host of critics of urban sprawl. The author contends that many of the claims of anti-sprawl planning advocates are unfounded regarding the loss of open space. They also challenge the assumption that the general public is largely discontent with urban living and looking for alternatives. Further, the report counters that New Urbanist-inspired proposals that call for higher density compact development and greater reliance on mass transit would only worsen environmental problems.

Davis, Lisa Selin. "A (Radical) Way to Fix Suburban Sprawl." ***TIME*** **173 (24; June 22, 2009): 54–57.**

The article focuses on ways to redesign cities to reduce the effects of urban sprawl and to make them more environment- and people-friendly. The author uses Tysons Corner, Virginia as a case study where a public-private partnership and county planning agency work together to increase the city's density with additional housing units and mixed-use buildings.

Emerson, Chad D. "All sprawled out: how the federal regulatory system has driven unsustainable growth." ***Tennessee Law Review*** **75 (3; Spring 2008): 411–451.**

In this article, the author argues that urban sprawl is not simply a problem of bad design or planning. Rather, it is a symptom of federal laws and regulations that have facilitated development patterns in the United States that are neither fiscally sound nor physically sustainable. He focuses on federal tax, transportation, and housing policies that have promoted sprawl and argues that, if these are modified or repealed, the United States can move toward a more sustainable land development strategy.

Fox, David. "Halting urban sprawl: smart growth in Vancouver and Seattle." ***Boston College International and Comparative Law Review*** **33 (1; Winter 2010): 43–59.**

Can smart-growth policies actually make a difference in halting low-density, land-consuming, noncontiguous development on the fringe of settled areas? This paper offers an analysis of these policies and their impact on two cities in the Pacific Northwest, offering comparisons and contrasts between the way these issues are being addressed in the United States and Canada.

Hilts, Stew, Smith Lone, and Melissa Watkins. "Saving the land that feeds us: how to revitalize our near-urban farmland and curb sprawl." ***Alternatives Journal*** **34 (3; August 2008): 8–12.**

What is the impact of urban sprawl on food production in Canada? The authors of this article make an impassioned plea to protect Canadian farmland from exurban housing, and the commercial and industrial development it spawns. They cite the need not only the priority of preserving the livelihoods of farmers, but also the importance of locally grown food as a key element in promoting a sustainable future.

Ingram, Gregory K., and Yu-Hung Hong. *Evaluating Smart Growth: State and Local Policy Outcomes*. Lincoln Institute of Land Policy, 2009.

The Lincoln Institute initiated this research project in 2006 to evaluate the effectiveness of smart-growth policies over the decade from 1990 to 2000. The analysis draws attention to four states with comprehensive statewide programs (Florida, New Jersey, Maryland, and Oregon), and four other states with local-level approaches to land management (Colorado, Indiana, Texas, and Virginia). The findings of this research are summarized and recommendations offered by the authors, both of whom believe that smart growth is possible, although it must take different forms in the context of each state where it is attempted.

Knaap, Gerrit-Jan, Yan Song, and Zorica Nedovic-Budic. "Measuring Patterns of Urban Development: New Intelligence for the War on Sprawl." *Local Environment* 12 (3; June 2007): 239–257.

There has been a great deal of controversy in the academic community over defining urban sprawl and how to precisely measure it. The authors of this article compute a variety of measures of urban sprawl in five study areas in the United States and use this data to question the utility of sprawl indexes for entire metropolitan areas. In the end, they offer mixed results for advocates of "smart-growth" policies.

Lewyn, Michael. "You can have it all: less sprawl and property rights too." *Temple Law Review* 80 (4; Winter 2007): 1093–1134.

The debate over urban sprawl has often been polarized between two groups with competing visions of suburban development—the "smart-growth" view which critiques automobile-dependent suburban sprawl, and the "property rights" view which emphasizes individual freedom. The article then shows that these visions are to a great extent reconcilable, by discussing a variety of legal reforms which can both reduce suburban sprawl and enhance landowners' property rights.

Ming Yin, and Jian Sun. "The Impacts of State Growth Management Programs on Urban Sprawl in the 1990s." ***Journal of Urban Affairs*** **29 (2; May, 2007): 149–179.**

Since 1961, fifteen states in the United States have adopted some form of growth management programs to curtail the impacts of urban sprawl. The authors examine the effectiveness of these programs in containing sprawl through some innovative indices for 294 metropolitan areas studied between 1990 and 2000. Their results demonstrate that these programs did in fact promote more compact development in terms of population density and land-use mixture.

Office of the President of the United States. ***Building Livable Communities: A Report From the Clinton-Gore Administration.*** **1999.**

This report provides a detailed summary of federal initiatives launched under President Bill Clinton's "Livable Communities" program. Its aim is to "provide communities with tools, information, and resources that they can use to enhance their quality of life, ensure their economic competitiveness, and build a stronger sense of community." Based on the findings of the Community Empowerment Board and the President's Council on Sustainable Development, the Livable Communities program pulls together resources from more than a dozen federal agencies that influence patterns of urban growth by helping to ease traffic congestion, preserve farmland and other open spaces, and revitalize declining urban neighborhoods. These initiatives were in included in President Clinton's fiscal 2000 budget proposals.

O'Toole, Randolph. "The Folly of Smart Growth," ***Regulation,*** **Fall 2001.**

A conservative economist examines Oregon's statewide growth management policy strategies and comes to the conclusion that they create worse problems than they were intended to solve. The author argues that a variety of different anti-sprawl measures have failed to accomplish goals, and further hinder the functioning of markets and are an unpopular attack on the suburban lifestyle preferred by most Americans.

Pendall, Rolf, Robert Puentes, and Jonathan Martin. "*From Traditional to Reformed: A Review of the Land Use Regulations in the Nation's 50 largest Metropolitan Areas.*" Brookings Institution Metropolitan Policy Program, 2006.

This survey of local land-use regulations is unusually comprehensive and very helpful in classifying a wide variety of regulatory systems into four broad typologies that are found in the 50 largest metropolitan areas of the United States. These range from exclusionary and restrictive to innovative and accommodating, and the authors find such laws produce a variety of effects on metropolitan growth and density, and on the opportunities afforded to the residents.

Resnik, David B. "Urban Sprawl, Smart Growth, and Deliberative Democracy." *American Journal of Public Health* 100 (10; October 2010): 1852–1856.

Although there is considerable evidence that urban sprawl has adverse affects on public health and the environment, smart-growth policies have been controversial, making implementation difficult. The author offers suggestions as to how to use deliberative democracy to overcome controversy among stakeholders affected by urban planning policies.

Salkin, Patricia E. "Squaring the circle on sprawl: what more can we do? Progress toward sustainable land use in the states." *Widener Law Journal* 16 (3; December 2007): 787–837.

This assessment of growth management policies at the state and local levels indicates that there is no one best model adaptable to all 50 states. Rather, the tremendous diversity in local government structure, cultural relationships of people to the land, and differences in geography and a sense of place have led to many different policies, programs, and regulations. The author concludes that much more can and should be done to stem the negative impacts of urban growth across the United States.

Smart Growth America and the National Association of Realtors. *2004 American Community Survey. 2004.*

These two organizations that represent often divergent positions on growth management issues jointly sponsored a survey on

Americans' preferences for the type of communities they want to live in and the policies they support for creating those communities. The survey offered valuable insight about three main points. Americans favor smart-growth communities with shorter commute times, sidewalks, and places to walk more than sprawling communities. The length of people's commute to work holds a dominant place in decisions about where to live. And finally, Americans want government and business to be investing in existing communities before putting resources into newer communities farther out from cities and older suburbs. The public's priorities for development include more housing for people with moderate and low incomes and slowing the rate of development of open space. Many Americans also express the desire for more places to walk or bike in their communities.

Smart Growth Leadership Institute. *Smart Growth Implementation Kit*, 2007.

The SGLI developed this tool for communities based on their implementation Assistance Program activities. This utilizes a scorecard to examine proposed projects, identifies "smart" sites for future development, and evaluates zoning codes, approval processes, and design protocols that help advance smart-growth strategies.

Staley, Samuel. *The Sprawling of America: In Defense of the Dynamic City*. Policy Study No. 251. Reason Public Policy Institute, 1999.

This report offers a critical re-evaluation of state growth-management programs that have been designed to protect farmland and open space from sprawl. The author offers a thorough review of the debates on these issues along with some of his own original research on land-use patterns in the United States. He concludes that low-density development and suburbanization do not significantly threaten the quality of life for most people, and makes a case in favor of relying on real estate markets rather than comprehensive planning to bring about the best outcomes for society.

Staley, Samuel. "*Statewide Growth Management and Housing Affordability in Florida*." James Madison Institute Backgrounder, 2007.

This study examines the impact of Florida's statewide growth management law on housing affordability in the state. The report offers strong evidence that this law has contributed to a crisis in affordability, and makes the case that the best way forward is to reform the planning process in ways that allow the private housing industry to meet the state's growing housing needs.

Torrens, Paul M. "A Toolkit for Measuring Sprawl." ***Applied Spatial Analysis and Policy*** **1 (1; April 2008): 5–37.**

Experts are divided over how to precisely define and measure the urban growth phenomenon of urban sprawl. The author notes that the literature is often narrative and subjective, with piecemeal and largely data-driven measures. In response, he offers an alternative approach to diagnosing sprawl, looking across the full range of its characteristic attributes and applies this methodology to the case of Austin, Texas.

United States General Accounting Office. ***Community Development: Extent Of Federal Influence On "Urban Sprawl" Is Unclear,*** **April 1999.**

This report was prepared by the General Accounting Office in response to a request by the U.S. Senate to research the origins of urban sprawl, explore to what degree federal programs have on this phenomenon, and make recommendations for federal policy. It acknowledges that a great deal of anecdotal evidence exists tying federal government policies with the influences of urban sprawl through specific programs, taxation, and regulation. However, the report does not recognize existing quantitative research as conclusive, and therefore does not uniformly endorse such claims. Rather, it states that "the level of federal influence is difficult to determine."

Urban Land Institute. ***Growing Cooler: The Evidence on Urban Development and Climate Change,*** **2007.**

This publication is based on a review of existing research on the relationship among urban development, travel, and the CO_2 emitted by motor vehicles. Urban Land Institute researchers find that urban development is both a key contributor to climate change and an essential factor in combating it. It provides evidence on and insights into how much CO_2 savings can be expected with the adoption of smart-growth principles that emphasize more compact development. Highlighted in the study is the concept of building "walkable neighborhoods" and how these could significantly reduce the growth in the number of miles Americans drive, shrinking the nation's carbon footprint.

Weitz, Jerry. *Sprawl Busting: State Programs to Guide Growth.* American Planning Association, 1999.

As public concern over the effects of sprawl grows, planners, developers and public officials alike are talking about the potential merits of "smart-growth" laws. Can we learn from the experience of state laws that have already been in place for decades? This book provides a thorough review of four state-wide growth management programs in Oregon, Georgia, Washington, and Florida. For those seeking to advocate growth management elsewhere, the author seeks to provide lessons on how to craft legislation, set up administrative structures, and build political support among local and county governments for state mandated land-use planning.

Developed World: North America, Europe, and Asia

Books

Couch, Chris, Lila Leontidou, Gerhard Petschel-Held, eds. *Urban Sprawl in Europe: Landscapes, Land-Use Change and Policy.* New York: John Wiley and Sons, 2008.

This work offers a comparative perspective on urban sprawl as it is being experienced in Europe today. Looking at a variety of diverse cases from the entire region, the authors consider definitions of sprawl, current theories of this phenomenon, and explore trends. Measuring the impacts of urban growth on the environment, social structure, and economies are all important themes. Different policies for the regulation of urban sprawl and the roles of different stakeholders are considered as well.

Czaplicka, John, Nida Gelazis, and Blair A. Ruble, eds. *Cities After the Fall of Communism: Reshaping Cultural Landscapes and European Identity.* Baltimore, MD: Johns Hopkins University Press, 2009.

This series of essays seeks to trace the new directions underway in East European and Russian cities since the fall of communism in

1989. New identities are found through an analysis of architecture and urban planning of evident in a wide variety of urban places that include Vilnius, Novgorod, Wroclaw, Tallinn, Odessa, Sevastopol, Kaliningrad, Kharkiv, Lviv, Lodz, and Szczecin. In each case, these studies demonstrate how culture is being selectively reimagined nostalgically toward older forms of Habsburg, Baltic, Imperial Russian, and Germanic culture, as well as new urban identities grounded in ethnic-national, European, Western, and global contexts.

Goetz, Stephan J., ed. *Land Use Problems and Conflicts*. New York: Taylor & Francis, 2009.

This collection of conference papers presented at the Northeast Regional Center for Rural Development draws together some of the most up-to-date research on the causes, consequences, and control of land-use change in advanced industrialized societies. Sections are devoted to problems in the United States and Europe, the consequences of such problems, land-use-related data and alternative solutions to conflict. A particular focus of this volume is the conflict over the development of rural land and efforts to protect rural landscapes and farmland.

Hall, Peter, and Kathryn Pain, eds. *The Polycentric Metropolis: Learning from Mega-city Regions in Europe* London: Earthscan, 2009.

This book studies urban growth in Europe through the framework of "polycentric city-regions" or "megacity regions" and the role these serve as locational anchors to the wider processes of globalization. These clusters of cities and towns that are physically separate, but intensively networked in a complex spatial division of labor are described and analyzed in eight different regions: South East England, the Bassin Parisien, Central Belgium, the Dutch Randstad, Rhine-Ruhr, Rhine-Main, Northern Switzerland, and Greater Dublin. A particular interest of the authors is showing how businesses communicate and function together within each region, between them, and with the wider world. Among the subjects covered are spatial planning, regional development and policy ramifications and outcomes for infrastructure, transport systems, and regulation.

Hamilton, F. E. Ian, Kaliopa Dimitrovska-Andrews, and Natasa Pichler-Milanovic, eds. *Tranformation of Cities in Central and Eastern Europe: Towards Globalization*. New York: United Nations University Press, 2005.

The essays explore the new directions evident in postcommunist cites of Eastern Europe. Readers gain perspective on past socialist models of urban development, and learn how contemporary forces of globalization, foreign investment, and European integration are restructuring urbanization throughout this dynamic region. Case studies drawn from a diverse number of capital cities that include Berlin, Warsaw, Budapest, Prague, Ljubljana, Sofia, Moscow, and the Baltic states help to illustrate how these forces are at work.

Karen, P. P., and Kristin Stapleton, eds. *The Japanese City*. Lexington, KY: University Press of Kentucky. 1997.

This edited work brings together a wide variety of perspectives on urbanization and urban living in Japan. A central theme of the book is to explore what forces have been shaping the ongoing development of Japanese cities. Larger themes of urban growth are reflected in studies of the way Japan's great urban centers handle the premium on space in this very crowded environment together. Additional attention is given to government policies that regulate land-use planning and commercial development in the context of economically depressed mining and industrial communities are featured as well.

Nivola, Pietro S. *Laws of the Landscape: How Policies Shape Cities in Europe and America*. Washington, DC: Brookings Institution, 1999.

There has been much interest in the United States about the experience of European urban growth and planning. This book addresses the issues of U.S. urban development and sprawl from a comparative perspective, noting that many other industrial societies struggle with similar growth patterns. Most importantly, the author explores why policies designed to control suburban growth have actually helped induce greater sprawl in the United States, but not in Europe. He offers a critical analysis of traditional smart growth-inspired controls in light of policies in Europe, where more compact forms of development have long been fostered by government planners. He concludes with a series of recommendations based on both the successes and failures of European experience that include implications for tax reform, transportation policy, crime policy, education, small business development, fiscal policy, energy policy, and immigration.

Phelps, Nicholas A., Nick Parsons, Dimitris Ballas, and Andrew Dowling. *Post-Suburban Europe: Planning and Politics at the Margins of Europe's Capital Cities*. New York: Palgrave Macmillan, 2006.

Much has been written in the United States about "edge cities" that have emerged in the midst of sprawling urban developments around the distant fringes of large metropolitan areas, but how well does this concept apply to Europe? Are Europeans experiencing the same sense of "placelessness" common to U.S.'s suburban residents? The authors of this book explore the theoretical and policy context for postsuburban growth in contemporary patterns of urbanization in Europe. The broader analysis of this phenomenon is supplemented by a comparison of examples in Greece, Spain, Paris, Finland, and Britain.

Richardson, Harry W., and Chang-Hee Christine Bae, eds. *Urban Sprawl in Western Europe and the United States*. Burlington, VT: Ashgate, 2004.

Much of the best writing about urban sprawl has been devoted exclusively to the United States. This book offers a truly comparative perspective on this phenomenon by including the United Kingdom and France into the discussion. General patterns of population and urban growth are described for each country along with the United States, but the real contribution of this book is the examination of policies that have led to both similar and different outcomes in each. The authors conclude that planners in the United States have misunderstood what is happening in Europe, finding that there is much more convergence in urban growth patterns than divergence.

Sorenson, Andre. *The Making of Urban Japan: Cities and Planning from Edo to the Twenty-First Century*. London: Routledge. 2002.

This book traces the patterns of urban development of Japanese cities from the 1600s to the present day. It provides a thorough, systematic chronicling of the evolution of Japan's built environment in the context of Japan's severely limited land resources and traditions of tightly-knit urban communities and mixed land uses. Particular attention is given to the weak, overly-centralized tradition of urban planning, lack of local land-use regulations, and strong tradition of individual rights of ownership that has given advantage to wealthy and politically well-connected interests. Since the end of World War II, these traditions have been challenged by growth in civil society movements and greater democracy.

Articles and Reports

Baing, Andreas S. "Containing Urban Sprawl? Comparing Brownfield Reuse Policies in England and Germany." *International Planning Studies* 15 (1; February 2010): 25–35.

This paper identifies factors explaining differences in the success of such strategic brownfield reuse policies in England and Germany. To do this, the paper explores the underlying spatial development paradigms in both countries as well as differences in planning policies and institutional settings.

Basse, Ellen Margrethe. "Urbanization and growth management in Europe." *The Urban Lawyer* 42 (4; Fall 2010): 385–407.

Managing urban growth is a serious issue in Europe, where more than a quarter of all land is impacted by urbanization and approximately 80 percent of EU citizens will be living in urban areas by 2020. This article explores the policy challenges of reducing air pollution, limiting the impact on natural areas, and creating more efficient transportation systems in a part of the world with increasing levels of consumption and travelling activities.

Chou, Tsu-Lung, and Jung-Ying Chang. "Urban sprawl and the politics of land use planning in urban Taiwan." *International Development Planning Review* 30 (1; March 2008): 67–93.

Rising levels of affluence in Taiwan have placed increasing pressures on limited land resources. In this study, the authors discuss and analyze the relationship between the local politics of land-use planning and inefficient sprawling patterns of land development. While urban sprawl in Taiwan is tied to the country's rapid economic growth, it has been aggravated by politically motivated decisions by those with responsibility for land-use management.

Couch, Chris, Jay Karecha, Henning Nuiss, and Dieter Rink. "Decline and sprawl: an evolving type of urban development–observed in Liverpool and Leipzig." ***European Planning Studies*** **13 (1; January 2005): 117–136.**

Does urban sprawl follow a different path in Europe as compared to the United States? Much of the empirical research on urban sprawl has been carried out in North America, so the authors of this study make use of two European cities to explore whether the process of urban sprawl is somehow specific in a situation of urban decline and what its outcomes might be for both urban form and urban policy.

Couch, Chris, and Jay Karecha. "Controlling urban sprawl: Some experiences from Liverpool." ***Cities*** **23 (5; October 2006): 353–364.**

British and European planners usually consider the issue of urban sprawl from the standpoint of urban containment and the search for compact cities. This article considers the development of policies for the control of urban sprawl within the British planning system and examines their implementation and effectiveness within one city region: the Liverpool conurbation. Despite the considerable achievements of British policy in controlling urban sprawl and encouraging urban regeneration over the last two decades, there remain some doubts as to how much further market forces can be directed towards the production of more compact cities.

European Environment Agency. ***Urban Sprawl in Europe: The Ignored Challenge*****, 2006.**

This report documents the sprawling urban development patterns evident across Europe and offers a critical analysis of the impact this will have for the future of the region. It makes direct links between sprawl and EU policies and provides policy advice to decision-makers.

European Environment Agency. ***Land in Europe: Prices, Taxes, and Use Patterns*****, 2010.**

This European Union study analyzes the interaction between land prices and land-use changes as a means to better understanding the way in which these forces shape overall urban development patterns in Europe. The report finds that taxes, tax relief, and urban pressure are the main drivers influencing land values. It also suggests that land prices can function as an early warning indicator of urban sprawl patterns and environmental threats.

Geurs, Karst T., and Bert van Wee. "Ex-post evaluation of thirty years of compact urban development in the Netherlands." ***Urban Studies*** **43 (1; January 2006): 139–161.**

What kind of impact do strict land-use regulations like those in place in the Netherlands have on urban development? The authors of this study measure the effectiveness of Dutch compact urbanization policies implemented between 1970 and 2000, concluding that urban sprawl in the Netherlands would likely have been far greater, along with greater car use, as well as more detrimental emission and noise levels in residential and natural environments and wildlife habitat fragmentation.

Hortas-Rico, Miriam, and Albert Solé-Ollé, Albert. "Does Urban Sprawl Increase the Costs of Providing Local Public Services? Evidence from Spanish Municipalities." ***Urban Studies*** **47 (7; June 2010): 1513–1540.**

The impacts of urban sprawl have become a major concern for Spain, which has experienced the highest rates of rapid, low-density urban expansion in Europe. The authors develop measurements for urban sprawl in this article to test the impact of this growth on municipal budgets. Their research confirms that low-density development patterns lead to greater costs for local public service providers.

Lewyn, Michael. "Sprawl in Europe and America." ***San Diego Law Review*** **46 (1; Winter 2009): 85–112.**

Is suburban sprawl an unavoidable byproduct associated with rising levels of consumption and prosperity in all societies of the world, or can its effects be mitigated by government policy? The paper challenges the assumption that sprawl is an inevitable universal phenomenon by comparing the cities of Europe to the United States. While European cities have been decentralizing and becoming more dependent on automobile transportation, they have been far more successful at limiting sprawl.

Næss, Petter, Teresa Næss, and Arvid Strand. "Oslo's Farewell to Urban Sprawl." ***European Planning Studies*** **19 (1; January 2011): 113–139.**

This case study from Oslo, Norway offers some excellent perspective on how some urban regions in Europe are successfully combating the impacts of sprawling development patterns. Since the 1990s, Norway has implemented a series of policies that promote concentrated and compact urban development, especially within the municipality of Oslo. This has contributed to a reduction in growth in car traffic.

Patacchini, Eleonora, and Yves Zenou. "Urban Sprawl in Europe." ***Brookings-Wharton Papers on Urban Affairs*** **(Issue #10 2009): 125–142.**

How universal is the conceptual framework developed in the United States to study urban growth patterns known as "sprawl?" This article explores the differences in the way in which U.S. and European academics study cities, urban growth patterns, and the causes of sprawl and identifies distinctive patterns of growth and decline evident in the cities of Europe.

Samaruutel, Annal, Steen Selvig, and Arild Holt-Jensen. "Urban sprawl and suburban development around Parnu and Tallinn, Estonia." ***Norwegian Journal of Geography*** **64 (3; September 2010): 152–161.**

This article describe the prevailing spatial development patterns of Estonian cities after the fall of communism. They are characterized by patchy patterns of urban sprawl, with little regard to infrastructure, public services, location of workplaces, and preservation of agricultural productivity. This case study offers an excellent perspective on wider patterns found throughout Eastern Europe since 1991.

Tschopp, Martin, and Kay W. Axhausen. "Transport infrastructure and regional development in Switzerland: Accessibility, spatial policy and urban sprawl during the last fifty years." ***Journal of Transport History*** **29 (1; March 2008): 83–97.**

The authors are interested in demonstrating how transportation infrastructure can impact the spatial development of municipalities and regions. Their case study of the evolution of Swiss transportation planning since the 1950s show how accessibility does influence spatial development, but differs considerably over time and space in rural and alpine areas.

Travisi, Chiara M., Roberto Camagni, and Peter Nijkamp. "Impacts of urban sprawl and commuting: a modelling study for Italy." ***Journal of Transport Geography*** **18 (3; May 2010): 382–392.**

Italy has experienced rapid urban development over the past 30 years. This paper connects prevailing urban sprawl patterns to automobile commuting for seven major Italian urban areas, comprising in total 739 municipalities. Empirical results confirm the expectation that sprawl is accompanied by intensive travel movements and associated environmental effects.

Developing World: Africa, Asia, Latin America, and the Middle East

Books

Brown, Denise Scott and Christina Crane. ***Asia Beyond Growth: Urbanization in the World's Fastest-Changing Continent,*** **San Rafael, CA: ORO Editions, 2010.**

The spectacular growth of cities of Asia that extend from Dubai to Shanghai is chronicled in this book, which offers both a visual and analytical exploration of the way these cities and their inhabitants are being impacted by this rapid change. A particular interest of the authors is to help the reader understand how diverse environments are adapted to the pace of population growth. In this regard, the fast-growing urban centers of Asia's emerging economies offer a testing ground for radical urban design proposals, several of which are reviewed in this book. The first part of the book provides an overview of statistics on population, consumption, and environmental impact, and the latter section details specific cities and projects.

Alexander, Catharine, Victor Buchli, and Caroline Humphrey. ***Urban Life in Post-Soviet Asia*** **London: Routledge, 2007.**

This book examines the changes in urban life since the collapse of the Soviet Union from an ethnographic perspective. Four cities: Tashkent, Almaty, Astana, and Ulan-Ude are examined for the purpose of illustrating how each has responded in different ways to the fall of the Soviet Union. Nostalgia and memories of the Soviet past remain powerful in the context of rapid change in the present. Privatization is giving rise to new social geographies, while ethnic and religious sensibilities are creating emergent networks of sacred sites. *Urban Life in Post-Soviet Asia* provides a detailed account of the changing nature of urban life in this region, clearly elucidating the centrality of these urban transformations to citizens' understandings of their own socio-economic condition.

Beall, Jo, and Sean Fox. *Cities and Development*. London: Routledge, 2009.

Most future urban growth will take place in the cities and towns of low- and middle-income countries, and this book seeks to understand the consequences of this massive shift. Demographic pressure is already straining the capacity of governments to manage urban change beyond manageable limits; hence a significant percentage of this growth will take the form of slums. Will our future be dominated by megacities of poverty and despair, or can urbanization be harnessed to advance human and economic development? *Cities and Development* highlights both the challenges and opportunities associated with urban change by examining historical patterns, the role cities play in economic growth in a globalizing world, the complexities of managing urban environments, and the possibilities for utilizing urban planning, governance, and politics to shape city futures.

This book offers a useful review of debates about cities and highlights strengths and weaknesses of current policy and planning responses to the contemporary urban challenge. It includes research orientated supplements in the form of summaries, boxed case studies, development questions, and further reading.

Davis, Mike. *Planet of Slums*. New York: Verso Press, 2006.

This widely acclaimed book offers a thorough examination of the growing urban pattern of substandard housing and slum neighborhoods in cities throughout the developing world. Ranging across many countries, the author chronicles how these slums have grown in a way that has been disconnected from industrialization, setting forth new patterns or urban development that are far less sustainable than similar processes a century ago. In the midst of these communities is an informal urban underclass that has the potential to organize and push for greater attention or possibly take a more violent path toward revolution. These urban trends are not isolated from global trends, but are rather closely tied to the activities of multinational corporations as well ill-conceived development and aid policies promulgated by the World Bank.

Durand-Lasserve, Alain, and Lauren Royston, eds. *Holding Their Ground: Secure Land Tenure for the Urban Poor in Developing Countries*. London: Earthscan, 2002.

Land tenure security among the urban poor is a significant problem for rapidly developing cities in Africa, Asia and Latin America. Based on extensive research, this book presents and analyses several case studies that offer a comparative perspective on urban land tenure. It looks at how solutions can be found and implemented to respond to the demands of urban residents of informal settlements, and analyses how urban stakeholders, under particular social, legal and economic constraints, are devising and employing innovative and flexible responses.

Dutt, A. K., A. G. Noble, and G. Venugopal, eds. *Challenges to Asian Urbanization in the 21st Century*. New York: Springer-Verlag, 2003.

A diverse group of contributors that include geographers, engineers, and urban planners who represent the United States, India, Germany, Sri Lanka, and Canada, tackle various aspects of urbanization in Asia. The diverse landscape of Asia provides many different contrasts in physical environments, historical backgrounds, social, economic, and political conditions. Case studies come from such diverse cities as Colombo, Hong Kong, Tokyo, Jerusalem, Delhi, and Kaohsiung in Taiwan.

Grant, Richard. *Globablizing City: Urban and Economic Transformation of Accra, Ghana* Syracuse, NY: Syracuse University Press, 2008.

Much has been written about the impact of globalization on cities in the advanced industrial countries of Europe, Asia, and North

America, but little on most other parts of the world. The author draws on ten years of empirical research in the city of Accra, Ghana to illustrate how African cities are being shaped by these forces. He helps to the way in which international, transnational, and local forces are operating on the urban landscape of Accra, from the gated communities of the elite, to the poorest squatters in the slums. Through interviews and extensive field work, we learn how foreign companies, returned expatriates, and native Ghanaians work out strategies to succeed in a rapidly changing globally connected world

Hsing, You-tien. *The Great Urban Transformation: Politics of Land and Property in China*. London: Oxford University Press, 2010.

China is currently experiencing almost unprecedented leaps in its economic development and expansion of its cities. This book offers a perspective on how these forces of growth are impacting people at the local level, with a particular focus on the urban fringe where important agricultural land is being consumed by development. Here, the author offers a close-up account of how people's lives are being changed—some for the better, but many others facing loss of a way of life and a bitter future. This, in turn, is triggering political upheavals and pressures on the state. Urban expansion is seen as platform for the process of capitalist accumulation, the restructuring of state power, and the changing relationship between state and society.

Keiner, Marco, Marina Koll-Schretzenmayr, and Willy A Schmid, eds. *Managing Urban Futures: Sustainability and Urban Growth In Developing Countries*. London: Ashgate, 2005.

This volume brings together leading experts from around the world to explore the policy challenges that result from patterns of rapid urbanization in developing countries. The various chapters of this edited work focus on population growth, rural-urban migration, and expansion of urban areas in developing countries. The comparative focus of these contributions help to provide perspective on how these challenges are impacting Africa, Latin America, Asia, and the Pacific in different ways in the context of competing policy frameworks.

Koonings, Kees, and Dirk Kruijt, Editors. ***Megacities: The Politics of Urban Exclusion and Violence in the Global South.*** **New York: Zed, 2009.**

The contributors to this book take a critical look at life in "megacities," urban places in the developing world that are experiencing growth on a massive scale. Using a framework derived from the tradition of class analysis and political economy, the authors see megacities as complex sets of relationships which link poverty and exclusion to urban politics, power relations, and public policy. It is a political environment in which the urban poor are confronted with inequality, deprivation, and violence. Particular attention is given to large Latin American cities, where low-income squatter settlements confront violence from drug-related gangs, from private armed militias and corrupt police forces. The book examines the ways that the urban poor devise strategies to confront and overcome this violence. There are important explorations of citizenship rights and how the evolution of democracy might be facilitated. Additional analysis is provided on the Middle East and Southern Africa.

Kramer, Mark. ***Dispossessed: Life in Our World's Urban Slums.*** **London: Orbis, 2006.**

This book relates the struggles of the urban poor in a number of large cities of the developing world that include Manila, Nairobi, Bangkok, Mexico City, and Cairo. The author reviews extensive statistical information about urbanization and growth trends culled from UN documents to inform the reader about current conditions and future trends. We learn about the reasons behind the rapid growth of slums around the world and assess long-term consequences. In addition, it also offers valuable personal accounts and stories that bring forth the reality of daily life in squatter communities in these locations.

Laquian, Aprodicio A. ***Beyond Metropolis: The Planning and Governance of Asia's Mega-Urban Regions.*** **Washington, DC: Woodrow Wilson Center, 2005.**

Asia is home to some of the world's largest metropolitan regions. The author offers an analysis of the planning and governance in several a diverse number of "mega-urban regions," with a particular focus on the management of water resources, transportation and mobility, housing and basic urban services, as well as better integration with the urban periphery. This latter aspect is of particular importance, since in every case, development has sprawled into the surrounding countryside, enveloping villages, towns, and small and medium-sized cities that now constitute "extended metropolitan regions." Data from twelve cities in Asia with populations over ten million are included in this study: Tokyo, Mumbai, Kolkata, Dhaka, Delhi, Shanghai, Jakarta, Osaka, Beijing, Karachi, Metro Manila, and Seoul.

Laquian, Aprodicio A., Vinod Tewari, and Lisa M. Hanley, eds. *The Inclusive City: Infrastructure and Public Services for the Urban Poor in Asia*. Washington, DC: Woodrow Wilson Center, 2007.

Delivering essential urban services such as transportation, trash disposal, water, and sanitation to the poor in Asia is hindered by a host of difficulties. The authors argue that these problems will not be overcome with traditional, top-down approaches. The premise of this book is that the most successful municipal governments have developed strategies that directly involve the poor themselves in improving their access to urban services. Case studies are drawn from the large cities in India, Bangladesh, Pakistan, China, Indonesia, and the Philippines. The contributors to this volume are scholar-practitioners from Asia as well as Australia, Canada, and the United States.

McGee, Terry, George C. S. Lin, Mark Wang, Andrew Marton, and Jiaping Wu. *China's Urban Space Development Under Market Socialism*. London: Routeledge, 2007.

China's urban growth is unparalleled in the history of global urbanization, and will undoubtedly create huge challenges to China as its modernization continues at a rapid pace. Adopting an interdisciplinary approach, this book presents an overview of the radical transformation of China's urban space since the 1970s, arguing that to study the Chinese urbanization process one must recognize the distinctive political economy of China. After a long period as a planned socialist economy, China's rapid entry into the global economy has raised suggestions that modernization in China will inevitably result in urban patterns and features like those of cities in developed market economies. This book argues that this is unlikely in the short term, because processes of urban transition in China must be interpreted through the lens of a unique and unprecedented juxtaposition of socialism and the market economy, which is leading to distinctive patterns of Chinese urbanization. Richly illustrated with maps, diagrams, and in-depth case studies, this book will be an invaluable resource to students and scholars of urban economics and policy, geography, and the development of China.

McGregor, Duncan, David Simon, and Donald Thompson. *The Peri-Urban Interface: Approaches to Sustainable Natural and Human Resource Use*. London: Earthscan, 2006.

This book focuses attention on one of most important aspects of urban growth in developing countries: the peri-urban (rural-urban) fringe. This is where the most intense growth in informal settlements (slums) is taking place today, and thus where the most pressing shortage of critical services such as water, sanitation, and urban planning is evident. Additional concerns relate to the degradation of agricultural land and severe environmental threats. These areas, home to hundreds of millions of people, face unique problems and need unique and innovative approaches that are reviewed by the authors of this work. Topics include resource sustainability, livelihoods, agriculture, urbanization, planning, governance, and future action plans for research and problem solving. Material is drawn from Africa, Asia, Latin America, and the Caribbean.

Murray, Martin J., and Garth A. Myers, eds. *Cities in Contemporary Africa*. London: Palgrave Macmillan, 2007.

The societies of Sub-Saharan Africa are experiencing the most rapid rates of urban growth in the world. This book offers a broad range of scholarly interpretations of the evolving forms and changing dynamics that characterize contemporary African cities. Importantly, it wrestles with questions concerning how large numbers of people crowded into Africa's cities find ways to survive and even prosper in the absence of conventional forms of employment, inadequate housing, and substandard city services. Multicity comparisons help to provide perspective on culture, political economy, work livelihoods, urban planning, and governance.

Naik, N. T. K., and S. Mansoor Rahman. *Urbanization of India*. New Delhi: Serial Publications, 2007.

The slum population in India is increasing at much faster rate than the total population, a situation which calls for serious attention as the supply of urban infrastructure lags behind the exploding demand. The authors of this text explore the concept of urbanization and discuss its development in India over the previous 100 years, and then offer a detailed case study of urbanization in Andhra Pradesh state and Kurnool district to illustrate.

Neuwirth, Robert. *Shadow Cities: A Billion Squatters, a New Urban World.* London: Taylor & Francis, 2006.

This is an account of one journalist's personal journey as he lived among squatter communities in Rio de Janeiro, Mumbai, Nairobi, and Istanbul. It is an impassioned, insider's view of squatter life that takes the reader away from official rhetoric of development agencies and government officials and places them in and among those who have found remarkable ways to survive and succeed in the tough urban environment. In addition, this book offers an exploration of different policy options that face rapidly growing cities of the developing world, and concludes that those policies that offer squatter settlements an opportunity to build upon their own carefully constructed economies, supported by solid, sustainable indigenous institutions are the most promising.

Sivaramakrishnan, K. C., Amitabh Kundu, and B. N. Singh. *A Handbook of Urbanization in India.* New Delhi: Oxford University Press, 2005.

This is a comprehensive analysis of the socio-economic and spatial characteristics of urbanization in India. Among the subjects covered are migration and urbanization patterns evident at the inter-state, state, and district levels of government. The authors acknowledges the big challenges associated with managing urban areas, and assesses the nature of the policies and programs required for better urban governance

UN-Habitat. *State of the World's Cities 2006/2007–The Millennium Development Goals and Urban Sustainability: 30 Years of Shaping the Habitat Agenda.* London: Earthscan, 2006.

The year 2007 marked the first time in history that over half of the world's population were living in urban areas. In recognition of this significant shift, and in light of efforts underway towards achieving the UN Millennium Development Goals, this volume considers a wide range of the issues which affect the lives of urban dwellers. Of special concern are slums and the challenges of addressing inadequate provision of water and sanitation, shelter, malnutrition, disease, education, and employment. Research from UN-HABITAT offers a harsh picture of many urban areas of the developing world that have failed to reduce poverty, hunger, child mortality, and HIV/AIDS rates in slums. The scale and distribution of slums worldwide is analyzed, along with progress of key indicators such as tenure, living space, and sanitation, showing regional differences and the impacts of slum conditions on health, employment, and security. The final part of the book evaluates the past thirty years of slum and urban policies.

UN-Habitat. *State of the World's Cities 2010/2011–Cities for All: Bridging the Urban Divide*. London: Earthscan, 2010.

This edition of the State of the World's Cities uses the framework of "The Urban Divide" to analyze the complex social, political, economic, and cultural dynamics of urban environments in developing countries. An important feature of this volume is legal rights associated with urban life, and an analysis of the many urban dwellers are excluded from public services. Overall, this book provides a thorough examination of the links between poverty, inequality, slum formation, and economic growth.

UN Millenium Project. *UN Millennium Development Library: A Home in The City*. London: Earthscan, 2005.

This volume acknowledges the challenge of more than 900 million people currently live in urban slums in the developing world and calls upon countries to improve the lives of this rapidly rising population. Proposed are specific investments and policy changes at both the local and national levels that will help to create a vibrant, equitable, and productive urban environment. It underscores the need for close strategic partnerships between local authorities and organizations of the urban poor for slum upgrading and improved urban management. From adopting citywide strategies and establishing adequate and affordable infrastructure and services, to building effective public transport and constructing low-income housing, this work offers valuable insights into ways to address slum formation.

Zhang, Li. ***China's Limited Urbanization: Under Socialism and Beyond.*** **Hauppauge, NY: Nova Science, 2003.**

Based on research conducted at the geography departments of the Universities of Washington and Honk Kong, this study seeks to explain the unique patterns of Chinese (under)urbanization and link them to patterns observed in other nominally socialist countries. It examines the impact of elements of the economic system, particularly "state-biased" development, the terms of trade between agriculture and industry, and irregular patterns of investment in different sectors and activities.

Articles and Reports

Arimah, Ben C. ***The Face of Urban Poverty: Explaining the Prevalence of Slums in Developing Countries.*** **United National University: World Institute for Development Economics Research Working Paper No. 2010/30.**

Attention has focused on the rapid pace of urbanization as the sole or major factor explaining the proliferation of slums and squatter settlements in developing countries, but there are other factors whose impacts are not known with much degree of certainty. This paper accounts for differences in the prevalence of slums among developing countries using data drawn from the recent global assessment of slums undertaken by the UN Human Settlements Program. The empirical analysis identifies substantial intercountry variations in the incidence of slums both within and across the regions of Africa, Asia as well as, Latin America and the Caribbean.

Arku, Godwin. "Rapidly Growing African Cities Need to Adopt Smart Growth Policies to Solve Urban Development Concerns." ***Urban Forum*** **20 (3; August 2009): 253–270.**

Is the "smart-growth" concept developed to contain the impacts of urban sprawl in the United States a worthwhile policy model that could be adopted by rapidly growing African cities? The author argues that the influx of rural residents to urban areas in Africa could be better managed if current urban development patterns dominated by unlimited outward extension, low-density residential developments, and haphazard patterns were contained through adherence to smart-growth principles.

Butala, Neel M., Michael J. VanRooyen, and Ronak Bhailal Patel. "Improved Health Outcomes in Urban Slums through Infrastructure Upgrading." ***Social Science & Medicine*** **71 (5; September 2010): 935–941.**

What policies work the best in alleviating the conditions experienced by poor slum dwellers in cities of the developing world? This study shows that an innovative slum upgrading project that combined using microfinancing and public-private partnerships in Ahmedabad, India led to a significant decline in waterborne illness incidence among local residents.

Cali, Massimiliano. ***Urbanization, inequality and economic growth: Evidence from Indian states.*** **Overseas Development Institute, November 2007.**

India is undergoing rapid rates or urbanization. This important research reports on the impact of this mass movement of people from rural areas to the cities on larger measures of social inequality and economic growth.

The author concludes that at least in the Indian context, the rate of urbanization (i.e., how fast a state urbanizes) and the rate of economic growth are negatively correlated.

Cho, Jaeseong. "Urban Planning and Urban Sprawl in Korea." ***Urban Policy & Research*** **23 (2; June 2005): 203–218.**

South Korea represents an interesting case study of a developing country that has matured into middle-income status over the previous thirty years. The author documents patterns of urban sprawl developing in the Seoul Metropolitan Area at the beginning of the 1990s and in other cities around the country. It analyzes the causes of urban sprawl and especially the failure of planning systems. The article also offers planning alternatives to prevent further urban sprawl in the future.

Dupont, Veronique. "The Dream of Delhi as a Global City." ***International Journal of Urban and Regional Research*** **35 (3; May 2011): 533–555.**

Since the liberalization reforms of the 1990s, Delhi has experienced rapid growth that has enabled it to become a truly global metropolis. The urban landscape has been transformed with the appearance of export processing zones, modern infrastructure, high-end residential complexes and shopping malls. And yet the city has also experienced negative consequences. Slum clearance has exacerbated socio-spatial polarization and inequality has increased.

De Wit, Joop, and Erhard Berner. "Progressive Patronage? Municipalities, NGOs, CBOs and the Limits to Slum Dwellers' Empowerment." ***Development and Change*** **40 (5; September 2009): 927–948.**

It has become conventional wisdom that any effort aimed at urban poverty reduction and service delivery improvement in slums must involve some form of community participation by the slum dwellers themselves. This study of cases from three Indian cities takes a critical look the "partnerships" between municipal agencies, nongovernmental organizations, and slum organizations and suggests that the poor, facing conditions of scarcity and competition, still rely heavily on vertical relations of patronage and brokerage. Rather than being vehicles of empowerment, these partnerships can even block progress, controlling or capturing benefits aimed at the poor and misusing them for private interests.

Joshi, Sharadbala, and M. Sohail Khan. "Aided self-help: The Million Houses Programme–Revisiting the issues." ***Habitat International*** **34 (3; July 2010): 306–315.**

The self-help approach to housing aims at creating an enabling environment in which occupants of a piece of land build their own homes. This article reviews the successes of the innovative "Million Houses Program" implemented by the government of Sri Lanka, which incorporated community participation into the planning, construction, and financing of the project.

Nsokimieno, Eric, Chen Shouyu, and Zhang li Qin. "Sustainable urbanization's challenge in democratic Republic of Congo." ***Journal of Sustainable Development*** **3 (2; June 2010): 242–255.**

Like all of the countries of Africa, the Democratic Republic of Congo is experiencing very rapid rates of urbanization. This study of the capital city of Kinshasa chronicles the story of chaotic urban growth characterized by social inequalities, poverty, environmental degradation, open spaces loss, socio-economic tension, spontaneous unplanned settlements and sprawl. The authors argue that sustainable urbanization is a priority issue and calls for the mobilization resources at local, national, and global levels.

Owusu, George, Samuel Agyei-Mensah, and Ragnhild Lund. "Slums of hope and slums of despair: Mobility and livelihoods in Nima, Accra." ***Norwegian Journal of Geography*** **62 (3; September 2008): 180–190.**

Many misperceptions exist around the livelihoods and living conditions of slum communities. This study of Nima, a slum community in Accra, Ghana helps to demonstrate the enormous socio-economic and cultural differences that exist. The authors' research documents the multiple strategies, migration patterns, and the changing character of slums that highlight both negative and positive aspects of these urban places.

McDonald, Robert I., Pamala Green, Deborah Balk, Balazs Fekete, Carmen Revenga, Megan Todd, and Mark Montgomery. "Urban growth, climate change, and freshwater availability." ***Proceedings of the National Academy of Sciences of the United States of America*** **108 (15; April 12, 2011): 6312–6317.**

With nearly 3 billion additional urban dwellers forecasted by 2050, cities will be hard pressed to provide adequate water supplies in the context of unprecedented hydrologic changes due to global climate change. The authors utilize a detailed hydrologic model, demographic projections, and climate change scenarios to estimate per-capita water availability for major cities in the developing world. They conclude that many cities in dry regions will struggle to find enough water for the needs of their residents and will need significant investment if they are to secure functioning freshwater ecosystems.

Martinez, Javier, Gora Mboup, Richard Sliuzas, and Alfred Stein. "Trends in urban and slum indicators across developing world cities, 1990–2003." ***Habitat International*** **32 (1; March 2008): 86–109.**

To what extent is a person's general health and household vulnerability to illness impacted by residence in a slum and what difference to slum improvement programs make? This paper analyses trends in the living conditions of slum and nonslum populations over the period 1990–2003, using data from UN-Habitat's Global Urban Observatory database for 188 cities. The study provides evidence of a general improvement in various slum indicators, such as durable structures, access to safe water, and access to improved sanitation.

Rolnik, Raquel. "Democracy on the Edge: Limits and Possibilities in the Implementation of an Urban Reform Agenda in Brazil". ***International Journal of Urban & Regional Research*** **35 (2; March 2011): 239–255.**

The return to civilian rule in the 1980s and 1990s in Brazil offered the possibility that urban growth and develop could be managed in a more equitable manner that involved all diverse constituencies in the country's fast-growing cities. This article assesses the institutional advances in the areas of housing and urban rights, including the recognition of the right to ownership of informal urban squatters and the direct participation of citizens in urban policy decision processes. Of particular interest are two policies: the National Cities Council and the campaign for Participatory Master Plans.

Sridhar, Kala Seetharam. "Determinants of City Growth and Output in India." ***Review of Urban & Regional Development Studies*** **22 (1; March 2010): 22–38.**

The sheer size of India, as the second largest country in the world, makes its experience with urbanization an important topic. The author investigates the agglomeration effects associated with urban population growth and economic growth in India using several empirical methods.

Takeuchi, Akie, Maureen Cropper, and Antonio Bento. "Measuring the Welfare Effects of Slum Improvement Programs: The Case of Mumbai." ***Journal of Urban Economics*** **64 (1; July 2008): 65–95.**

Can slum improvement programs really make a difference in improving the lives of the poor? The authors of this study evaluate the impacts of both in situ slum upgrading and relocation programs using data for 5,000 households in Mumbai, India.

World Bank. ***Approaches to Urban Slums: A Multimedia Sourcebook on Adaptive and Proactive Strategies.*** **World Bank, 2008.**

In the next 30 years, the number of people living in slums is estimated to double. This report draws from a large body of research and knowledge available through nonprofit organizations on how to improve the lives of slum dwellers while simultaneously planning for new urban growth. It offers a user-friendly multimedia approach in easy-to-understand language. Adaptive approaches seek to improve the existing conditions of slum dwellers through upgrades and improvements of public services, as well as establishing tenure rights. Proactive strategies that anticipate future growth are identified in the report as being far more effective, affordable, and easier to implement than retroactive measures that simply adapt to existing conditions. Case studies are drawn from Tanzania, Ecuador, Vietnam, Brazil, Afghanistan, and Mauretania.

World Bank. ***Systems of Cities: Harnessing Urbanization for Growth and Poverty Alleviation.*** **World Bank, 2009.**

Recognizing that cities account for 70 percent of global GDP today, the World Bank offers support in this report for a new paradigm that embraces the critical role urbanization is playing in promoting rising productivity, new opportunities for employment growth, and greater access to global markets. It argues that cities need to be equipped with tools and resources necessary to harness the vast potential of their fast-growing cities to improve national development, and has pledged greater attention to financial support and technical assistance to meet these needs.

UN-HABITAT. ***UN-HABITAT'S Strategy for the Implementation of the Millennium Development Goal 7, Target 11.*** **2005.**

This report gives an overall vision of the strategy that was adopted by the UN Human Settlement Program (UN-HABITAT) to ensure that 100 million of the world's urban poor would have significantly improved lives by the year 2020. An analysis of the extent of global urban poverty is followed by a variety of different ways in which this UN agency will seek to implement and monitor progress on fighting urban poverty. This includes the promotion of research, raising public awareness, and coordination of specific anti-poverty programs to be implemented with member state governments and nongovernmental organizations.

UN Millennium Project. ***A Home in the City: Task Force on Improving the Lives of Slum Dwellers.*** **2005.**

This report makes a strong case that the urban context is critical to understanding and meeting all of the objectives of the Millennium Development Goals. Improving the lives of slum dwellers is vital in combating HIV/AIDS, improving environmental sustainability, reducing gender inequality, and addressing poverty. This urban challenge dictates a much broader and more ambitious approach than the improvement of a portion of the world's estimated slum dwellers summarized in target 11 and subsumed under Goal 7. Slum upgrading, improved urban planning and design, and the provision of adequate alternatives to new slum formation must become the primary focus of local and national governments supported by international development agencies. Ample evidence over the past 20 years shows that the urban poor themselves can provide the central impetus for change toward good governance. Governments, especially local governments, have also demonstrated that they can develop the capacity to use their mandates and resources for sound and participatory urban development policy, if such policies are rooted in a political leadership that is committed to a democratic and equitable vision of civil society in all spheres of government. What is needed is the vision, the commitment, and the resources to bring all actors together.

Zhao, Pengjun. "Sustainable urban expansion and transportation in a growing megacity: Consequences of urban sprawl for mobility on the urban fringe of Beijing." ***Habitat International*** **34 (2; April 2010): 236–243.**

The effect of urban expansion on transportation in growing megacities has become a key issue in the context of China's current development. Examining the case of Beijing, this article analyzes the policy implications of urban growth management for sustainable transportation in China's megacities. To achieve sustainable urban expansion, the author argues for stronger metropolitan development management measures.

Nonprint

Websites

There are dozens of websites accessible today that offer a rich and abundant selection of perspectives, opinions, data and analysis on the topic of urban growth around the world. Thankfully, much of this information can be access free of charge. A thorough sampling of what is available today online can be found in the list of organizations located in Chapter 7 of this volume, all of which have a presence on the web. The list of electronic resources that follow below provide especially helpful, easy-to-access, and free information and data on global urban growth.

American Farmland Trust. "Farm Information Center"

http://www.farmlandinfo.org/. Accessed June 29, 2010.

The Farm Information Center is a clearinghouse for information about the loss of U.S. farmland to urban sprawl, and provides additional information about its protection and stewardship. The site is provided in partnership with the USDA Natural Resources Conservation Service.

American Planning Association. "Growing Smart Guidebook"

http://www.planning.org/growingsmart/index.htm. Accessed June 29, 2010.

States and their local governments have practical tools to help combat urban sprawl, protect farmland, promote affordable housing, and encourage redevelopment. The American Planning Association provides substantial information about these tools in this hands-on resource.

Brookings Institution. "State of Metropolitan America"

http://www.brookings.edu/metro/StateOfMetroAmerica.aspx. Accessed on June 29, 2011.

The State of Metropolitan America portrays the demographic and social trends shaping the large metropolitan areas of the United States and discusses what they imply for public policies to secure prosperity for these places and their populations. The report is highly informative and freely available for downloading.

Central Intelligence Agency—World Fact Book "Land Use"

https://www.cia.gov/library/publications/the-world-factbook/fields/2097.html. Accessed June 29, 2010.

This entry contains the percentage shares of total land area for three different types of land use in all the countries of the world.

Cities Alliance. "Cities Without Slums"

http://www.citiesalliance.org/ca/news_events. Accessed June 29, 2011.

This multimedia resource offers access to a variety of different means to access and learn about slums in the developing world, issues related to city development, cases and strategies to advance slum upgrading around the world.

The Citistates Group. "City Wire"

http://citiwire.net. Accessed June 29, 2011.

Free access to a variety of different articles and useful links to publications from the Citistates Group of authors and experts on diverse topics related to global urban growth, economic trends, and policy perspectives.

E Magazine. "Cities of the Future"

http://www.emagazine.com/magazine/issue/122. Accessed June 29, 2010.

This special issue of *Environment Magazine* offers several excellent articles on the topic of urban growth and the environmental impact this is having.

European Environmental Agency. "Urban sprawl, 1975–1990–2000"

http://www.eea.europa.eu/data-and-maps/figures/urban-sprawl-1975-1990-2000. Accessed on June 29, 2011.

An interactive resource with searchable data base that offers a look at the extent of urban sprawl in the member states of the European Union over the previous 35 years.

Globalis. "Interactive World Map"

http://globalis.gvu.unu.edu. Accessed on June 29, 2011.

Globalis is an interactive world atlas where the visitor to the website decides what is to be displayed on an interactive global map. This resource helps to illustrate the impact of the construction of cities and roads and how these factors decrease the natural value and the biodiversity of the environment. The site allows comparisons with human impacts over time.

Heritage Foundation. "Smart Growth"

http://www.heritage.org/Issues/Housing/Smart-Growth. Accessed on June 29, 2011.

This webpage offers links to a variety of different reports and opinions published by the Heritage Foundation that question the fundamental assumptions of the "Smart-Growth" movement. Topics range from analyses of federal and state budgets to housing, growth management, and transportation policies.

Indexmundi.com. "Country Facts"

http://www.indexmundi.com. Accessed on June 29, 2011.

This is a data portal that gathers facts and statistics from multiple sources and converts them into easy-to-use visuals and offered free to the general public. The site has numerous fully searchable databases, and offers convenient summaries of data via maps, charts, and tables. Several variables covered in the data are useful to those seeking to learn more about global urban growth and related policy issues. Highly recommended.

Land Trust Alliance. "Find A Land Trust"

http://findalandtrust.org. Accessed on June 29, 2011.

Land trusts are a vital means of preserving environmentally sensitive land from urban encroachment and development. This free interactive map feature allows users to research all of the land trusts operating at the local, state and national levels in each state of the United States and learn more about them.

Lincoln Institute of Land Policy. "Resources and Tools"

http://www.lincolninst.edu/resources. Accessed on June 29, 2011.

The Lincoln Institute of Land Policy offers this resource to researchers, practitioners, policymakers, and the media who are seeking to learn more about urban growth and policy issues. It provides access to case studies, model representations, and best practices, and extensive information resources in the form of databases.

NASA Science. "Urban Sprawl: The Big Picture"

http://science.nasa.gov/science-news/science-at-nasa/2002/11oct_sprawl. Accessed on June 29, 2011.

This site sponsored by the National Aeronautic and Space Administration (NASA) describes an ongoing research project through which satellite-generated mapping is being utilized to analyze urban growth patterns and trends.

National Geographic Magazine. "The American Dream: Urban Sprawl"

http://ngm.nationalgeographic.com/ngm/data/2001/07/01/html/ft_20010701.3.html. Accessed on June 29, 2011.

National Geographic Magazine assembled this resource in 2001 to educate the public about prevailing urban growth patterns in the United States called urban sprawl. It offers access to articles, multimedia resources, and links to those interested in learning more about this phenomenon.

Nationmaster.com. "Welcome to NationMaster"

http://www.nationmaster.com/index.php. Accessed on June 29, 2011.

NationMaster is a clearinghouse of data that allows the user to compare nations of the world on dozens of different measures that include urban growth-related topics. The site brings together information from reputable sources that include the U.S. government, the United Nations, and OECD. This interactive site allows visitors to generate maps and graphs.

NewUrbanism.org. "New Urbanism: Creating Livable Sustainable Communities"

http://www.newurbanism.org. Accessed on June 29, 2011.

This website serves as an easy-to-understand guide to "New Urbanism." A variety of different articles help promote the design philosophy, which promotes the creation and restoration of diverse, walkable, compact, vibrant, mixed-use communities as well as environmentally sustainable public transportation policies.

NumbersUSA Action. "Urban Sprawl"

http://www.numbersusa.com/content/issues/urban-sprawl.html. Accessed on June 29, 2011.

This site offers information and access to data bases on population and urban growth in the United States. The sponsoring organization seeks to help the public better understand the linkages between immigration and urban-related policy challenges.

Planetizen. "Features"

http://www.planetizen.com/features. Accessed on June 29, 2011.

The Planetizen website serves as public-interest information exchange for the urban planning, design, and development community. It offers access to a variety of different articles, multimedia resources, and links for urban planning news, commentary, interviews, event coverage, book reviews, announcements, jobs, consultant listings, and training.

Plannersweb.com. "Sprawl Guide"

http://www.plannersweb.com/sprawl/focus.html. Accessed on June 29, 2011.

A helpful webpage from the *Planning Commissioners Journal* that provides background information on defining sprawl, analyzing its causes, assessing its impact on transportation and environmental conditions, and reviewing potential solutions.

Population Reference Bureau. "Data Finder"

http://www.prb.org/DataFinder.aspx. Accessed on June 29, 2011.

The Population Reference Bureau, a private nonprofit research foundation, offers free public access to a very comprehensive, fully searchable population data base on the United States and all the countries of the world. Search themes include population characteristics, education, health, transportation, housing, family structure, reproductive health, and other topics.

Post Carbon Institute. "Post Carbon Cities"

http://postcarboncities.net. Accessed on June 29, 2011.

This is the companion website to the book by Daniel Lerch titled *Post Carbon Cities: Planning for Energy and Climate Uncertainty* that offers access to a database on local government, news and resource archives as well as information on the book, presentations, and the author.

Science Daily. "How Does Your City Grow? A View of Urban Sprawl from Outer Space."

http://www.sciencedaily.com/releases/2006/04/060426182328.htm. Accessed on June 29, 2011.

This website, which offers scientific information to the general public, reviews the findings from a University of Toronto-based team of researchers who used satellite data and aerial photography to create a grid of 8.7 billion data cells tracking the evolution of land use in the continental United States. Several links offer additional insights on the topic. See http://www.sciencedaily.com/releases/2007/12/071217171404.htm for a follow-up story from the same resource.

Sierra Club. "Stopping Sprawl"

http://www.sierraclub.org/sprawl. Accessed on June 29, 2011.

This site is maintained as a resource in support of the Sierra Club's "Challenge to Sprawl Campaign" and offers a wide variety of reports, guidebooks, multimedia resources, and other useful information to the general public. It seeks to inform the public about the organizations opposition to poorly planned development while offering support for smart-growth communities that increase transportation choices, reduce air and water pollution, and protect natural places.

Sprawlwatch.org. "SprawlWatch Clearinghouse."

http://www.sprawlwatch.org/frames.html. Accessed on June 29, 2011.

This website offers access to a variety of different books, reports, websites, and organizations that share the common concern about urban sprawl. The extensive information about state growth management policies is extremely thorough, but has not been updated in recent years.

UN Department of Economic & Social Affairs, Population Division. "World Urbanization Prospectus."

http://esa.un.org/unup. Accessed on June 29, 2011.

This site provides access to a fully searchable database on urban and rural population statistics with a special focus on annual growth rates and cities. It covers each region of the world as well as individual countries.

UN Development Program. "Slum Population in Urban Areas"

http://data.un.org/Data.aspx?d=MDG&f=seriesRowID%3a711. Accessed on June 29, 2011.

This site maintained by the United Nations permits the visitor to view data on the numbers and percentage of populations of all countries of the world that are residing in slums over time. This data is part of the larger UN Millennium Development Goals program. More information on this can viewed at http://www.un.org/millenniumgoals.

UN-Habitat. "UN-Habitat Around the World"

http://www.unhabitat.org. Accessed on June 29, 2011.

This is the main web platform for the UN Human Settlements Program. It offers the richest and most comprehensive set of free resources on the cities of the developing world available today. These include e-library and e-learning tools, publications, reports, photos, multimedia presentations, surveys, and urban indicators data. This is without question the single most important resource on this topic available today.

U.S. Department of Agriculture Natural Resources Conservation Service. "National Resources Inventory"

http://www.nrcs.usda.gov/technical/NRI. Accessed on June 29, 2011.

The NRCS conducts regular statistical surveys of land use and natural resource conditions and trends on all U.S. non-federal lands. This information is made available at this website, along with a variety of related reports and useful policy analyses that provide key insights into urban growth in the United States.

U.S. Environmental Protection Agency. "HUD-DOT-EPA Partnership for Sustainable Communities"

http://www.epa.gov/dced/partnership/index.html. Accessed on June 29, 2011.

The Partnership for Sustainable Communities website enables visitors to find resources and grant announcements and to learn about the Partnership. The website includes contact information for each federal agency's sustainable communities office, ongoing project updates for sustainable community grantees around the country, and recent news and grant information from the Partnership.

U.S. Geological Survey. "Land Cover Institute."

http://landcover.usgs.gov/nalcms.php

The website maintained by the USGS Land Cover Institute (LCI) provides maps and analysis on land use and land cover surveys for both the United States and the entire world.

U.S. Geological Survey. "About the GAP Analysis Program"

http://www.nbii.gov/portal/server.pt/community/program_info/1849. Accessed on June 29, 2011.

This website sponsored by the U.S. Geological Survey offers access to a rich array of maps and data to assist in efforts to monitor to what extent native animal and plant species are being protected. The data can be accessed at a state, local, regional, or national levels and offers abundant insight into urban growth-related pressures.

USATODAY. "A Comprehensive Look at Sprawl in America"

http://www.usatoday.com/news/sprawl/main.htm. Accessed on June 29, 2011.

In 2001, USATODAY undertook a detailed analysis of information from the 2000 U.S. Census for the purpose of measuring the extent and impact of urban sprawl across the United States. While this information is dated, it remains today as one of the most insightful surveys of urban growth patterns and related pressures available.

Wendell Cox Consultancy. "Demographia"

http://www.demographia.com. Accessed on June 29, 2011.

This highly informative website is maintained by Wendell Cox, a leading authority on urban policy and free market advocate. The site provides a massive quantity of data and reports on urban growth, transportation, economic trends, land-use policy, and other topics as they relate to the United States and the rest of the world. There is also analysis and commentary provided by the author and other free-market advocates.

World Bank. "World Development Reports"

http://www.wdronline.worldbank.org. Accessed on June 29, 2011.

Each year since 1978, the World Bank has produced a comprehensive survey called the *World Development Report* that offers a detailed analysis on the state of progress in human development for all countries of the world. These report collate and analyze a variety of different information that is useful in better understanding policy issues related to urban growth. Each report is available for downloading free of charge on this website. Highly recommended.

Yale University. "Environment 360"

http://e360.yale.edu. Accessed on June 29, 2011.

Yale University offers a variety of opinion, reports, and analysis of regional and global data on the state of the environment and related urban policy challenges on this multimedia website that is free of charge to users.

Glossary

adequate public facility ordinance A growth management tool used by urban planners that require real estate developers to ensure that electricity, water, sewerage, and roads are in place before they are permitted to sell plots.

American Institute of Certified Planners An organization for qualified professional planners, affiliated with the American Planning Association. To become a member requires passing an examination after having demonstrated some practical experience working as a planning professional.

brownfields Abandoned, idled, or underutilized industrial land that cannot be redeveloped due to serious environmental contamination. A significant reason for why commercial and industrial development has failed to materialize in many economically depressed inner city communities in the United States.

central business district A designation given to an urban area that has an historic status as the commercial and political center of the community. Typically, such areas are the traditional focus for retail, commercial, and office land uses in cities.

cluster zoning In an effort to protect vulnerable open space from development, development restrictions are waived in other more suitable areas in order to encourage more compact, higher-density land use.

community A collection of people who share a common sense of identity and knowledge about the place in which they reside. In its strongest sense, it implies regular interaction among people, accountability, and shared sense of shared commitment to civic ideals.

compact development Exists where buildings are situated within close proximity to one another, and may apply to either residential housing, commercial developments, or a mixture of both. This kind of development is often preferred by planners and environmentalists because it enables people to get around by walking, uses less land, and can foster a greater sense of community.

comprehensive plan A plan prepared by the citizens of a community to guide current and future land-use development in their locality. These plans commonly incorporate elements such as economic goals, environmental protection, health, public safety, traffic circulation, and fiscal stability. All states have enabling legislation permitting local governments to create comprehensive plans, although these plans have only an advisory status in most.

concurrency A growth management technique that disallows new real estate development unless adequate road, utility, and other publicly funded service infrastructure is already present or funded so that it will be completed at the same time as the development.

conservation easement This is an agreement between a landowner and an outside party to restrict the future development of that land to certain specified uses (as farmland or in an undeveloped state) in return for compensation. Such easements can be negotiated and paid for by government or by private, nonprofit trusts seeking to preserve open space and scenic landscapes.

density In the context of urban planning, this term is used to refer to the number of buildings per mile or acre. Higher density leads to more compact development on less land, while lower density contributes to sprawling development on greater amounts of land.

edge cities Large suburban communities located on the periphery of metropolitan areas that have evolved into growth points that function independently of the traditional central city of the region. These cities have attracted the highest share of business investment, new residential housing and commercial development over the past 25 years, often to the detriment of central cities that cannot compete with the low taxes, cheap undeveloped land, and close proximity to low-density residential neighborhoods.

enterprise zones An urban redevelopment policy whereby local governments offer lower taxes, less regulation, and other inducements to attract new businesses and investment to stimulate the local economy.

exclusionary zoning Land use rules that make the construction of affordable housing difficult if not altogether impossible to achieve by imposing regulatory costs that are unjustified from the standpoint of conventional health or safety considerations. Exclusionary techniques include imposing unreasonably large minimum lot sizes, prohibitions on multifamily dwellings and mobile homes, and other measures that keep low-income citizens from residing in the community.

exurb Rural areas located miles outside of defined metropolitan regions and suburbs. Many of these unincorporated areas that have been undergoing rapid urban growth as new highway interchanges are built that enable commuters to reach them in a day's journey to and from work.

gated community A residential development or *housing estate* set apart from the surrounding urban area by controlled entrances and closed perimeter walls and fences.

Geographic Information Systems (GIS) GIS comprises a variety of software and hardware computer systems that relate and display geographic (spatial) data. Information can be incorporated into these databases from a wide variety of sources, and typically includes geologic, ecological, land use, demographic, transportation, economic development, and other components. The capacity of GIS to quickly overlay new information on top of existing data and to display it in diverse graphic presentation formats had enabled land-use planners, business developers, governmental officials, and many others to make more rational decisions regarding present and future land use.

green belt An integrated system of open land that surrounds a metropolitan region. It is protected from urban and incompatible rural development. Greenbelts can consists of a variety of lands that might include parklands, natural preserves, state forests, and protected farmlands.

growth management Attempts by communities to regulate the amount, timing, location, and character of current and future land development. Communities undertake growth management planning to avoid experiencing tax increases that result from new housing and commercial development, mitigate traffic congestion, and prevent other socially unacceptable burdens created by urban sprawl.

impact assessment A formal study that uses a variety of measures to determine whether a proposed land use will impose acceptable costs and burdens upon a community. Areas usually addressed in these assessments are fiscal, traffic, public facility, and special impacts such as air quality, noise, and exposure to other hazards.

impact fees A one-time fee levied on real estate developers by local governments. These fees are designed to mitigate the otherwise onerous impact of expanded public facilities and infrastructure that are necessary when new homes or businesses are located within a community.

infill development Real estate investment that occurs in a depressed urban area that has suffered from a lack of business and job opportunities. This type of urban revitalization is often cited by planners and activists as a preferred alternative to the ongoing commercial and residential development of open spaces located at the periphery of metropolitan regions.

land invasion A strategy in which a group of landless people take possession of undeveloped land for the purpose of settlement. Normally, some kind of tacit approval already exists from politically influential people to minimize the possibility of eviction or reprisals by local authorities.

land trusts These are nonprofit voluntary organizations that work with landowners to protect natural, scenic, and agricultural lands that are threatened by urban development. Land trusts use a variety of tools to conserve open space that include obtaining conservation easements that permanently restrict land use, outright purchases of land for conservation, and the facilitation of estate planning.

leapfrog development A situation that occurs when real estate developers and home builders bypass established suburban communities that have imposed strong growth controls and development restrictions, locating their projects in ever more distant unincorporated areas. This urban growth pattern perpetuates the problem of urban sprawl.

master plan See **comprehensive plan.**

megacity An extremely large urban metropolis that is usually defined as having a population above 10 million. In 2011, there were 21 metro regions with this designation.

metropolitan government A government that has been granted limited powers over in a multijurisdictional region. In the United States, these agencies have often involved county-level governments merging select services with municipal governments, but may go even further as in the case of Portland's Metro government.

Millennium Development Goals Eight goals were identified at the Millenium Summit in 2000 under the auspices of the United Nations as being the most critical in advancing human well-being throughout the world. Among these goals is a commitment to "improving substantially the lives of at least 100 million slum dwellers, while providing adequate alternatives to new slum formation" by the year 2020.

new towns Large-scale planned urban communities established in Great Britain at the end of World War II to shift population growth away from overcrowded industrialized areas. Over a period of three decades, 28 "new towns" were developed in a fashion that has been mimicked by many other countries across the world facing similar conditions.

New Urbanism A school of design founded on the conviction that planners and architects have the responsibility to construct socially diverse and environmentally sustainable communities. They favor more compact neighborhood designs, with denser housing clustered around mixed-use commercial zones, a reliance on mass transit, preservation of open space, and neotraditional civic architecture.

NIMBY An acronym for "Not In My Backyard," this is an attitude that commonly finds expression among homeowners who find a proposed change to existing land use to be objectionable due to the detrimental impact they perceive it to have on their own property values and quality of life.

open space Land that lacks any substantial buildings or residential uses and therefore, imposes few burdens upon a community to underwrite the cost of public services. Such land is either left in its natural state as a preserve, set aside for passive recreational use purposes as a public park, or is being utilized for some agricultural purpose such as cultivation or grazing that does not greatly alter the existing natural landscape.

overurbanization A term used to refer to cities of the developing world that struggle to provide adequate public services for fast-growing populations associated with by rural-to-urban migration. Conditions associated with overurbanization include extensive slum housing, overburdened public transit, crowded streets, inadequate provision of public utilities, and lack of education facilities.

performance zoning Local codes that stipulate what real estate developers and builders may or may not do in terms of end results. This is an alternative to more exacting regulations that tend to bog the process down in red tape and often fail to accomplish larger community goals.

planned unit development Land-use regulations that permit relaxation of the zoning standards for a specific district so as to provide flexibility in the placement of buildings in exchange for an overall development plan for the property. Under an approved plan of this type, the local community has in effect entrusted a real estate developer with the task of developing a substantial tract of land in a responsible and beneficial manner.

planning board An appointed or elected body of citizens who exercise authority over the orderly use and development land within a local government. Responsiblities include overseeing the implementation and enforcement of zoning bylaws, and developing long range land-use plans.

primate city A large urban center that indisputably holds the leading position in all economic, political, and cultural affairs in a country. This is a common feature of the urban hierarchy in most developing countries of the world and is often attributable to the impact of European colonization on prevailing urban patterns.

privatization Any policies that aim to allow privately owned entities to displace governments in the provision of public services even if these must be sold off through the market.

property rights In the context of land-use issues, this refers to the exclusive right to possess, use, and dispose of land (i.e., real property) that any owner enjoys, as recognized by common law and upheld in the courts of the United States.

purchase of development rights An arrangement where a farmer voluntarily sells the development rights of farmland to a state or local government, receiving compensation for development restrictions placed on the land thereafter. The goal of these programs is to keep land in agriculture or preserve open space. Under these agreements, the farmer retains title to the land and can sell or pass along the land to others, although development restrictions remain.

regionalism An agenda built on the belief that cities and their surrounding metropolitan areas are best able to address shared problems through regional governmental cooperation, rather than independently derived disjointed policies.

regulatory taking The loss of market value that occurs when a piece of real estate is affected by development restrictions imposed by environmental regulations. Restricts are likened to the loss of land due to an eminent domain taking by government. Property rights proponents maintain that such "takings" are unconstitutional under the terms of the Fifth Amendment unless just compensation is offered by the government.

regularization A policy that allows for the legalize acceptance of formerly unauthorized settlements by local government. These policies offer the possibility of slum dwellers gaining some form of legal title to the land they occupy, and may also make way for the formal establishment of public services (water lines, electricity, etc.) in these communities.

reurbanization A process in which the rate of population loss previously experienced by the inner core of an urban area is reversed.

right-to-farm laws Most state governments in the United States provide farmers with legally defensible protection from nuisance lawsuits in defense of standard farming practices. Such laws arise when residences and commercial properties complain about the noise, odors, chemicals, etc. associated with farming.

road pricing Policies that seek to reduce traffic congestion in crowded urban areas by increasing the price of commuting by private vehicles.

rural-urban migration The movement of people from low-density, natural-resource dependence settlements to higher-density, built urban environments. This process is stimulated both by the relative attractions of the city as well as the lack of opportunity and other constraining factors associated with rural life.

security of tenure The status of ownership over land generally attained through legal procedures that result in obtaining a title or some other certificate of occupancy. Security of tenure is a fundamental right that is often absent in the cities of the developing world.

shantytowns see **slums.**

site plan review A community vests its planning and/or zoning agency with the responsibility of granting building permits based on a review of new land development, taking into considerations building safety, lay out of utilities, internal circulation, adequacy of parking, and buffering from adjacent land uses. This is the principle tool that most local governments possess for regulating land use.

site and services schemes A government policy in which local authorities set aside an undeveloped site for settlement by low-income inhabitants, grade the land, establish home sites, and extend some public utility lines (electricity, water, sewage, paved roads, etc.) in advance of settlement. While these projects have much to offer the urban poor, they are often situated far outside of cities in places where long daily commutes and other hardships pose a barrier to those they are intended to serve.

slums A term that universally refers to poverty-stricken neighborhoods. In the cities of the developing world, slums are usually unplanned, illegal settlements that are located in undesirable places (e.g., floodplains, steep hillsides) that are underserved by municipal governments and may even face the regular threat of harassment and even eviction by the authorities. Slum dwellers remain in these places because they offer an affordable and convenient location that is usually within close proximity of workplaces.

slum clearance schemes A policy in which municipal authorities seek to eradicate all problems usually associated with unplanned illegal urban communities (crime, poor sanitation, fire hazards, etc.) by simply bulldozing all built structures. In most cases, there is a plan in place that will offer the cleared land to business elites to redevelop the land for other uses.

slum upgrading A policy in which municipal authorities seek to improve conditions for those who live in slum communities by extending water mains and sewage lines, paving roads, building schools, and a variety of other improvements.

smart growth A strategy that seeks to overcome the historic deadlock between pro-growth and anti-growth forces. Advocates hope to achieve economic development while recognizing the need for communities to better the quality of life of existing residents, preserve open space, and contain costly fiscal burdens associated with rapid, unplanned commercial and residential development. Smart growth presupposes that carefully planned development derived through inclusive process of consensus-building is the best way for communities to grow.

smart roads A proposal to issue electronic devices known as transponders (or smart tags) that compute mileage charges for drivers for use of roads by the mile. The charge for mileage would be higher for trips during daily rush hours as an inducement to drivers to either commute at less congested times, or share the cost of a ride with another person.

socio-spatial segregation Circumstances where people reside in separate communities based upon social characteristics such as income level, race, ethnicity, and religious orientation.

spontaneous housing Houses constructed of rudimentary building materials that may literally appear over night as the result of squatters moving in to claim the land for their homes and businesses. Allowing this kind of activity is in effect, an alternative form of "housing policy" since it relieves any burden municipal authorities might otherwise have in attempting to provide affordable quarters for poor and homeless migrants who wander their streets in seek of shelter.

sprawl This term refers to both the outward spread of commercial, industrial, and residential development into open spaces located on the fringes of urban centers, and the detrimental side effects that this kind of development pattern imposes upon citizens. Negative effects of sprawl include the loss of productive agricultural lands and other natural landscapes, increasing tax burdens associated with the need to underwrite the expansion of urban services to newly developed areas, rising traffic congestion on existing road networks, overcrowded public schools, and a general loss of community identity in the midst of automobile-dependent, low-density subdivision housing.

squatters Individuals who occupy undeveloped urban land illegally for the purpose of building homes and businesses. This may begin as a short-term survival strategy to meet immediate needs, but may over time become a permanent residence through more secure tenure.

stakeholders That collection of people and organizations that share an interest in the present and future development of a community. Stakeholders interested in land-use decisions typically include individual residents and landowners, civic and religious organizations, business associations, environmental and conservation groups, and governmental agencies at all levels.

strip development Planned commercial developments where buildings re located along a heavily traveled road or highway corridor. Such developments are faulted by planners for being wasteful of open space, create significant traffic congestion, and accessible only by automobile. Strip developments can be contrasted with compact commercial development, which situate buildings close together within easy walking distance of transit.

structural adjustment programs Policies in which heavily indebted governments are required by the International Monetary Fund to cut domestic spending drastically in order to qualify for more generous loan repayment schemes established by lenders. Mandated cuts in social services, infrastructure, education, housing, and the like have had a devastating impact on urban conditions in the fast-growing cities of the developing world.

subdivision The process by which a tract of land is split into smaller parcels, lots, or building sites so that the parcels may eventually be sold and developed. Regulation of subdivision by agents of local government serves the purpose of controlling the process so that substantial changes to existing land are compatible with the wishes of the larger community.

suburb An urban community that is located outside of the environs of an older city. Suburbs have a separate political jurisdiction, tax base, school system, and other services from that of the traditional city center. Suburbs also often possess a different racial and ethnic composition from the center city.

sustainable communities Living places that are able to accommodate the needs of present-day economic development while preserving nonrenewable resources and ensuring that the future quality of life for residents is not compromised.

sustainable urban development Growth of cities that meets the economic needs of living generations without spoiling assets for the generations that follow.

technoburbs Suburban communities that have grown around the location of high technology office parks.

traditional neighborhood development An urban architectural design in which the basic unit of planning is the neighborhood district, which is limited in size, with a well-defined edge and focused community center. The design reflects a deliberate attempt to foster community interaction through a network of interlinking street patterns, gathering points, and shopping districts that are arranged within walking distance of densely arranged homes.

transferable development rights A program in which development rights on farmland may be sold to real estate developers, providing a financial incentive for landowners to remain in farming. The developers then have clearance by the community to use these development rights in other specified areas previously designated for high-density urban and commercial land use.

transit-oriented development This exists where regional urban plans call for new housing or commercial development that will accommodate mass transit by bus or train. Transit-oriented development usually involves such elements as high housing density, concentration of commercial activities in a compact center, and pedestrian amenities that facilitate movement to and from transit stops. This kind of planning reflect a concern for limiting private automobile use, and thereby contribute toward a decline in local traffic congestion and air pollution.

UN-HABITAT The name used to identify the UN Human Settlements Program. UN-HABITAT has been given the mission to promote "socially and environmentally sustainable towns and cities" with the goal of providing "adequate shelter for all." Its budget is derived mostly from contributions by multilateral and bilateral partners, and is supplemented by governments, private foundations, and the UN general budget.

urban development corporations A private nonprofit agency that obtains authority to use both public and private resources to stimulate positive change in poverty-stricken communities through the provision of affordable housing and other benefits.

urban land An area classified as having sufficient population density to be considered a town or city. In the United States, an urbanized area must have a population of at least 2,500 people per square mile, and adjacent areas must have a density of 1,000 people per square mile.

urban growth boundary Lines that are mapped out by planners as a means to contain sprawling urban development that is encroaching upon green spaces located beyond city limits. They mandate that all development must be concentrated in land area within a boundary, usually with allowances for greater density and mixed use.

urban renewal Any type of coordinated effort that combines public subsidies with private sector investment capital to revitalize a deteriorating and economically depressed urban area.

urban service area A defined area where water, sewer, roads, and other public services will be extended by government to facilitate urban residential and commercial development. The purpose of these areas is to limit development to the confines of such zones, and thus prevent sprawl growth into the countryside.

urban social movements Citizen-level organizations that form among disadvantaged city residents seeking to bring about some kind of change to government policy that will improve their quality of life and collective welfare.

urbanization A process in which the size of a built-up, high-density area of human settlement expands outward both by natural population increase and migration from other places.

zoning Refers to rules governing land use in a community. Such rules are designed to control the type of use, building height, minimum lot sizes and building setbacks, parking, signage, landscaping, and other considerations of interest to citizens, and are adopted through the democratic process under the authority of a zoning ordinance.

Index

Page numbers followed by f indicate figure
Page numbers followed by t indicate table

About the Author

Dr. Donald Clyde Williams is a professor of Political Science and Geography in the Department of History and Political Science at Western New England University in Springfield, Massachusetts. Dr. Williams received a Ph.D. in Political Science and a Graduate Certificate in African Studies from the University of Florida in 1991. His doctoral research concentrated on state-society relations in Africa and the politics of land reform in Nigeria. He is the author of *Urban Sprawl: A Reference Handbook* published by ABC-CLIO in 2000. He has published numerous academic works on land use policy and democracy in Africa, and also has served as an elected official on the Planning Board in the town of Wilbraham, Massachusetts. He is married and has three children.